PREVENTING

AND

ENDING

DOMESTIC ABUSE

BY

ALAN VENUS

Copyright©2026 Alan Venus

ISBN: 978-1-7642329-0-6

All rights reserved. No part of this publication may be reproduced, stored in a retrieval system, or transmitted in any form or by any means—electronic, mechanical, photocopying, recording, or otherwise—without the prior written permission of the author, except in the case of brief quotations embodied in critical articles or reviews.

This book is classified as a hybrid work, blending elements of philosophical reflection, creative nonfiction, and practical guidance. It is intended to empower, inform, and inspire readers through its interdisciplinary approach.

While every effort has been made to ensure accuracy, the author and publisher assume no liability for the use or misuse of the information contained herein.

ACKNOWLEDGMENTS

This book is dedicated to my mother, **Barbara Venus**, pictured above whose poignant portrait shows her at the tender age of just six years old, whose legacy of teaching empathy through love, respect, and compassion made this book possible. A woman who experienced a twelve-year gap between herself and the first of her five siblings having learned very quickly the virtues of motherhood at a young age. A pillar of strength, who continues to enjoy life as I write, her presence and influence will always remain entrenched in those who know her, forevermore woven throughout the pages of this book.

Love you, Mum.

To my beautiful teenage granddaughters, who unknowingly provided further inspiration for this book—

'In the hope they may live their lives free from abuse'.

And finally, to the love of my life my wonderful wife Lynn who continues (trying) to keep me in line after fifty years. Love you HB.

❀ ❀ ❀

PREFACE

Author's Note-

This book is the result of freewriting—spontaneous with honest intention. Every word came as it felt.

Domestic abuse is a shadow that too often lingers behind closed doors—silent, out of sight and unspoken.

This book exists to cast light into that darkness.

Qualified trainer assessor/health and safety, the author has seen first-hand how providing the skills and knowledge, support, and awareness can empower lives.

How to *Prevent and End Domestic Abuse* is the culmination of years spent listening, learning, and equipping others with the tools to stand strong against cycles of harm.

Although this book was written predominantly with women in mind—who statistically bear the brunt of domestic abuse—it speaks to everyone, and anyone who has felt diminished, afraid, or unsure of their worth, regardless of gender, age, or background. Abuse does not discriminate, and neither does hope. It's time for a shift.

For too long, many women have been expected to endure, to stay quiet, or to manage the impossible without the tools they need to protect themselves. That must change. It is high time that practical skills—rooted in real-world safety, self-awareness, emotional resilience, and legal understanding—are placed in the hands of those most vulnerable. What women need is not just sympathy but a toolkit that empowers them to live with safety, freedom, confidence, and respect.

Here you will find strategies rooted in safety and self-advocacy, scenarios that echo resilience, and clear guidance on recognizing early signs, navigating complex emotions, and reclaiming autonomy. Whether you're seeking a relationship, experiencing abuse, maybe someone concerned about a loved one or simply committed to fostering a safer society, this book invites you to imagine something better, by turning that imagination into reality.

Beyond its practical strategies and protective frameworks, this work is a guide toward personal transformation. It invites readers to rise above their current circumstances and step into self-reinvention. Through understanding one's own fortitude, that quiet indomitable spirit of strength that resides within - even amid adversity, instills the direction for you to shape your future defined not by past harm, but by present empowerment.

Change begins when silence ends—Let's get started.

Table of contents

INTRODUCTION 1
DATING 22
    ON-LINE DATING 41
COURTSHIP 54
ENGAGEMENT 69
MARRIAGE 85
DIVORCE 146
LIVING ALONE 163
CONTROL AND COERCION 170
SEXUAL ABUSE 190
    RAPE 216
DYSFUNCTIONAL FAMILIES 240
THE ELDERLY 299
DRUGS AND ALCOHOL 318
FORTITUDE 359
SINGLE MOTHERS 370
CONCLUSION 388
EPILOGUE 391

INTRODUCTION

This Self-Help Book has been written primarily to offer advice, guidance, and to provide the skills and knowledge along with recommended, practical and realistic safe solutions to identify and ultimately...

– Prevent and End Domestic Abuse –

But also, to encourage and inspire females of all ages into first recognising and understanding the basis for making better informed decisions, through a more intentional process. The focus of this book is to end domestic abuse in both non-committed and committed relationships. Along with safety awareness for those women in different circumstances outside of relationships covering - 'Single mothers', those 'Living alone' and the 'Elderly'.

PREVENTING DOMESTIC ABUSE: Covers chapters on Dating, Courting, and Engagement. This looks at periods where no domestic abuse has yet surfaced, with emphasis on the processes that every female should consider adopting. That's to ensure their date or partner doesn't harbour underlying traits or show any characteristics that could become the catalyst for different types of domestic abuse in the future.

ENDING DOMESTIC ABUSE: Covers chapters on Marriage, Divorce, Sexual abuse, Drugs and Alcohol, Control and Coercion, along with Dysfunctional families—not limited to. Here we identify domestic abuse having infiltrated the relationship, the reasons why, and the suggested steps to remediate. This will be accomplished by following the recommended procedures through careful planning, during the process of either preventing or ending domestic abuse.

Again, regardless of your reason for reading this book, whether you are currently experiencing some form of abuse, concerned for your own safety, suffering emotional stress, or about to date for the first time, this book will provide practical guidance. This self-help resource is relatable and written in everyday layman term language for people of all backgrounds, age groups, and levels of understanding.

Honesty

Should this self-help book resonate with you, it's important to be honest with yourself from the outset. Starting with how you represent yourself as a human being, either in or when looking for a relationship. Having your own indiscretions in life without taking ownership first and expecting to resolve issues by finger pointing will not end well.

Acknowledging any shortcomings you have now will make your journey more reassuring. Therefore, as you read the passages within this book allow yourself to accept change rather than protecting any indiscretions and remaining in denial.

Are you ready to become inspired?

Reading this book will give you the opportunity to privately gather your thoughts. The guidance and suggested remedies will acknowledge your situation and prompt your thought process. Assisting you with questioning the present, learning from the past, and focusing on your future. It will support you in all important future decisions coming through unharmed, whereby you will take greater care of your well-being, finding happiness and peace of mind- forever more.

The idea for this self-help book also came about from a genuine belief there's a serious lack of former education amongst those women that have had no previous guidance when seeking a relationship. Together with the skills and knowledge in understanding how to address both the prevention and ending domestic abuse. This is evident, due to worldwide statistics that show the high numbers of female casualties and divorce rates. Yet alarmingly, we generally only hear about domestic abuse 'after the fact',

Introduction

usually when a serious incident has already occurred, followed by the report of another female fatality.

In the workplace, employers have a responsibility to carry out a risk assessment for any proposed task by understanding if potential hazards exist. This process involves identifying hazards and then evaluating the level of risk by considering two key factors: the likelihood of the hazard occurring and the severity of the potential consequences. Although the assessment is partly subjective, once these elements are evaluated, appropriate control measures are then implemented to eliminate or reduce risks to an acceptable level. Safeguards must be practical, straightforward to apply where possible, and regularly monitored to ensure they remain effective- 'what's the connection you might ask'.

Unfortunately, when contemplating starting a relationship most men and women do not have such thoughts about putting safeguards in place. This is because human beings are driven by emotion and rarely think about the inherent risks.

Therefore, women are not prepared against the potential of becoming subjected to domestic abuse. Without safeguards or boundaries in place, these women remain in vulnerable situations, exposed to consequences that could have been mitigated had initial processes and controls been put in place.

All too common scenario

Take the woman who has an abusive and aggressive husband because of his alcohol abuse and wants to let him know she will not put up with his behaviour any longer. What are her options: wait for him to come home to talk to him, leave him a note, or show up unannounced at the place where he drinks? Or should she first think about the level of potential risk associated with each of those scenarios, along with the type of potential consequences? Therefore, ensuring appropriate safety controls are in place, before making her decision.

It's important to understand, there would be significantly more females alive today, had they thought more about their personal safety before carrying out any type of confrontation.

This is achievable by having made proper thought-out plans, before addressing any type of domestic abuse issue, or carrying out any type of confrontation. By adopting a very important strategy and complete understanding - there's a time and place', which we will take a closer look at.

Overdue regulations

Having raised the point of the risks associated within the workplace, it could be argued that a woman's home should be recognised as her place of work. Whereby she would be entitled to the same protective measures under the health and safety act that every other type of worker enjoys. Covering issues such as verbal and physical abuse, sexual harassment, bullying and psychosocial behaviour. Putting every male on notice, adding an extra layer of overdue protection for women who are currently fighting the great cause for defeating domestic abuse in their own home.

Every husband or partner would soon become aware they are now accountable through another legal framework that comes with severe consequences.

— A significant game changer against domestic abuse —

On average five women are killed every hour somewhere in the world at the hands of domestic abuse; this terrifying statistic demands that all women, regardless of relationship status, remain one step ahead of the danger.

— That's a staggering forty-thousand deaths per year —

As mentioned, a major concern is a lack of education that results in failure to identify and remedy domestic abuse so desperately needed, particularly for all males and females. Other than by the current widely accepted statistic whereby a staggering 48% of marriages fail leaving couples no choice but to learn from their mistakes — but do they?

Introduction

An all too familiar adage – 'Putting the cart before the horse'.

Sound the alarm

Let's be clear, if you are in a distressed state because of domestic abuse and finding it difficult to cope, you owe it to yourself to go straight into a police station and make a full report. Then ring the many available domestic abuse and charity hotlines to receive the help you need, as there are caring people out there waiting to hear from you.

(See Epilogue to find contact details and further help).

Capabilities & goals

It's very important that you become realistic regarding your capabilities and goals, in terms of your limitations during any intervention and or confrontation. Therefore, adopt a new strategy whereby- before you act, first Pause, Reflect, then Engage- that's your new mantra, which we will also explore further.

It's imperative you establish each other's true feelings towards one another, and if you are unsure you wish to remain in this relationship, then this book will provide you with good reasoning, one way or another.

Far too many women remain unstable in a relationship for a variety of reasons, which we will again discuss throughout the following pages, by addressing how to first avoid, but also to resolve. Although it can be frightening for many women to even think about going down this path, it is very achievable. So, by taking on the suggestions and following the recommendations you will reach your goals, even when feeling like you can't.

Verbal abuse

Let's look at a common scenario—verbal abuse, under the category of 'Ending domestic abuse', where this type of behaviour has now entered the relationship.

These women, many of whom are newlyweds now endure the added burden of being verbally abused whilst maintaining the household.

This includes raising and getting the children off to school, then going off to work by herself concealing her secret, whilst having to contain that nauseous feeling inside. These women neither draw attention nor complain.

For many, they disguise this living hell of being abused by acting out a charade of normality whilst being denied a normal and happy life. That's because young wives become so overwhelmed by marriage they feel they have an increased sense of duty. Domestic abuse remains a taboo subject and responsible for a multitude of tragic and hidden atrocities.

Being abused by the very person who up until recently confessed their love for their partner only compounds on a young woman's mind, further complicating the world she now lives in.

There's a further pressing problem and it's not just the sheer weight of the mental anguish she must endure. It's the sense of failure which in part, is caused by the perception of social status and disappointing the extended family.

— But at what cost to your mental health —

Some young mothers believe they can solve this type of abuse through their own self-abuse, a tragedy within itself. Turning to drugs and alcohol in a futile attempt to hide the pain and remain in denial. This signifies the mental anguish associated with domestic abuse that can become soul-destroying, usually behind closed doors.

These young women should never accept this type of behaviour from their spouse, not now, or at any other time. Instead, they need to end this mental torture and get their life back, before any further escalation in abuse takes place.

Yet as mentioned there's a need for women to believe they must conceal and cover up this type of behaviour. This only exacerbates the situation, almost as if the perpetrator programmed her to do so.

Sadly, for a variety of reasons many women fail to read the signs of their man's behaviour before they enter into a marriage. However, it may also be the case he only became abusive once they were married. Either way, we will also address these issues and put into place planned practical procedures along with safe solutions. All of which will hopefully be specific to your needs and situation, putting an end to the abuse so you can become the person you always wanted to be.

So, if you can relate to this common scenario, then now is the time to make this self-help book your new best friend and constant companion. There are other readers who, just like you are having to deal with different types of abuse. You are not alone.

This self-help book illustrates the immense daily pressure on the many women with scenarios just like this one. So regardless of your circumstances, I invite you to join a new crusade. It may be the case you're already in the mindset of, enough is enough', therefore the time has come for you to put some other important relationship issues into proper perspective. Therefore, a woman wanting change must also realise that change starts with herself—change doesn't just materialise.

Taking ownership

Many couples overlook a crucial issue—the need to take personal responsibility for any indiscretions they may harbour, instead of shifting blame onto others. These matters must be addressed both individually and through open communication with one another. Unless both partners are willing to confront and acknowledge any shortcomings—and make amends earnestly and honestly—resentment will build, that often escalates into verbal abuse.

By embracing this approach you'll begin to restore your self-respect. This sets off a natural chain reaction rediscovering your self-confidence, experiencing renewed optimism, finding relief, and discovering true sense of self-worth and belonging. You'll notice a new spring in your step—energized by the awareness that you're on the right path, moving ever closer to a life of genuine fulfilment.

– Holding on to indiscretions will hold you back –

Taking advice

There is seldom anything in life, more volatile than domestic abuse, that's why it's important you remind yourself there is both a right and a wrong way in handling 'off course' relationships.

Unfortunately, there will always be circumstances that cannot be resolved, either in a timely manner or in a willingness, which can sadly end in tragedy. So, consider taking the following advice seriously with willingness.

There are many everyday abusive situations females have witnessed, lived through, aware of, or heard about. However, receiving advice is one thing but accepting, comprehending, believing, agreeing, or having the fortitude and capability to do something about it, is altogether different. We all have our own reasons for doing what we do, however it's how we go about doing those things that we need to take a closer look at.

– Consider adopting your own personal approach before any knee jerk reaction, and again—pause, reflect, before engaging, as part of your mantra and discover how your decisions and choices take a different course. –

Some suggestions within this book will resonate with you, as you have most likely had the same thoughts yourself, but perhaps wondering how best to deal with them. However, for others some recommendations won't, for personal reasons only they will ever know. We all make multiple decisions daily, usually without any adverse consequences, usually because of their simplicity. However, due to the complexities and specific nature of domestic abuse, a completely different approach must become part of your new thought process. An area we will explore at length a little later.

Self-worth

Whether you're suffering from some type of abuse or not, in life it's best to maintain a cheerful disposition, as you can't afford to be consumed or become overwhelmed by personal circumstances. This book will explain how to appreciate yourself more and learn to be kind to yourself, and by doing so you will start to appreciate your self-worth. It's part of what it means to be human, something far too many women in strained relationships overlook.

Find inspiration by thinking more about your principles and values and you will soon reconnect with your goals and regain your sense of belonging. If you have a young family, then think more about the children and how they should be living in a happy family environment. Along with the satisfaction of knowing that your extended family and friends will admire you for your resilience, and let's not forget, the most important person on planet earth- is you.

By making a full commitment to follow through and accomplishing what you're about to undertake, you will restore your faith in human nature. This process is also character building, which is important in maintaining your overall well-being. So regardless of your age, acknowledge that any abuse you may be suffering from must end, and your redefined mindset will keep you better focused.

Exchange any negative thoughts you may have with positive ones. Bring to the surface that vibrant person you know you can be, rediscovering the confidence you once had. You will soon begin demonstrating how to become forthright with your use of discipline and willpower, by using your strength and courage, and to follow through, it's all there for the taking.

With that in mind, along with knowing your family and close friends are right behind you—however for the time being it's best to stay quiet on the matter. Reminding yourself of the utmost importance of carrying out the right processes, with further emphasis on what we have already discussed. That is, 'there's a time and place' to address and resolve issues as mentioned, as failure to do so has resulted in far too many cases ending in tragedy, even death.

Being prepared

Never feel pressured to make any immediate decision or choices about anything. Instead, take the time to distinguish between your options and put them to one side for now. Then further analyse their relevance toward your goals, ensuring they are well-suited to what you aim to achieve while prioritising your safety. – Every step of the way.

As an example of what to expect when we move into real-life scenarios, when deciding it's time your partner understood your grievances. You therefore plan to confront him when he arrives home from work.

However, because of your specific situation, you made the wrong decision on several fronts. You know your partner displays aggressive outbursts, therefore deciding to confront him at home was not in your best or safest interest. Also, the timing was wrong, since you approached him when he walked through the door after he had been consuming alcohol. These seemingly simple scenerios place you in a dangerous and vulnerable situation. After all, you are all alone with him at home in the confines of four walls.

Because of these types of complexities, it's important to do as much research on him as you can. That goes hand in hand with carrying out your personal risk assessment we discussed earlier, weighing up the potential risk you are exposing yourself to before you confront him.

Don't allow the word 'Confront' or 'Intervene' scare or put you off. Remembering there are other ways to confront someone without the need to be face-to-face, again understanding your capabilities and limitations as a woman, cannot be over emphasised.

That is why you should never act 'like a bull at the gate, instead you will take a different approach based on your calculated risk, before taking any action. These thought processes play a crucial and important role in life, particularly when deciding on whether to enter into a relationship. Once you do, you should continue to discover all you can about this man before making any fulltime commitments.

So now it's time to become assertive with yourself if in a troubled relationship, and stop accepting that notion and saying, "It is what it is", because it's not, and it doesn't have to be. Instead, it's long overdue to do something about it.

More than awareness — an awakening.

If you have a different reason for reading this book and haven't been looking for answers regarding domestic abuse then you will become

Introduction

inspired in other ways, as this self-help book offers so much more than just providing solutions. Again, it's more than awareness, but an awakening that can so easily result in your complete transformation - if you what it to be.

— You may even become inspired and motivated to become a champion for those women you suspect are suffering from domestic abuse. It may be a case where you want to help children you also suspect may be the subject of other types of abuse, which we will also address in later chapters. —

Hopefully, younger women will come to understand that while confidence and independence are strengths, even the wisest of women can badly misjudge a situation. It's easy to dismiss advice when you're young, but no one is immune from ending up in a place they never imagined, especially when danger wears a charming face. Many older women once stood self-assured, carefree, and certain they were making the right decision—only to discover too late, that safety isn't guaranteed by good intentions alone. Therefore, it's not just believing that by demonstrating confidence alone will keep you safe, it's about being wiser than your adversary.

— Therefore, for the younger ones—unless you are prepared to take early advice, then chances are your immaturity and heightened emotions can potentially lead you in the wrong direction, resulting in a lifetime of uncertainty, unhappiness and regret. —

Primates

We describe human beings as being civilised since there are many who show love, respect, compassion, and consideration. However, humans are also extremely complex primate creatures with many capable of barbaric wild savagery.

Let's not forget that humans have evolved over thousands of years without any serious intellectual rivalry. Therefore, they possess the autonomous cognitive ability to demonstrate abusive traits at will. This systematic unleashing of calculated, callous, and heinous acts where domestic abuse is concerned, on many occasion results in women suffering both mentally and physically, even death.

— Where does domestic abuse stand in society? —

Preventing and Ending Domestic Abuse

We should all acknowledge as mentioned, when domestic abuse is highlighted on the news it's usually to report another female has sadly lost her life. Other than that, there is little coverage. Unlike the reporting of the more trivial crimes that choke our TV screen almost on a daily basis.

Therefore, the sooner females accept the undeniable fact that the authorities expect couples in relationships to resolve their own problems, the sooner females across the world will acknowledge their fate is in their own hands.

Hence the ongoing need to emphasis the urgency of educational training that provides essential skills and knowledge from an early age.

It is therefore high time every woman understood and accepted that they only spend a small amount of quality time with their partners. As a result, humans still find the time to get on one another's nerves. This is when a woman should never underestimate her ongoing vulnerability when in the company of her man, particularly when he has shown signs of being abusive.

Domestic abuse inevitably places women and children at the forefront, trapping them unwittingly as participants. Having to listen and witness vulgar, threatening verbal and physically aggressive behaviour. In constant fear without the male comprehending both the immediate and future effects of emotional abuse.

– One of the main reasons behind high domestic abuse is arguably the result of the male unable to control his emotions. As a result, allowing himself to become frustrated over something that could otherwise be an easy fix. Instead, he becomes agitated and bad tempered looking on for an easy target to take his frustration out on. His mindset, now corrupted by this process, targets the most vulnerable, the very people he would have you believe he loves - his wife and family-.

It's the nature of the beast, however in contrast a woman has a much better temperament and resolve when handling her own frustrations. Having already learnt how to deal with life's difficult and sometimes arduous matters, she prevails, while the male looks for a scapegoat and continues with the blame game.

Introduction

It's how males control that frustration that will define who they are, and what they become, as they go through life. Through their demeanor and natural disposition, it becomes clearer what they truly represent.

Emotional toll

The toll on people who witness domestic abuse is nothing short of horrendous, as their minds and souls have been subjected to shock. This type of event requires time for healing for the human body to reinstate itself to its natural form. The repetitiveness and pervasiveness of the abuse extend overtime to psychological stress disorders. The likes of which have traumatic consequences on individuals that ripples across the whole of society.

That's because children who are witness to this ongoing abuse are within the solitary confines of four walls—out of sight and out of mind— with far more reaching implications, resulting in greater suffering, both in the short and long term.

In many countries there are government department initiatives to assist with domestic abuse, however the fact remains, there is very little the authorities can do unless the matter is reported or provided with an early tip off. It's for that reason you should become more in tune with who you are and what you're getting out of life. That's in contrast to maintaining that almost robotic style of existence within a relationship that so many women seem to just accept and continue with, almost as if under some type of male induced hypnotic spell that has a magical hold on you.

Traits and Attributes

By ensuring her partner is not an abuser in any shape or form, therefore by making it very clear to him from the very beginning that she will not tolerate any type of abuse is the number one aim. This means he will know from the outset that should he become an abuser; she will dissolve the relationship.

It's how that woman goes about discovering a man's traits and attributes that define the type of risk she is taking. The first three chapters explore these topics. This should be every woman's goal, and every man's understanding, by acknowledging long before allowing the relationship to fully blossom. Doing so gives the relationship the very best opportunity for long-term survival and success.

How many women have spoken such powerful words to the person they are in a non-committal relationship with from the outset, so that the male is under no illusion how he will need to behave? Particularly if he should continue wanting to pursue this woman, knowing only too well what her principles and values are. Furthermore, will he still be around to sweep her off her feet, if so, then this woman has given herself a better-than-average head start, which is what every woman should want to achieve.

After all, is there anything wrong with a woman being upfront and honest when pursuing a relationship, setting a man straight from the outset, and possibly saving herself from all the heartache of future abuse? –Business before pleasure.

There are many women throughout all walks of life who are in a committed relationship with a male, now finding themselves having to put up with his abusive behaviour, a far less-than-ideal position in life to be in.

The psychological difference between a non-committed and committed relationship in a marriage, is that once committed the male now holds the certificate of marriage, his now prized possession. He believes his home is his castle, therefore what happens in the home stays in the home.

Is it about mentality?

That's how the male's mentality with abusive tendencies works, believing it's his business and his alone, and therefore he can't be challenged. A different mindset to the one he had before, when in a non-committal relationship, when he knew he had to tread carefully being aware she could so easily walk out the door. Again, that's the mindset of the conniving male, one who believes he is well ahead of the game to that of his partner- when planning the type of long-term relationship he wants.

Not unlike many marriages, the woman had never given it much thought, nor had she been inclined to examine the details closely. Without that

Introduction

mindset from the outset, she lacked the skills and awareness needed to understand what she was potentially getting into.

Throughout these chapters try opening your mind and looking further into what we as human beings were all born with, something that makes us all so unique, yet for many they seldom think about it- their fortitude. When called upon it provides all the tools, we need to handle ourselves in almost every situation. As a result, it provides human beings with a much better outcome, had they not reached out and taken complete advantage of, as intended.

Human fortitude, that inner strength is available to us all, at will, through our natural cognitive ability, of which there are many natural faculties. Now, before you think you're about to be given a lesson on neurophysiology, you're not. It is, however, a salutary reminder of what you were born with. More importantly, it awakens you to the defenses you have at your disposal, in challenging many adversities, including abuse.

While your conscience discerns what is right and wrong, it is your fortitude that transforms thought into action—enabling you to embrace learning, adapt to change, and grow through challenge. This inner strength enhances problem-solving and decision-making and empowering individuals to navigate complex situations with clarity and resilience- *Will you rise to the challenge?*

Domestic abuse can be a debilitating depressant, showing little signs to the outside world. It's a devastating situation that holds women to ransom, through time itself. Again, these women must be reminded they only need to bring to the surface those tools provided by their fortitude that secures their defenses, giving them guidance. By engaging and exercising those tools in their entirety, you forge your own pathway as life intended. Doing so allows you to customise your own unique character and personality, your own lifestyle, complementing the justification of being a civilised human being.

– Come along on this journey and trust that it will change your perception of what life can offer and discover what you are capable of –

When suffering domestic abuse, you miss out on the many things that life has to offer, and you're less likely to experience natural moments of showing empathy and humility. Don't allow this hideous depressing style of existence stand in your way of maintaining a sustainable level of happiness and wellbeing.

Integrity - the ground beneath your feet

Using and leveraging our fortitude encompasses the moral ground we walk on, that every woman in abusive relationships should stand firm on. Humans have unrivalled intelligence, being a formidable force. Unfortunately, many people cannot appreciate what they were given to fend off evil. In times of difficulty people choose to have no resolve and easily roll over, when they could have otherwise made such a profound difference in their lives.

Human emotions are both powerful and highly sensitive, which makes them difficult to control. They are among life's most unpredictable forces — capable of giving us joy one moment and grief or sadness the next.

These tools -we will refer to- are freely provided by our fortitude which are interchangeable with one another, again allowing you to accomplish just about anything you desire, including ending domestic abuse. This will occur naturally when you're conscientiously calling on them, making proper assessments of your circumstances then putting them to good use. But when you're not in control of your emotions, you're more likely to remain complacent, almost like being in cruise control, operating and functioning by instinct. As a result, you may not reach your true potential, failing to achieve your goals.

It will also pay to remember that every ounce of work you put in now, regardless of how exhausting you may think it to be, may just be your greatest achievement, whether you're in a relationship or not. The day will come when you reflect upon all that time and effort you put in, as being almost inconsequential, compared to the work you would have been required to carry out, had you lived a lifetime of abuse. With the resulting mental health issues, sadness, loneliness, along with regret, it is not a

Introduction

pleasant thought is it. However, for many women it's an all-too-common outcome.

As you turn the pages and acknowledge that it's finally making sense, you may well become a little overwhelmed and realise that this is the journey you need to be on. Therefore, you deserve a different type of partner, one that will never abuse you, a partnership that's empowering and for all the right reasons - your diary.

With all the positives associated with keeping a diary, there is but one area that can provide you with the answers you will look for. That being, on reflection, when reading over previously written events then suddenly and inexplicitly find the answer you have been looking for. It's during this time when it just suddenly becomes clear, showing you the way forward, and realising the direction you need to take. – A truly enduring moment.

– You will no longer be in any doubt as to what you must do, as your natural thought process will trigger your fortitude into providing you with confidence, courage and determination. –

The fallout or aftermath of domestic abuse can be far-reaching, resulting in an enormous number of resources, involving the police, ambulance, hospitals, doctors, specialists, psychologists, physiatrists, solicitors, councillors, courts, probation officers, family services and rehabilitation, and sometimes sadly the coroner. Whilst there may be consequences involving some criminal charges against the male the sad reality for many women is, there remains a gross injustice. Many women feel trapped having nowhere to go other than charity shelters, or a home belonging to friends and family. However, the authorities may provide you will temporary accommodation- if you're lucky.

In many households, abuse persists unchecked because it is seldom confronted. This is deeply troubling, as perpetrators often evade accountability until it's too late—usually with a report that another female has lost her life.

Therefore, the abusive male's mentality will remain the same, whilst women choose to remain quiet, obedient and loyal. Many factors cause this behaviour and although deeply concerning, it stems directly from many inadequacies in a woman's self-esteem. This is due largely to the level of man's dominance that produces fear, branching out creating a whole range of psychological impacts, including intimidation, control, coercion, and financial deprivation. Not limited to.

For many women, this leads to that terrible feeling of worthlessness, self-loathing, hopelessness and guilt, which leads many to just want to give up.

Should that be the case, the time has arrived to discover the many avenues that are available to you. Although this is achievable, we must also acknowledge the need to make compromises and be flexible. Humans are creatures of habit and don't take to change easily. Again, they are often reluctant to take on board any suggestions and recommendations, even when they are constructive, well balanced or well intentioned.

Is your diary close at hand?

Comforting yourself is the name of the game, and there is no better way than to confide in your diary. Even if you think it will be of no use, it will prove to have been the best decision you ever made. Start by highlighting this paragraph and continue to do so throughout this book anything that resonates with you, because it offers the inspiration you inadvertently look for.

Again, this is an excellent way to start, so it is best not to look at making entries into your diary as a chore, instead have some fun documenting your memoirs as your personal salvation. Consider your entries as your new lease on life, because it offers something very special, a secret place to express your most inner secrets. As mentioned, when you re-visit your diary and read on reflection, you implicitly find that elusive answer you weren't aware of. Therefore, it's so important for you to believe that only positives can come out of becoming proactive, but only whilst remaining a believer.

By reading through the chapters within this book, you will also find topics, and scenarios that you will relate to. Again, try to remain open-minded, as naturally there will be some digression, subjectiveness, and of course repetitiveness to both emphasize and make the same point, yet in different scenarios. Again, the context is in layman's terms to help with any barriers, whether related to learning difficulties, age, or cultural background.

—Everything you mention in your diary will assist you, particularly when decisions need to be made, perhaps even by the authorities, because without it, it's your word against the world. —

So, take some time now to focus on what's important, by sparing a thought for those millions of women somewhere throughout the world who are never likely to be given any learning skills. Instead, they will continue to believe they must continue with their current circumstances.

If you are experiencing abuse, you can choose to either remain in your current situation or use the advice in this book to resolve your issues and even reinvent yourself. The opportunity is here; the choice is yours.

Stop procrastinating and start doing

There are many women who have fallen into the category of wanting to 'end domestic abuse', having had many years of experience living with it. Who now, with the benefit of hindsight, wish they had received the help and advice we are now discussing.

When you read through the passages within this self-help book you may well experience a lightbulb moment. However, that moment may not necessarily come entirely from the pages within this book, instead of a combination of something that's been waiting to surface.

SUMMARY

- Try to have a positive outlook and remain open-minded when reading the following chapters, as this is an opportunity for genuine discovery and positive change.
- Remember the importance of being honest with yourself, which will assist your mental health and your overall well-being, when moving forward.

- If you're new to finding a relationship, also have fun with this book, but take note of the sections that influence you, then make your own decisions.
- Highlight areas within this book that you resonate with and write down what you were thinking about at that very time in your diary. Be sure to set goals in your diary by forwarding reminders to get things done and be sure to follow through. You don't want your diary just to be a memoir and end up in a bottom draw somewhere, you want it to talk to you, a driving force in reaching your goals.
- Every type of reference you make in your diary can and will play a major role, either as reassurance through reflection, action, decision and choice making, or as evidence.
- Believe in your fortitude. You possess inner strength and untapped potential waiting to be unleashed.
- Start by finding the desire to refresh your self-esteem and self-respect, allowing them both to build on your new foundation.
- Don't allow yourself to be consumed by your circumstances because of your relationship.
- Start to re-invent yourself and become pro-active.
- Defeat any negativity in overcoming any personal indiscretions by using your new tools to make any necessary positive changes.
- Remind yourself of your goal and settle for nothing less than long-term happiness, and remember, we all have dirty laundry that can be cleaned and aired.
- Share your thoughts only with a trusted confidante, such as a family member, friend, or professional, to ensure confidentiality.

Introduction

- Remember – loose lips sink ships; therefore, your diary is your one and only true confidante—as long as it's well-hidden.

DATING

As we begin the first chapter on dating, some may say, "What does dating have to do with domestic abuse?" While the link may seem of little relevance at first, we must recognise the vulnerability of all females—even in the early stages of a relationship - dating. Thus, the potential power dynamics and risks that arise during dating are not unlike those encountered in established relationships. Therefore, should you be looking for a date you may like to consider the following…

Stepping out

Dating, as we know it, is one of the oldest traditions in the world and for good reasons. It's a time to have fun, and who knows you might discover and fall in love with a potential lifetime partner.

It's also an opportunity to scrutinise others in a close and intimate way, if you choose. It's during this period when humans naturally explore and express themselves, to even show off a little, inadvertently seeking out that all important connection between two people.

Dating

For humans, it's the ultimate experience, the inexplicable chemistry between a man and a woman which serves as the foundation for discovering and defining both love and compatibility.

Unless you're in a group, your first date is ideally best suited being in public view, so never compromise your personal safety by going to a secluded location. You probably know very little about this person, so it's best to make some enquiries about your date beforehand, if you can. Ask around for people who know him or maybe have heard about him.

Always notify a family member or close friend of your location, your plans, your date's identity, and your expected arrival time home.

– Safety must always be your number one priority –

As tempting as it might be to change your arrangements, failing to let someone know is a big mistake. This could be his opportunity to groom you through charm, alcohol, and drugs, sometimes with tragic consequences.

Ques: "Isn't that being a little overcautious?"

Ans: "Perhaps, but it's a good learning curve you will come to appreciate."

Always remain mindful of that adage – 'When fools rush in'…. As a young female, you are perhaps not always aware of what's happening to you both mentally and physically.

Little red flags!

Assuming you become somewhat attracted and impressed by your date you may feel you would like to see him again; therefore, there's no time like the present to have some subtle questions, at the ready.

– Expressing your principles, values, beliefs and aspirations, puts your friends and indeed your date on notice that you're a woman of substance. –

Unless you discover what lies beneath that charming exterior, in a timely manner, you're aligning yourself with a potential long-term disappointment, as many females later discover. Ending a relationship isn't as easy as you might think, therefore reiterating the absolute necessity of discovering as much as you can about this person before making any type of commitment. While your date appears to be a decent human being, it may be that he has little in common with you.

—The types of red flags you need to identify early with, as there are individuals who may project one character and personality while their true self is altogether very different. -

However, it's just a date and whilst you may well be looking for a relationship, never feel obliged to see him again. If you feel a little bad about it, that's fine, it's driven by emotion. Under these circumstances it's unwise to cater to someone's feelings and to be too accommodating as it may prove to be counterproductive.

Ques: "I've been dating for a while and haven't had much luck meeting anyone that I want to go out with long-term. Now I'm asking myself what I'm doing wrong?"

Ans: "Probably nothing, it can take considerable time to meet that someone special. So, remain patient with the mindset that it will happen, but only when fate plays its hand. If you're out socialising perhaps pay more attention to the type of venues you visit and never drop your guard by accepting a lift home from a stranger."

A common scenario – despite the red flags you continued to have more dates with the very person you told yourself you didn't want to see again. As a result, the two of you eventually became intimate, then falling pregnant, having now become married and raising children.

The memory of that time you didn't want to see him again continues to haunt you, a constant reminder of the mistake you made. You now feel trapped in a marriage, living within a cycle of domestic abuse - having manifested from the time you showed no love or admiration for him, a situation he remains all too aware of.

– Was that a result of a young woman unnecessarily pressuring herself at such a young age to find a husband and to have children. Or was it the result of her inability to control her sexual appetite and her emotions, instead of remaining patient and true to herself? –

Reasoning

Failure to act on sound reasoning affects many young women, so isn't it better to understand the circumstances you might find yourself in and give yourself a head start in looking closely at relationship boundaries to begin with.

It's a significant moment in a young female's life, when she feels she must question herself over whether she wants to see him again or not. If you're not sure, then the safest thing to do is to give yourself time, since you have plenty of it and allow things to evolve naturally.

Ques: "I stopped dating, not for all time, but to try something different, asking myself if I'm on the right track?"

Ans: "By doing so you are giving yourself more time to form meaningful friendships, without the burden of feeling you should follow the status quo like so many people do. This phase of your life provides more opportunities with less anxiety, so why not allow your destiny to happen naturally, making discoveries when you least expect it."

Dating to find a partner should be about spreading yourself around, exploring, discovering and remaining open-minded, without restraints, or timelines. However, here lies the dilemma for too many young females, again being the lack of patience, emotional control and maturity. With very little understanding of both what they are potentially getting themselves into, and indeed the man inside the man.

When you discover the staggering rate of divorces throughout the world, what you come to realise is the number of relatively brief marriages. It therefore raises the question as to why so many couples would want to get married so soon.

Am I falling in love?

But what about love, that all important feeling of being emotionally charged, that intense attraction, the undeniable and inexplicable chemistry.

The longing for someone special to be a part of your life, the only one you would ever want to hold your affection for, in passionate meaningful intimacy.

Is this what you truly feel? Do you have the same desires and share the same principles and values as one another? How about being in tune with one another without having to try, making simultaneous remarks, laughing at the same jokes, that unique gift that could never be quite the same or ever replicated with another.

– Think you're in love? How much of the above do you honestly relate to? –

> **Awareness**- Whilst dating can be a lot of fun, it has the tendency to take on a journey of its own, unless you maintain discipline and willpower, remaining steadfast to those all-important principles and values. Otherwise, you could become just another statistic or worse - casualty, making the most common mistake of all, *getting married to the wrong person, at the wrong time.*

Ques: "But I'm not really thinking about getting married, am I?"

Ans: "Maybe not, but nor were all the previous and countless other young women just like you, who were initially only looking for a date, who have now found themselves in an abusive marriage."

So, your first date has you a little curious and you decide you want to see him again, so how far will you go by giving out your personal details? By far, the safest course of action is to ask him for his phone number and not give your phone number out. This allows you to take control from the outset, giving yourself the time to decide whether to see him again, without any recourse.

Expression

Now that you have organised a second date with this same male, you feel more relaxed this time round, whereby you might open up a little more, and express yourself. You become more confident when making conversation, talking about your interests, your goals, likes and dislikes, and more importantly your principles and values. Expressing your dreams and aspirations for the future provides your date with the understanding from the get-go that you are ambitious and not someone who hasn't thought about where they intend to go in life.

By conducting yourself this way early in the piece will produce interesting results, since your date now realises, you're a young woman with ideas and convictions. This narrows the gap - and indeed the field - between being a woman of substance, and a woman that exposes her vulnerabilities. The latter can give the male the perception his date can be easily controlled and manipulated.

As a result, many of these women simply get married, not understanding why, only to live a sub-standard life, filled with insecurities and intimidation, being unhappy and abused. All because they never thought about what they themselves stood for and failing to make it very clear from the beginning who they were, and again what their dreams and aspirations are.

Perhaps you're someone who has not thought about their future in any detail, and that's perfectly ok, however by establishing what you stand for early in life it will set you apart.

Ques: "I'm only young, so do I really need to think about what I want in life when dating?"

Ans: "There's no time limit, being young doesn't mean you have to decide what you want in life and dating doesn't have to lead to a relationship or marriage. However, just be mindful of what you want, should you be looking for a relationship."

Self-analysis

Although a date is just a date, it's a golden opportunity for women of all ages to discover more about themselves at the very same time.

We can assume, that for whatever reason there are women who accept their partners for who they are, what they stand for, and tragically in many cases, for who and what they become. As a result, these women see no wrong, then find themselves having to live a life with the cards they dealt themselves.

— If you are living with a carefree attitude, you are in a unique position to reflect on your current life and compare it with how you may feel after reading this book. You might decide to shift your current beliefs and ideas about relationships, adopting a different perspective and taking a more serious approach. This could involve questioning how you see yourself, coming to terms with who you are now, and envisioning the person you perhaps would like to be. Such is the complexity of human nature when emotions intertwine with the naivety of what could be perceived as life's trappings. —

Ques: "I've realised that I'm susceptible to being easily led and have been more a follower when I'm out with my friends, usually just going along with what they do. Maybe this is a good time for me to take charge of my own life?"

Ans: "An excellent decision, whether it's peer pressure, shyness, or if you are somewhat introverted. True fulfillment comes from having a balance of overseeing your own destiny with life's uncertainties, with everything else coming second. If that means embarking on a relationship then all the better, as you're now on track to handle anything life throws at you, having put yourself first."

Let's assume your interest in your current date gathers momentum, with your mindset telling you that a more formal relationship is your calling. So now is a good time to raise your awareness antenna on all fronts, remembering what we discussed earlier, that is, ensuring your reasoning, emotions and patience are kept well under control.

Is he right for me?

Let's remind ourselves of what we are discussing here, and that is, 'preventing domestic abuse', being your number one goal. Nothing compares to doing your research, no matter how long it takes, in finding out if he is right for you.

If you are considering future dates with this man, it is essential that during your conversations, you make observations gathering as much insight as possible to identify any behavioral patterns you both like and dislike. These patterns should influence your decisions and help you decide whether to continue your discreet observations, in potentially uncovering more.

Making notes in your diary is extremely important, referencing what you see in him, from both good and bad. This again will provide times of reflection going over past thoughts to your present ones. This process helps you make more informed decisions, often uncovering truths that are otherwise difficult to find.

Therefore, never underestimate the importance of the amount of care and patience needed when building a relationship. Again, take the time to ensure genuine compatibility exists long before committing to a potential lifetime of marriage. Overlooking early warning signs during this crucial discovery phase can lead to significant future challenges later. However, this period also offers a valuable opportunity to learn, grow, and evaluate whether the partnership is the right fit for you. If the signs suggest otherwise, it's much easier to part ways amicably than to face potential difficulties or worse in a committed relationship later in life.

When dating, you are in a prime position. There's no pressure, as you are playing the field with no obligation for any attachment. You're now feeling more upbeat and alive with more confidence, all because you have now shown your date that you're a woman going places. This is when a woman is at her best, knowing she has the self-confidence along with her self-esteem, without having to feel the need to throw herself at anyone too early, but rather show restraint and play a little hard to get.

For many young males when out looking for a female the initial excitement is the hunt and ultimately the overall conquest being their number one goal and not necessarily interested in anything afterwards. That is why for every fired-up testosterone fueled male, you need to ensure if it's right for you and not just become another statistic. Sexual pleasures can turn to sexual abuse and unplanned pregnancy, turning your future goals on their head.

Since you have now expressed your views on life, it's fair to assume at this stage—since he hasn't run off—he wants to continue seeing you. This provides a bigger opportunity to find out more about this person and the direction this relationship could take. Being a young woman, you may very well be setting your future sights on a marriage and raising a family, and if you follow that path, you will be embarking on one of the most recognised institutions on earth.

Although that above paragraph hits on that warm fuzzy feeling of thinking about marriage, raising a family, and living happily ever after. It should also act as a reminder of how all-too-often life can go so terribly wrong.

> **Awareness** - It's understandable that many young women don't either comprehend or contemplate their future, as life for them is all about fun and enjoyment. However, the previous paragraphs are important, and although there's no need to dwell on them, consider taking it as seriously as you can, by following some simple processes and procedures early on.

It's fair to assume that what you see on the surface is what you get: his looks, mannerisms, attire, hygiene, and, of course, his character and personality. The potential problems lie in what you can't see. This is where you need to take a different approach, again discovering the type of man, within the man.

Let's not forget and remind ourselves of the many women throughout the world who would say to this very day…

— If only I had received the skills and knowledge to make better-informed decisions and life choices, had I controlled my impatience and emotions, I wouldn't have rushed into marriage. If only I had thought more about the impact of getting it so wrong, and the effect it would have on myself and my children. Particularly since I now know, had my marriage been without domestic abuse my children would have had a very different upbringing, and I would be in a much safer place than where I am today. —

Think of dating as a mere steppingstone in providing the experience to one day make better-informed decisions along with all those other life choices, which should be every woman's consideration before entering into a long-term relationship.

Beyond the surface

CAUTION – Try to establish what his true intentions are.

- Does he show genuine physical affection towards you?
- Does he want a family?
- Does he like children and animals?
- Is he ambitious, adventurous, kind, giving, and intelligent?
- Does he show you love, compassion and empathy?
- Is he a man of moderation?
- And the big one—is he respectful towards you?

Showing you he possesses these above attributes should leave no doubt in your mind that you're having good first impressions of this person, even if it turns out to be simply a friendship. It's fair to say that humans can so easily fall victim to the – 'we see what we want to see', when we run our eyes over someone for the first time, which in many cases it turns out not to be in our best interests.

Because it's so much easier and so much more fulfilling in wanting to believe that something is good, rather than worrying about whether it's bad, then having to deal with it. This is a common mistake in human nature, whereby we can find ourselves in serious trouble, all because of our lack of due diligence.

However, some people take a more calculated and meritorious approach, by saying, "There's something about him I can't quite put my finger on". They may well be right in their assumption, as there will never be a better time in your life to be sceptical than when dating. By understanding the innate characteristics of someone, their inner qualities and what makes them tick, you can gain valuable insight, particularly if someone should become more than just a friend.

Ques: "What if I get it wrong about him?"

Ans: "There's always that chance in life, when in any doubt take a pause from your date. By doing so affords you time and patience to make a better-informed judgement, making comparisons to your beliefs and discovering what is really the truth."

By following these simple yet vitally important processes in discovering what you can about someone, may not provide all the immediate answers you were looking for, however it can establish both satisfactions, leaving some doubt in your mind. You can improve on this by continuing your process of discovery and ongoing scrutiny, identifying what it is you see in him and whether he has anything that aligns with your principles and values. So, let's not underestimate what we are discussing here even though you might say, but it's only a date'.

Or does he harbour underlying traits like being moody and getting angry easily, tends to raise his voice, is self-centered, controlling and impatient. These are just some of the areas you must pick up on and remain aware of as early as possible.

– Isn't it far better to seek out someone who shows the natural attributes you're looking for, as opposed to try and turn someone around to your preferred way of life? –

Refocused

Is he, or does he come across like someone with the 'bad boy image' with an attitude to match, portraying himself as smug and arrogant? Is he unintelligent and foul-mouthed? If so, ask yourself this: What's the attraction? And is he the type of person you want to be with, to one day possibly father your children?

Too many females, particularly the young ones, fall into the trap of thinking the bad boy image is somehow cool or fashionable, well it's not. It raises the bar to fast tracking towards a life with domestic abuse, unhappiness, and regret – a real hell on earth.

Ques: "I go out with a guy who admittedly acts that way, and looks rough around the edges, mixing with people I don't particularly like that much, but I know he is a good person inside. That's how I feel, is that so bad?"

Ans: "Sounds like you're asking yourself. When you're young it's understandable you can feel that way, again remembering your emotions and immaturity can lead you astray. So, ask yourself something meaningful, - if you were to fall in love with this person, how long would it take for you to adopt his type of attitude".

In the event you are dating someone with these traits, then look deeper at what the attraction really is and be honest with yourself. It may be based on your infatuation and nothing more.

Knowing when it's time to move on!

It's important to note that having male friends who don't align with your long-term expectations isn't inherently wrong. However, if you're a young woman actively looking for a partner, it's worth questioning yourself whether you should remain in certain social circles with people you can't aspire to. By maintaining anything beyond being a casual acquaintance with individuals you don't share your principles and values with, is unguarded temptation, in ways that could well hold you back, – forever.

-This delay can stall your natural progression toward flourishing amongst like-minded people, something you will do well to remember-.

Sociological warfare is everywhere. It operates in subtle ways, influencing attitudes and behaviour's without humans fully realizing what's happening around them. Again, think carefully about the people you surround yourself with. Ask yourself why you're drawn to certain individuals. Is it because you feel needy and crave attention and wanting acceptance? Are you simply being friendly, or do you find yourself liking someone without understanding why? Perhaps there's no clear reason at all. –Take control !

By simply letting go of your thoughts and feelings and writing them down in your diary can be incredibly rewarding and stimulating. Your diary acts as a confidante, your own personal sounding board for future reflection, a space to process emotions tied to situations that demand thoughtful consideration.

Ques: "Can my diary really help me?"

Ans: "More than you can imagine. It allows you to express yourself freely, without fear of persecution and opposition— your best friend who won't reveal your secrets. With consistent entries you can capture recent events, your likes and dislikes, providing a snapshot of your emotional landscape. Better still, your diary becomes a tool to bolster your self-esteem and help you grow into the person you want to be. By revisiting past entries, you may uncover answers or discover patterns of behaviours that had previously gone unnoticed, forgotten, or just had you puzzled."

Being friendly is a wonderful attribute, but it's wise to hold something in reserve. Knowing when to move forward or step away is crucial. Remember, control and intimidation aren't confined to relationships; they can appear in many forms throughout your life. Recognizing these dynamics is essential not only to preserving your sense of self, but also in building the kind of meaningful, respectful relationships you truly deserve.

Casual sex

Another significantly bad choice is for young women to allow themselves to accept sexual advances on the first date. Because by doing so potentially lowers the respect that these women need to be shown from the outset. Particularly if that male becomes their future partner. If it's unguarded pleasure, then it potentially becomes problematic that can cause a different set of consequences altogether usually with deep regret. See chapter on 'Single Mums'.

Ques: "Then why does it appear that everyone I know seems to sleep around?"

Ans: "Base your mindset on what you feel comfortable with, by allowing your conscience to determine when is right and when it's wrong and never allow coercion or peer pressure to influence your decisions."

Isn't it far better for a woman to show a male she's not easy and that he needs to earn his place alongside you. Because by making your date wait a little longer, demonstrates to him you are no walk over. Doing so puts you into that all important category from the outset, of being shown the lasting respect you deserve. There's no suggestion here that you should wait until marriage to have sex, far from it. However, when that time comes, it should come with your consensual agreement and timing.

Standing your ground and denying any early sexual advances will cause some contenders to walk away, in which case you have wisely narrowed the field. In contrast to the one who has been understanding and patient, it is he who has shown you early respect.

Many females who take the risk of falling pregnant whilst still young and single should realise their life would no longer be theirs to do as they please, certainly not in the short term. Consequently, you will then have the type of responsibilities of motherhood that would have otherwise been in the future. A time when you would have become more worldly, and more mature, possibly with a good man at your side.

That's not to say the father of the child isn't a good person, but is he right for you? Where's your security? Where will you live? Will he be there for you when you give birth? For any young woman who hasn't thought things through, this is the reality. These young mothers then burden their own mothers with the responsibility of becoming more than just grandmothers.

- A topic we will further discuss during a later chapter on 'Single Mothers' -

Again, as difficult as it is for some young people to grasp, if the attraction both physical and mentally isn't there after a few starts then chances of a compatible long-term relationship aren't there either. Best to part ways, sooner than later.

True Colours

Ending any prior involvement with a male requires serious consideration, particularly if you know he wants to see you. However, that's not always as easy as first thought, when a woman has given out her personal details. Therefore, as mentioned, never give out any personal information until you feel completely comfortable, which can only be accomplished through time itself.

Because in this scenario he feels somewhat jilted, and resorts into leaving abusive messages, thereby showing his true colours. In your response you have messaged him asking him not to do so. If he continues sending text messages, trolling, phoning, calling round to your residence unannounced then he is stalking you.

– Do you wish you had kept your personal details to yourself? –

The consequences can be dire, as it's only now that you understand the potential danger you find yourself in, since you now feel all alone, scared, and feeling completely helpless.

Ques: "I went through this hell for a long time, ending up moving and starting over. At the beginning I was told by the police the matter had been dealt with, but he came around to where I lived and showed up when I went out. My life became unbearable all because I made the mistake of giving out my details, now I feel a little paranoid when I meet a male for the first time, is that normal?"

Ans: "Your safety is more important than anything else, and although moving was probably an inconvenience, you felt it was in your best interest. Your story also highlights how life can go from high to low in an instant, and the importance of having made difficult decisions. On the bright side it appears you're now safe, unlike the many victims, who paid the ultimate price. And no you're not being paranoid, only cautious."

If you are experiencing this type of abuse, make no further replies to the perpetrator, instead either block his number, or consider receiving his text without replying and downloading the contents so you have an account of his behaviour. Contact your parents or friends and head home straight away, or ring the police, as you don't know what his intentions are.

Your personal protection

Remain in a safe environment and explain to your parents or close friends what is happening and don't allow anyone to tell you that you're overreacting. There are too many people in this world today who live with the daily reminder of losing a loved one, having shown poor judgement by doing very little in a similar situation, which continues to weigh heavily on their minds

Your parents should then go to the police station with you to make a formal complaint and provide a written statement, asking the police to issue the perpetrator with e.g. a 'banning notice', or a 'cease and desist order', both legal documents ordering the perpetrator not to make any further contact with you. Keep all duplicated copies for yourself safely stored away, providing you with some satisfaction in knowing you have a record of events for future reference, being so important.

Ques: "Do I really need to take this matter to that extreme?"

Ans: "The value you place on your life will determine the emphasis you put on the meaning of something extreme."

In the event the situation worsens, seek professional advice, however, it's best to understand that at this point you only have pieces of paper, along with having explained your predicament to the authorities and nothing more. So never become complacent, - he is still out there.

The biggest problem we have in our society today when we discuss domestic abuse is the number of people who don't take these types of matters as seriously as the perpetrator does. It was earlier mentioned that we only hear about domestic abuse after the fact, so ask yourself, are you prepared to wait that long? No, of course you're not.

A cynical view perhaps, but one with merit since the perpetrator likely believes that he will receive some type of leniency if in fact the case ever goes to court? There's a good reason for why he thinks this way, since in many countries the justice system has turned a full circle to that of when the punishment was an accurate reflection of the crime.

Unlike in the past, today's trivial sentencing emboldens perpetrators, making the risk seem worth committing the crime. It's a grim truth, but one we must acknowledge and confront—because for too many women, by the time action is taken, it's already too late.

Do the authorities really look after me?

Hopefully, the scenarios we are about to discuss will not affect you directly. However, such challenges will persist unless women take proactive steps to safeguard themselves — by fostering strong support networks, seeking help from trusted individuals or organizations, and adopting personal safety measures. These efforts must go hand in hand with systemic action to hold perpetrators accountable.

Consider how this continuing scenario might unfold: the police respond to a report of domestic abuse, only to discover you are tragically deceased at the hands of the very individual they recently issued a warning to. Crimes against women persist because perpetrators disregard the law and evade meaningful accountability and consequences—a pattern of behaviour entrenched throughout modern society.

Ques: "If the authorities can't protect me, who can?"

Ans: "You can, just as a mother has a maternal instinct towards protecting her young family, you need to take measures to prevent yourself from coming to any harm. Think ahead, and do not wait until after the fact, whereby you will only receive token assistance. This is the hard reality of being involved in relationships whether you believed you were a willing participant or not."

Returning to our scenario— Again, no one at this stage is aware of his intentions other than the threats he has already made to this young woman, which may be a one off, then again it may not. The perpetrator may only prove to be a public nuisance; however, there's also a possibility he is premeditating something far more sinister.

In which case, it could become a very troubling matter, and although he may have stopped making contact, this person could be anywhere. Therefore, remain mindful not to become complacent and to always be in the company of someone else and for some time to come, especially at night. This may take some time to resolve even if the police explain to you, he has given his word not to make any further contact, so just remember to remain vigilant, because talk is cheap.

This type of situation is quite unnerving for anyone, particularly for a young woman who may now be in constant fear and feeling totally vulnerable. In direct contrast to the perpetrator who now enjoys his freedom, walks the streets free as a bird. Having convinced the authorities, he won't do it again.

– Unfortunately, this is an all too familiar pattern –

The longer a male remains angry and disgruntled his resentment grows, feeling betrayed particularly in the mind of the younger immature male. It's here where early education would have been so beneficial for this individual's well-being and future development. Sparing this young woman and possibly others from a traumatic experience.

Fortunately, in this case, the perpetrator relented; however, it may have just as easily ended with this young woman losing her life. Therefore, this should also act as a reminder for every woman that abuse has no boundaries, and not just in the marital home. It's the world we live in, the type of circumstances every woman could find themselves in.

Recognising the signs

It was merely a date between two initially consenting individuals that revealed the darker side of human nature, severely impacting one unfortunate person.

Therefore, further imagine how it is for the many women who never understood the early signs, who now believe they have no choice but to remain in their marriage. In all likelihood these women had the chance but never walked away when they should have. Having now experienced a further escalation in the abuse, feeling trapped, remaining unhappy, and further isolated.

Awareness – The above is more than a scenario; it's a life choice. It re-enforces the earlier advice — to make a conscious decision, discovering whether a male is of good moral character or not. Otherwise, you might find someone controlling you without your understanding, living a life like the one just described. Understand that the human body has a defensive mechanism, instinctive to alerting you to say - 'something's not quite right' so never ignore it.

Preventing and Ending Domestic Abuse

Ques: "How will I ever know if the signs are genuine or not?"

Ans: "Possibly never to its fullest extent, but you can shorten the odds by following the steps of discovery, as recommended throughout this book. First acknowledge you're receiving an alert, then act on what you are feeling at the time, it's intuitive. Your instincts often guide you more reliably than you might expect."

There are many types of abuse that human beings can fall victim to with the above scenario showing aggressive and abusive behaviour being no exception. Therefore, don't forget to control your emotions, become more aware of what is going on around you, and become less naive and gullible.

If you are now in a relationship having dated for some time, don't make the mistake of thinking you need to get married, instead continue going through the stages of discovery, embracing a period of courtship and engagement. After all, what's the rush? Better to try and get it right the first time when in a non-committal relationship, than to look back when trapped in a committed one.

SUMMARY

- Dating is all about having fun, discovering yourself and the opposite sex.
- Become familiar with sociological behaviour and never allow your principles and values to be compromised.
- With a first date, your safety could be in question, either remain in a crowd or stay in public view.
- Never give out your phone number and address on your first date. Leave details with family or friends to your whereabouts and expected time home. Make further contact when arriving home.

- When seeking a relationship, try to find his values and priorities that align with your future goals. Use your intuition and look for any indiscretions.
- Does he show any signs of being apathetic, or perhaps disingenuous, first impressions are important?
- Take your time, why be in a rush, instead discover the enjoyment and romance of dating without commitment, and remember, let him chase you.
- Hold on to your self-respect, integrity, and never give into any sexual advances until you are ready.
- You won't regret making your diary your 'newest best friend'. It will surprise you just how influential it is- in times of reflection.

ON-LINE DATING

(Sub-heading)

For better or worse, technology has given us the means and opportunity to meet people without the need for a formal introduction. Although this process is easy and convenient, there's no indication that it contributes to any more successful relationships to that of the more traditional dating methods.

Am I entering the artificial world?

This process, being a form of streamlined presentation, providing personal details for compatibility checks is questionably dangerous. Along with the costs involved when subscribing to dating agencies, if in fact they exist at all, and for the potential leak of your personal data.

It's also a known fact that whilst there are many people who are genuinely looking for a partner and conducting themselves ethically with integrity, there will always be those people who are insincere, having become cunning and conniving fraudsters, only in it, to get what they can out of it.

Ques: "So how should I start to protect myself?"

Ans: "You can cut to the chase by asking him for a police history report."

— That may seem somewhat heavy handed and intrusive, but let's be frank, you probably know nothing about this person, their past, or their behaviour. Should you be dealing with - let's say a confidence trickster, chances are you will immediately eradicate those who would like to be, from those that could be. —

As mentioned, it's the sheer simplicity and convenience of on-line dating—and to a degree laziness—that makes it so appealing. For all the right and wrong reasons, it continues to attract every imaginable type of person, from decent and genuine, to the undesirable. Therefore, many of whom feel comfortable hiding behind technology, because of its secretive appeal. By doing so it provides a convenient cover of anonymity shrouded in covert comfort that gives way to premeditated, brazen, fraudulent and cowardly behaviour.

Women of all ages remain vulnerable in these situations, often because of their genuine sincerity failing to recognize any impropriety. Under these circumstances, along with other challenging characteristics, immaturity, naivety, excitement, desire and possibly being a little nervous. But let's not forget the big one, our emotions, the one area that humans have trouble controlling especially when looking for love, becoming somewhat overwhelmed by the entire experience.

Is it better to be a little old-fashioned?

The undeniable fact remains that having been introduced by family or friends, or indeed an impromptu chance meeting, is by far the most natural, exciting and dignified way of meeting a stranger. It hasn't been the traditional method or as mentioned, old – fashioned, since the beginning of time without good reason, being more civilised and certainly more romantic. As it is more rewarding, allowing you to exercise your senses as life was intended.

– *That fleeting, peripheral awareness of an unfamiliar sighting—an implicit attraction that just occurred—serves as a dormant trigger, left to its own devices until mysteriously called upon, igniting an emotional awakening.* –

That unexplainable connection like no other, since the male on this occasion received the same type of telepathy, whereby you both instinctively glance and walk toward one another. Having never set eyes on one another previously, a truly unique moment, now seeing eye to eye in the flesh, whereby any pretense falls to the wayside. Could there ever be a more refreshing, exciting and rewarding example for a man and a woman to meet unscripted. That all too clear realism, those features, that scent, that attire, and that sexual desire, far exceeding the realms of any pre-arranged, curated digital on-line appearance, or indeed performance.

Not forgetting the prospects of an exciting future rendezvous that could never be digitally replicated, it's when worlds collide for all the right reasons. Unlike that digital process that so many humans now follow, having an air of artificial uneasiness about it, along with the unpleasantness and slightly intimidating process of looking at a screen or reading a text.

Online dating offers certain advantages for many women, such as the ease of meeting someone without socially awkward encounters, however it does allow deception to be easily concealed.

It's the convenience, comfort and security of perhaps being in your own home and feeling more relaxed during conversation, that you might otherwise find more difficult when face to face, adding to the appeal of being online.

Ques: "I'm only young, but I find dating sites easy and convenient. Is there anything wrong with that?"

Ans: "Not at all. Online dating provides great diversity and accessibility, making it easier to connect with potential partners. Again, we are still discussing preventing domestic abuse; therefore, whilst you may have good intentions, there is always someone, somewhere, just waiting for an opportunity to come along, whose motives are anything other than wanting a genuine relationship."

Being honest and up front in this delicate of situations has enormous advantages when gauging a potential partner. Since again, it's far better to ask some relevant perhaps pertinent questions that align with your beliefs, than to just make small talk and pretend to be some long-lost friend.

Adopting a bold approach will help to reduce the number of males who may feel somewhat intimidated by you, who fail to meet your standards, and instead end the conversation. In direct contrast to those males who remained confident while connected on-line and therefore handled your straightforwardness.

Isn't that what it's all about, narrowing the field to give yourself the very best possible opportunity to find the type of man you're looking for? This way you can learn to sidestep those males that failed to show that all important first impression, while maintaining control of your emotions.

Just bring it on.

Then there are those women who just aren't all that interested in scrutinising a potential date at any length whilst on-line. Instead, preferring to just bring it on—as they say, "they're not looking for a long-term relationship". However, that doesn't mean that your wellbeing is any less at risk.

While this online date is taking place—in the artificial world—the male person on the screen in front of you can continue to build on his assessment and evaluation of you. Doing so without giving away his real intentions, all due to the lack of sensory human perception that exists in virtual communication. As a consequent, he can conceal his style of demeanor that humans would otherwise become instinctively aware of during a normal, face-to-face encounter, – in the flesh.

Very possibly the type of male opportunist with conniving ulterior motives, again having no genuine interest in any long-term relationship. He's more likely interested in charming and coercing you into a sexual encounter, whereby you have no inkling of his real motives being both emotional and financial advantage.

Ques: "But surely everyone is aware of that?"

Ans: "Are they? at least let's hope so. But the facts speak for themselves, as even discerning women continue to be conned, scammed, abused, even killed, with the police having little to go on."

In the event you become a little overwhelmed and perhaps intimidated, and your intuition tells you, 'Hey, something's not right here." So best to pause, reflect before engaging, by either changing the narrative, or if need be, end the conversation and move on. Because you don't want to get carried away with this person by feeling you need to blurt out privileged and personal information, regretting it later, then finding yourself sleeping with the enemy.

Risky business

It's fair to say that while there are women who knowingly engage in risky behaviour when it comes to using on-line dating platforms, it will be the woman who carries that extra bit of caution with her when dealing with a stranger, that maintains a much higher level of wisdom and indeed safety.

It's understandable for a more mature woman to say, "It's just common sense when conducting yourself online", perhaps having had former experience. However, the facts are, there remains a prevalence of on-line grooming disguised as on-line dating. This is when it becomes far too easy for any young woman naively believing she will meet the person she thought she saw and spoke with during her on-line date encounter. But it wasn't to be, since the whole time she was unwittingly being groomed, coerced, then agreeing to meet with this stranger. No one ever saw or heard from her again.

— Don't think it doesn't happen, because it does —

Catfishing!

It's a known fact that physical attraction influences most people when they seek a date, but strangely enough they also attempt to seek out attraction while looking at a monitor on their digital devices. Such is the power and desire to find a companion that provides any perpetrator lying in wait with further credence into believing he can simply pretend, by appearing to be whoever he wants to be.

Once the pleasantries are over, particularly with first timers why not just get straight down to it, asking what he is looking for in a date? Whereby he may reply with "I'm only looking for a woman to go out socially with" or "I'm looking for a lifelong partner to settle down and start a family with", which all sounds rather noble, however, he may also be lying through his eye-teeth.

Make a man work for you—in the initial stages to begin with—which isn't asking too much, particularly since it's one of the most chivalrous of all gestures a man can do for a woman, particularly when looking for a potential partner. Of course, that may not always be as easy for some women as it is for others, simply because we need to remind ourselves of the untold stories out there. The high numbers of women who never mention the ordeal they went through. For many it's the embarrassment of failing to be as vigilant as they know they should have been when pursuing a date online to begin with.

This causes distress on several fronts, with the least being the female who ends the relationship almost immediately having met her date face to face putting two and two together, moving on, having learnt from her ordeal, while others weren't so lucky.

—Oddly enough many women find themselves in situations having no explanation or recollection of how it all came about in the first place, such is the power of human emotion-

By carrying out these self-styled safeguard initiatives early, they can and will save you valuable time, and possible heart ache, protecting you from potential future problems. Other than dropping your guard, becoming complacent or being forgetful, which is exactly what some on-line deviates rely on when playing the game. Again, using on-line dating for some is nothing more than a ruse for being deceitful to fulfill their fantasies and desires.

It's a sign of the times when the digital world went full steam ahead with little thought of both understanding and security, as do the many women who choose on-line dating. Jumping straight into the deep end, without the slightest thought or regard for their own security, safety and emotional well-being.

We should all treat on-line contact with extreme caution, along with the skepticism it deserves. These cowards remain hidden away behind their digital arsenal with an extra layer of confidence and abrasiveness, preying on emotionally charged females, of all ages.

Ques: "Don't dating agencies check the identity of the person chosen for this introduction?"

Ans: "To some extent, however, people can become whoever they want to be, particularly when conclusive checks and balances aren't in place."

This type of calculated individual can either strike hard and fast, then move onto his next victim, or he can methodically play the game with the same woman, over and over again. That way he can lie, cheat, steal, and have sex, all under the pretense of being the loving, decent person he is not—along with playing on your financial heart strings.

Domestic abuse isn't just verbal and physical violence, it comes in many forms and styles, all of which have one thing in common, resulting in severe emotional duress. As a result, many females suffer in silence, never reporting the abuse for reasons only they know—usually through lack of self-esteem.

— That doesn't mean you can't make confidential reports to the authorities —

Research first

Entrapment can go beyond the bounds of belief; because of the sheer callousness and depraved minds some human beings are in possession of.

A true story: In one such case a very beautiful and impressionable young woman connected to an animal welfare website who offered her a voluntary traineeship, by which she had naturally become excited about. Her parents were initially sceptical, yet after viewing the website they gave their daughter approval, allowing an apex sexual predator to take her life. The perpetrator and the website were fake, an incredible hoax. An elaborate and premeditated plan, to lure, trap and have his way sexually with this young woman before taking her life.

This drives home the point of the dangers that many females find themselves in, meeting with a stranger without having taken any appropriate precautions. Sadly, on this occasion it was a date with death, and all because this young woman who only wanted to help animals to explore and discover what life had to offer, sadly had no knowledge or the skills to protect herself.

Ques: "How do you find out if a website is bona-fide or not?"

Ans: "First, you establish doubt, then use the same technology as the website and expose the website details on social media asking for reviews, humans love to respond to on-line questions. If bad or no reviews, then stay well clear, remembering the adage – Curiosity killed the cat."

It would have only taken an astute and protective parent to be the guardian, as it should have been. Having carried out a little research, by making proper and thorough enquiries as to the validity of this animal welfare website. This would have raised alarm bells and exposed the perpetrator, preventing him from ever harming another person.

This young woman would have held the belief that since her parents had given their consent for her to become a trainee at an animal welfare center, that everything would be fine. Which proved to be quite the opposite and therefore should act as a stark reminder for all parents to become more involved by understanding the potential dangers associated with anything to do with the digital age in which we live.

— In most cases, perpetrators can carry out whatever they put their minds to; therefore, we all need to remain one step ahead. —

Such is the power of the human mind, not just capable of conjuring up wild and imaginative thoughts, but just as easily carrying them out, offering no suspicion, all due to…

— The overwhelming, emotional excitement human beings are prone to engage in. —

The desire to believe in what we see and read often clashes with the truth. Verifying the facts requires diligent research, double-checking, obtaining clarification.

— Have you ever come across someone in real life that you have seen on television or at movies, only to become surprised and perhaps a little shocked at how they look in the flesh? Well, it's potentially the same dilemma you face when you go from looking at a monitor screen when staring at your potential date, then meeting him for the first time, - Smoke and mirrors! —

As explained in the earlier passages on 'Chapter 1: Dating', a situation between two people can go from being seemingly perfectly amicable one minute, to threatening behaviour the next. Therefore, anyone contemplating using online dating agencies and apps is no exception. By understanding that the initial like-mindedness and all the fraternising that took place on a digital device, again could well have been nothing more than a staged performance.

Remember, you must have control measures in place to get a degree of protection, because no one, including the police, friends or family, can provide it for you, particularly when you need it the most.

— Again, would it be money well spent to have someone's background checked, especially if you later find that it was your best investment ever? —

Ques: "Without drawing his attention how can I find out about someone's potential criminal past?"

Ans: "As mentioned, ask the person outright or call the clerk of court's office and try applying for a criminal history report or background check on the individual. If you have any doubts, simply end any further interaction. However, having the confidence to question him in ways he doesn't suspect your motives, you can attempt to catch him out. During appropriate times ask him some questions, i.e "What type of hobbies do you like?" "What sort of work are you doing?" And "Have you travelled much?" Now you can ask him some further pertinent questions at a later stage, based on those previous answers he provided you with. During which time you might discover whether you are being played for a fool or not".

If you're inclined, then by all means use on-line dating and have some fun with it, however, do some research first and always remain sceptical. Learn how to maintain your anonymity until you feel you are ready to let a stranger possibly know too much about your personal details. This is one of the biggest problems with on-line dating, where people become too familiar with a stranger they know very little about.

There are people possibly just like you, who join dating agencies to get more than just one date. They want to be loved and spend the rest of their lives with that someone special. However, during this time, unfortunately allowing their emotions to spill over, so again, maintain that aura of playing a little hard to get. As mentioned earlier, make it clear you don't suffer fools. By doing so, you're contributing to preventing domestic abuse from ever entering your domain.

One day you may find yourself in a similar situation, whereby you now have the presence of mind to recall what you have read throughout this entire 'Chapter 1, on Dating'. Whereby, you now know how to risk assess before over extending – try before you buy.

SUMMARY

- When using on-line dating apps, consider the consequences when offering a stranger your private information.
- Keep your emotions in check. Remember, smooth talking hackers and scammers are prevalent.
- Always remain open minded, allowing your intuitive senses to guide you.
- Well-versed conversation carried out by a perpetrator can disguise his true intentions, leading you astray.
- Remain mindful of this person not being who he says he is, so ponder his questions and answers, and be ready to challenge him.
- Inquire about his hobbies, then research and test his memory and knowledge at a later date, studying his response.
- Hiding the truth and telling fibs are pre-requisites for the fake on-line perpetrator.
- Meeting someone in person offers a uniquely magical, undeniable experience; something digital interactions could never do.
- Continue reading chapters 1-3, on 'preventing domestic abuse' that falls into the non-committal bracket of relationships, before committing to a marriage.

PERPETRATOR

Why continue to portray yourself to be the genuine all-round good guy, when you know only too well, you're not? Consider reading the following passages whereby you may well connect with yourself and take a closer look at the off-path trajectory your mindset currently has you on.

Imagine the good you could do by using that imaginative mind of yours you currently use to lie and cheat your way through life and become someone who understands what life really has to offer. By remaining not only true to yourself but also to the person who could have possibly fallen in love with you, wanting to believe in you.

If you truly believe you get satisfaction from what you do, then you are short-changing yourself, since being deceitful is entering and remaining in the world of self-abuse. That's right, you're abusing yourself, therefore placing you in the unenviable position of being a coward, hiding behind technology, by portraying yourself as someone you are never likely to become.

– You may just as well dress up in the costume of your make-believe hero and live in fantasyland. –

Have you ever considered the personal satisfaction you could experience by dropping this childish bad boy image, regardless of your age, by allowing that special someone into your life. If she's the one, be prepared for that person to look after you and to love you, wanting to spend the rest of their life with you. —Is that not enough?

So, in comparison with what you currently have going for yourself, which appears to be very little, surely, it's not before time you come to realise you are missing out on a whole lot of what life has to offer. Denying yourself, self-respect, and again the love you would otherwise have found, if only you had remained true to yourself and your date.

This isn't the direction you really want to be heading in, you only think it is, because you have adopted the type of mindset many males like you have fallen into, with no logical explanation for it. The reason for this is because you are not in control, having never self-assessed yourself, identifying what you have become. By making simple easy adjustments you can become the man you're presently delusional about.

Dating

Therefore, just as easily as you went in the wrong direction to begin with, you can just as easily turn yourself around and head in the opposite direction. After all, it was only through making unplanned decisions to start with that has you in this ridiculous predicament you now find yourself in.

It's only then that you will truly discover what life really has to offer, unlike what you currently receive. It's utter madness, because the day will inevitably come when your conscience finally catches up and overwhelms you. Only then will you realise the only one you have been conning to such great effect is yourself, resulting in wasting your time and indeed your entire life. If that wasn't enough, remind yourself of the one you possibly allowed to get away.

Why not start now, and simply give it a go, and you will discover who you are really supposed to be? Instead of having these insecurities and this alter ego. You stand to gain more than you could ever imagine when you start treating yourself with respect, and regaining control of yourself.

When you do, you will end the emotional mental torture you presently inflict on innocent women, and yourself – which you know to be true.

It's entirely up to you!

COURTSHIP

Y ou have decided the time is right to move into the next phase of your relationship, having already had several months of dating one another.

These stages serve as the vital steppingstones on your path toward the possibility of marriage. The progression functions much like an apprenticeship—an intentional period of learning, development, and more important gaining insight into working relationships, and indeed into the man you are with.

By the time this process is complete, couples have usually come to know one another deeply enough—often without consciously realising it—to sense whether he is truly "the one." This kind of clarity rarely emerges on its own; it grows out of the deliberate, necessary preparation that gives a relationship its strongest chance of survival, over time.

Therefore, your single status is now in question and being challenged, since your heart maybe set on sharing the rest of your life with this man. There's a lot at stake, and although it's perfectly normal in the belief that as human beings, we have all the answers when we want them, the reality of life is we don't, so we learn as we go.

We have addressed what is necessary to discover about one another during these relatively early times, in terms of your man's characteristics, and of course, the physical and mental attributes of being attracted to one another. All this, and the feeling of compatibility and wanting to be with one another, allows you and your partner the comfort and mindset of wanting to move forward—but will it be enough?

Does he tick some, or all the boxes? Are you in love with him? Is he in love with you? Those questions are of no immediate urgency at this stage, as your non-committal relationship is still in its infancy. Meantime be content with continuing to live life, whilst remaining mindful to scrutinise both his behaviour, and that of your own.

Let's continue to analyse this courtship partnership, as there is no better way than to learn from each other through time itself, along with keeping a sharp eye on the direction your principles and values are travelling in.

Assessment

The best way to evaluate your progression and keep track is again to maintain your diary, constantly updating and reflecting on the direction your life is going in, and should be taking. Humans are like ants, busy, busy, and before you know it something that's relevant to your relationship can be overlooked, something worth noting. – Don't discard it.

By doing so, you continue to assess everything that's important to you now and for your future. Identifying, analysing, adjusting and remedying, whatever you see as a threat to your ongoing happiness, is so important. Reminding your man and yourself for the need to compromise and resolve any questionable behaviour in a timely manner. Such is the emphasis for understanding the necessity to again ensure your life is going in the direction you set your course on, without deviating or running aground.

Preventing and Ending Domestic Abuse

— Salvaging can be a costly exercise —

You don't want to discover your man only wants a woman to have his children, cook his meals, wash his clothes, and be at his beck and call. Difficult to imagine isn't it, but it happens all too often.

This type of mindset stems from primeval male instincts in pursuing females, all part of the conquest for male dominance. For many this behaviour is to then simply roam around and start all over again, irrespective of whether they are in a relationship or not.

— Sadly, not unlike the piped piper, finding yourself entranced by his tune happily following along, then finally getting married only to feel like you're drowning. -

A cynical view perhaps, however, since there's an element of risk in almost everything we do in life, there's nothing that could ever be compared to the risk we all face when looking for a lifetime partner. A simple, common-sense approach, outlined throughout this self-help book with everyday scenarios, drastically reduces those risks. Therefore, let's not forget the complexities of being in a relationship, thus the need for every woman to monitor her man, particularly whilst she continues building on the early stages of her relationship.

Although it's important that a woman invests in her man, of which sex is generally an important aspect, it's not the be all and end all. However, it is essential in keeping the relationship alive, particularly in the very early stages. All marriages take constant work, so remain mindful of how easy it is for any relationship to fall into a mundane like existence. If a cohesive effort from both of you isn't forthcoming naturally, it can become a recipe for the relationship to dissolve without warning.

Ques: "This is my third relationship, and I believe it's going along ok, since I believe my man in most regards is a decent human being. However, I have found sex to be a useful bargaining chip when he needs to be kept under control, is this a mistake?

Ans: "Until sex is no longer used as leverage, you can only hope he has adjusted at the same pace. Do any of his traits or indiscretions suggest that offering sex as a compromise is appropriate? Resolving issues requires meaningful conversation, accountability, sometimes with consequences however small, complete with a lasting resolution".

Working on your compatibility and thinking about doing things together, organising surprises, such as dinners, or weekends away. Showing compassion toward each other, all of which are areas that prolong relationships which inadvertently prevent domestic abuse.

– As long as it's reciprocal –

If your man shows early signs of apathy, then potentially you have a serious problem on your hands. Of which can manifest into the type of behaviour causing domestic abuse. These are the type of signs you need to identify and be aware of early, because chances are, being young, you won't be looking in the right direction. Being around someone who's unmotivated can put a serious strain on a relationship, maybe not in the short term, but certainly in the long term.

Perhaps he has made other arrangements when you suggest doing things together, it may just mean he wants to spend more time with his mates, so there is no need to panic just yet. Instead, do your thing in life and make an entry in your diary. Remembering, time, patience, and a pattern of his behaviour will provide you with the answers you are looking for.

Explore and identify

This is exactly what courtship is all about, to explore and identify, that will provide the information to make informed decisions and choices in the early stages of a relationship. Again, by doing so, you should pay particular attention to your man's characteristics and personality, identifying any of his possible hidden traits and secrets. Having become satisfied, you can then settle into a routine with your man, knowing you have gone above and beyond to find a loving and loyal companion. However, this is where so many women become far too complacent and unfortunately are now paying the price.

Ques: "How concerned should I be if I feel things only appear to be running smoothly?"

Ans: "If you believe your satisfaction is only based on the surface, ask yourself whether you need to look a little deeper. If so, use your imagination by working on one particular concern at a time, perhaps it's his change in tone, if so, respond by replying straight away, expressing your disapproval."

Fortunately for the man, it's the woman who has the strength, courage and the commitment to stay the course. That early maternal instinct to settle those day-to-day issues most men are less concerned or indeed take little notice of. Such a contrast between the genetics of a male and a woman where understanding and rationale are concerned. Therefore, never underestimate any immediate shortcomings you may have detected or overlooked that require an immediate remedy. The type of intervention required long before moving forward into the next phase of a more serious relationship with your man. Look at the next phase of your relationship becoming engaged as possibly the final frontier for your total freedom.

All too often, many couples simply end their relationship irrationally, packing their bags and leaving, essentially lacking the life skills to cope. Consequently, only to repeat the entire episode again, and again, having multiple relationships, and in some cases, multiple children. As suggested earlier regarding the use of your diary, start with what your goals are in life, referencing your principles and what you value most – is it having a husband and raising a family? If so, then write down your likes and dislikes about this courtship and make comparisons against your likes and dislikes about him. This will create a bigger picture, assisting you when you need to make future decisions.

Having concerns about your man and wanting answers can be daunting, therefore being direct—a situation that many couples prefer to avoid— is so important because by doing so causes him to provide an on-the-spot response which has its advantages. Especially since he must think on his feet and explain himself, thereby providing an answer you either believe, or you don't. Either way humans with a guilty conscience are less likely to be convincing, a telltale sign if there was ever one.

One way for you to make further discoveries is through cunning, without having to utter a word, by casually watching perhaps from a distance, making observations through his body language, being in earshot of conversation. Remember, you only need a pattern of behaviour to make any sort of accurate assessment, other than readily accepting assumptions.

To some people this may sound a little underhanded, however think of it this way, one day in the distance future having spent many happy years together, you can reflect on the earlier clandestine surveillance and intervention work you put into during your courtship. This should be the goal of every woman in a courtship that will produce the evidence for her decision to either continue with or end the relationship.

There is still some way to go

This type of mindset shouldn't be discounted, as the continuous learning and discoveries you make along the way can re-shape your future together. Providing you both with the importance of showing one another respect, whilst remaining in love and finding lasting happiness. This is where the proof will then be exposed, as to the true effectiveness of whether your compatibility and love for one another is working or not.

— Although your goal should be to keep domestic abuse at bay, be prepared for it anyway, because it's far better, he remains constantly aware and understands your continued opposition to any type of abuse from ever entering the relationship. —

Any woman can make the toughest of men see the errors of his ways, but only if she starts early enough in the relationship and not waiting for him to commence being abusive without your prior opposition or discussion on the matter. It could be argued that many successful relationships are the result of a woman at the helm, instinctively resolving matters. Something she should always acknowledge and embrace as part of her right and her role in sharing the load—for the sole purpose of maintaining a positive and peaceful relationship.

Preventing and Ending Domestic Abuse

There are basically two types of males in a relationship, the one who doesn't get annoyed with his woman when she voices her opinion, and respecting her for who she really is, and what she represents. This provides a woman with real purpose, and the belonging she deserves. Meanwhile her man understands his partner is nobody's fool, where they each bounce off one another in the most positive way.

Then there's the male who believes he, and he alone should be the decision maker on all matters. Since his mentality is, he knows best. Nor has he ever been challenged, allowing him to have his way while his suffering wife remains quiet, obedient, and submissive.

Ques: "That's how my mum was when we were kids, so isn't that just normal in most relationships?"

Ans: "Did your father show your mother the type of respect you expect to receive from your partner, if so, and you're happy with those arrangements in allowing your man to make the decisions, then so be it? However, isn't it worth considering having equal status now, before domestic abuse has the chance to enter the home, in part to your seemingly apathetic approach?"

When a male appears to show a genuine caring interest in any issue requiring a joint decision, and explains that he will take care of it, the woman is usually in agreement. Since she is acknowledging her partner is ensuring her best interests at heart, and that may just be the case. However, it is beneficial for a woman to understand and monitor control and coercion in the early stages of any relationship, which will be discussed in a later chapter.

Perhaps you're already experiencing one or more types of abuse, which we will also address in the 'Ending Domestic Abuse' chapters, starting with chapter 4 – 'Marriage'.

But for now, let's not forget we are discussing 'Preventing domestic abuse' within relationships during dating, courtship, and soon engagement. Therefore, we are acting on the presumption that no type of domestic abuse currently exists in your relationship and hopefully following these recommendations never will.

Early intervention!

Remaining on this notion that women should consider taking the lead, early in matters of intervention— but only when they are confident of their safety—particularly when she feels the male has no understanding of what he did or said. Therefore, unless you make the male aware and become accountable for his indiscretions, he will continue with this type of behaviour without consequences. As an example, the male having never been previously challenged becomes bemused and somewhat shocked by your confrontation. This is exactly the reaction you want, but how many women actually do this?

Going unchallenged only allows a male to become more brazen, leading to more aggressive forms of abuse. Therefore, this is where you would need to follow through, explaining what he has done, pushing the point home that you will not tolerate any type of abuse in the home.

Let's assume your partner has displayed a type of verbal abuse you haven't encountered before. In such cases, approach the situation rationally by saying, 'I haven't heard you talk like that before.' He might respond with, 'Sorry about that, I shouldn't have spoken that way." Use this opportunity to show some humility and not attempt to inflame the situation by further chastising him.

It's the behaviour of the male who responds with contempt and ridicule that you clearly need to recognize having now become your adversary— make no mistake about it. This cannot be ignored and is likely deeply entrenched, a situation that cannot continue and requires urgent intervention—either through an amicable resolution or by establishing grounds for possible separation.

Ques "Why do I have reservations about calling him out on some things he says?"

Ans: "Unfortunately, that's all too common, because many females falsely believe the male is the dominant one. To some extent he is, but certainly not in a relationship where both parties have equal status. Once you cross that line from indecision to becoming forthright, you will never return to the mental space you are currently in."

By taking this type of stance decisively, with ongoing monitoring against initial domestic abuse, is the ultimate course to take when in an early relationship when thinking of marriage. This is where the woman has consciously and systematically done all she can to put an end to something that had the potential to escalate into something far more destructive.

Unlike the abuse that was never addressed early enough, now affecting so many established relationships in marriages along with the children, that continues to destroy generations of people who unwittingly became affected.

Benefit of the dealt

In these early stages of a relationship, it's very possible the male will not understand what is and what isn't acceptable behavior, as difficult as that may seem to believe. Everyone has a different upbringing; therefore, everyone deserves the benefit of the dealt particularly in a relatively new relationship.

That said, you must only ever accept zero tolerance when discussing domestic abuse with your man. Explain to him just once, and if that fails and he continues with his abuse, you must consider your options without delay and not allow your emotions to get in your way.

This really is so important, so make sure it's not just an off-the-cuff remark you make when raising the issue of domestic abuse. Instead sit down with your man and explain the situation for him to understand that domestic abuse could undermine the relationship. Further explain the facts to him, that one in three marriages fail due to domestic abuse.

— Encourage your man to read the following section after this chapter, titled 'Perpetrator', as mentioned, there are perpetrator sections following chapters throughout this book. —

Couples who are progressing harmoniously often share their thoughts and aspirations, discussing future goals such as starting a family or securing a mortgage. However, a conversation on one of the most critical and relevant topics—domestic abuse—is rarely discussed. This is concerning given the sobering reality: because at the time of writing, statistics show one-hundred and one Australian woman were killed due to gender-based violence in 2024. That's according to *Australian Femicide Watch*, that's a thirty percent increase from the year before in 2023, truly alarming.

Tragically, this topic is almost taboo in the family home as human beings simply don't know how to deal with it, as a result, far too many are afraid to discuss. The biggest hurdle when debating domestic abuse is having the courage to speak up, when all it takes is for the two of you to sit down and talk it through. If only couples understood it's just like any other topic that needs to be addressed from time to time.

Ques: "But what if I'm not able to discuss domestic abuse with my partner?"

Ans: "In which case ask yourself why you are with this person and perhaps coming to terms with the fact that the relationship may be better if it were dissolved. Alternatively, face up to the facts of life when in a relationship having to make a stand at some point, but don't procrastinate.

However, we are all guilty at one time or another of staying quiet when we know we should speak up, mainly due to its sensitive nature and hoping it will just fade away. This is a big mistake since the perpetrator has been given a free rein resulting in no accountability and getting away scot-free.

— Again, avoiding this one major issue is a huge mistake when in an early relationship-

Now that you are courting, do not shy away from discussing with your partner the present-day divorce rate, which should act as a reminder to you both the relative ease marriages can end. All that hard work, having once confessed their love to one another, who now, after a relatively short time, have decided to drive a wedge between themselves and their happiness.

The golden rule

Strangely, but not surprisingly, many of the couples who do separate usually do so without having first spoken the golden rule, that is…

—In the event our relationship becomes so troubled that we discuss separation, we shall apply the same amount of time, energy and effort we afforded each other, when we first fell in love-

Many relationship failures have resulted from the most trivial of circumstances, such as pride, stubbornness, anger and spite, where a resolution was well within reach. What you are being asked to consider whilst in a non-committed relationship is minor compared to what could be expected of you. That is, should you experience domestic abuse in a committed relationship where it will take a lot more than just soul searching to resolve.

As mentioned, ask yourself, do I really want a marriage, a family life, raising children, a mortgage, and everything that goes with it'? If you struggle to answer honestly, then re-evaluate your goals. However, if you're certain you want to get engaged and married, you best also be certain of the responsibilities that affect both the good and the bad times.

— Just as long as you firmly believe you are making the right decision, firstly for yourself, your partner, and your future family. —

> **CAUTION** – But of course, it's not just a simple decision based purely on logic, because our emotions tend to throw a spanner in the works—it's just human nature— when feeling self-entitled, which can go against our better judgement, resulting in having to learn the hard way.

Should I, or shouldn't I?

Now that the courtship has run its course, it's time to reconsider your options, as follows– become engaged, perhaps put a plan together to reshape your man, or end the relationship.

If you believe you have accomplished and achieved all you set out to do, and you're convinced you and your man are as one, then there's no reason you shouldn't move forward into the next phase and become engaged. Properly structured stages when building a relationship are by far the best way for couples to have any chance of surviving in a long-term relationship.

View the next stage of engagement with equal excitement as dating, and courting, by remaining mindful of your final stages of being single. A milestone reached comes two-fold, with many women soon to find long lasting love and happiness, whilst for others it's a life of uncertainty and too often regret.

SUMMARY

- Using the steppingstone approach that involves dating, courtship, and perhaps soon engagement, is an effective and proven method for a more successful marriage. – Recommended over a five-year period.
- Maintain your diary methodically, as it will act as a purposeful reminder, along with a record of the time you spent in your courtship with your partner.
- Pay particular attention to any progressive and adverse pattern behaviours in terms of indiscretions he may have recently adopted.
- Pay further attention to where you currently stand by addressing any outstanding issues, long before thinking about moving on and becoming engaged.
- Are you in this relationship for the right reasons, and not because you feel obliged?
- Are you truly convinced he genuinely loves you? If so, how do you know, is it time to find out?

- Keep on track, stay the course maintaining a free domestic abuse relationship, watch for the signs and continuously act on your suspicions.
- If it wasn't to be, then as difficult it may be, move on, and consider what you have learnt, putting you in a much better position for making more informed decisions in the future.

PERPETRATOR

So are you or aren't you the person you portray yourself to be, perhaps you're neither here nor there in this relationship. Instead, preferring to allow things to just happen, a take it or leave it mentality.

Had you really been head over heels for this woman, it would have been so much different, wouldn't it? Whereby you would have been the one to feel the insecurities, worrying about how she really felt about you. But since that's not the case, you don't have to worry about the hurt of being jilted, because the truth is, you're only focused on yourself.

If you are the type of person described as—being a perpetrator—and somehow thinking you will benefit from playing emotional blackmail, then it's best you think again. Because the only person you are deceiving is yourself. It will catch up with you one way or another, as countless men can testify too—who like you, winged it the whole time.

Then finally getting married, readily accepting everything a woman willingly provides for her man, until at last, it all comes tumbling down. A time when a man's false demeanour and conscience turn on him, resulting in desperation and depression. As a result, falling into the depths of despair, looking for a way to escape, believing domestic abuse is the only way out.

This type of emotional abuse is no different to sticking a knife through a woman's heart, because it's the callous nature and not the usual writing on the wall scenario. Whereby a woman with knowledge of her man's deception could have made plans and moved on with her life. Unlike you keeping your cards close to your chest- is this how you would like to be treated?

A low act indeed, and now is the time to acknowledge one very serious matter, that is, you're about to go into an engagement, the final non-committed part of a relationship before marriage. So where do you fit in? Are you going through with this charade, or are you going to man up and explain the truth to your partner- that your hearts not in it?

Try questioning yourself regarding your failure to be in control and looking at the bigger picture, and when you do something will come over you, whereby you will stop beating yourself up, instead coming back to the real world where you belong. When you take back control of yourself and start being honest with yourself you will feel an enormous weight lift off your shoulders, and wonder what possessed you to become the way you are.

Deciding to end the relationship allows your partner to heal and move on with her life, or maybe you will realise what you had all the time. This wakeup call usually represents itself when you experience that empty, sickening feeling when thinking about life without her. So, is it now the time to act?

This is your opportunity here and now, to ask yourself why this type of behaviour is your preferred way. Like so many other foolish men in a relationship who go against the grain, having initially jumped through hoops to win her heart. You don't really know yourself, having never given yourself the time to understand love, to be loved, or to show love.

Instead, you're advocating a case of 'Que Sera, Sera'— 'Whatever will be, will be'—which is a very sad indictment and quite a flawed analogy when human pain and suffering are involved. The answer of course, is staring you in the face, your insecure a result of being selfish and self-centered, preventing you from discovering love and to be loved by someone else.

In other words, you're corrupting your own mind which you may never fully recover from or ever return to being the person with the character and the personality you were destined to have. Instead of being a fraud, why not challenge yourself to reinstate the good in you - it's there, just reach for it.

— *Unfortunately, there are women in love who can see no wrong in their man, yet their friends and family see you for what you are.* —

We all like to be different simply because we are, and we all like to do things that give us the most pleasure in life. Since making mistakes is a normal part of life, realising and learning from those mistakes is fundamental to who we are and who we become. Fortunately, wanting to change your ways is as easy as flicking a light switch, but only when your man enough.

TIME TO MAN UP

1. Speak Up Early
If you're not really in it for the long haul, say so. Don't keep quiet or pretend you're unsure just to avoid awkward conversations. That only ends up hurting her more.

2. Don't Fake It with Affection
Don't use hugs, kisses, or sex to cover up the fact that your heart's not in it. If you're emotionally checked out, being physically close sends the wrong message.

3. Ask Yourself Why You're Still There
Are you scared of being alone? Do you just like the attention? Are you trying not to hurt her feelings? Be honest with yourself—knowing your real reasons helps you do the right thing.

4. Don't Stay Just Because It's convenient.
If you're only sticking around because it's more convenient than leaving, that's a problem. Relationships need real commitment—not just comfort or habit.

5. Release

Releasing her is to release yourself.

ENGAGEMENT

Coming through those heady days of dating, having recently completed your courtship, you have continued pursuing your relationship with the same man and becoming engaged. A time for making further considerations towards the real possibility of a more entrenched relationship, particularly now that you have both agreed to live together. Couples who live together for the first time share a more intimate relationship and soon become even more familiar with each other, along with making new and surprising discoveries.

As importantly, does he continue to treat you with respect, because as mentioned, when living with someone for the first time it takes a lot of compromise since there are unforeseen forces at work? Such as unsuspecting personal likes and dislikes which may surface, which can be both enjoyable and problematic.

The latter produces the actions and habits that can cause both indifference and annoyance, that can manifest into different types of domestic abuse if left untreated.

> **CAUTION** – The above paragraph is so significant that it would be difficult for married women now living with domestic abuse not to agree with. Particularly for those women who were aware the signs existed early in the relationship yet did nothing about it. It's not only a reflection on the women who looked the other way, but also on their ingrained belief that such behaviour at that time was expected in a marriage. – But not anymore.

Could he be resting on his laurels?

This is not the time to take anything for granted, believing you're on the home run, because you're not. As a perfect example, the male can become all too complacent settling into life during this period of engagement with many believing they are already in a marriage.

Hopefully, it won't come to that, instead there's every chance you will continue to build on your relationship in a positive fashion, however we must be realistic as to what happens in the real world once relationships take on that better known adage…

– When familiarity breeds contempt –

Unfortunately, and in many cases it's the woman that sadly rests on her laurels by not following through on the last leg of her non-committed relationship. By failing to scrutinise and remedy everything she can, to ensure what she needs to believe in is in fact the truth.

Ques: I'm starting to think I ignored the signs because I was afraid of what the truth might mean for me?"

Ans: "Perhaps you did. Not because you're weak, but because facing the truth can be difficult. You wanted to believe things would get better, or maybe you were just in denial. Deep down though, you knew something wasn't right. Had you addressed the warnings at the time, then chances are you probably would never have made contact. But since you have, your now aware the truth doesn't just disappear."

As we will continue to point out, the male can easily escalate his confrontational methods from verbal to physical abuse at any time during transitioning from being in a non-committal relationship to a committed one. A fact every woman should learn to understand and constantly remain aware of. By acknowledging their equal standing and asserting their authority from the start, women can resolve most relationship problems in a timely manner.

Any inaction provides the male with the green light to continue with his behaviour, a trend that can produce long term disappointment.

I'm determined to have equal status

This is the correct thought process to begin with, because for too long too many women have held the belief that it's a man's world, but not anymore, that's all in the past. Times have changed for men and women to understand, for their relationship to work long term there must be a balance on equal terms.

Successful marriages understand that most challenges can be resolved with a willingness to work together. Couples need to recognise that the early stages of a relationship call for effort, commitment, determination, perseverance, and patience. When partners communicate openly, express themselves honestly, and treat each other with respect, they create the foundation needed to grow toward shared goals.

Ques: "Is there a better way than to just tell him I want equal status without causing any animosity?"

Ans: "It's unfortunate you feel that way about simple open communication. However, go about your business and from time to time in a forthright and confident manner and make off-the-cuff remarks in passing. Particularly regarding your preferences on issues, he would normally take for granted making decisions on. By doing so you are exercising one of your rights to equal status in front of your man. Key being never allow yourself to be roped into an argument, instead give him time to digest what you have said, and leave it at that."

When you were dating or during your courtship you generally made the most of each other's company, knowing that the time will soon come when you both have to part ways and head home in different directions. But now you're coming home each day, consciously aware of living together, which provides you with the awareness of these new types of living arrangements.

Discussing problematic relationship scenarios is one thing, but to remedy them is altogether different, particularly issues that have escalated beyond just annoyance. As an example, from trivialities to the more serious nature of his abrasive tone he now uses, but only when talking to you. This change in communication should be addressed promptly and resolved before making any marriage plans.

As this self-help book will continue to advocate, words cannot fully capture the magnitude of potential challenges you may encounter after crossing the threshold into marriage. Especially if you've avoided addressing any crucial matters with your partner, or indeed yourself. The answers might already lie within your diary if you take the time to recognize the significance of your entries and read between the lines. Entering marriage under such circumstances is a momentous decision—again one that carries the weight of considerable responsibility and a huge gamble.

Should I remain with this person?

We should consider a raised voice the exception rather than the rule; therefore, ongoing abusive tone is unacceptable, and that's where you must draw the line. Looking at the bigger picture, is this the real characteristics of the man finally coming into focus for the very first time, and if so, is the pressure catching up with him?

It's concerning, that whilst there are women who have the confidence and capabilities to prevent domestic abuse from entering their relationship, unfortunately there are many women that lack the vision, strength and conviction.

When the relationship is heading towards a potentially tumultuous point, your man will never remind you to chastise him about something he said or done. Therefore, unless you adopt zero tolerance with immediate intervention and find a solution, you are inadvertently providing him with the power to become more assertive and dominant.

Again, it's one thing to get a little hot under the collar, even to get frustrated and angry, and feeling the need to let off some steam, even to the point of an occasional verbal outburst. But it's an entirely different matter altogether when that male crosses the line, making his verbal attacks towards you, both personal and frequent.

Making the decision whether to remain with this person is a personal choice, made easier if he takes accountability for his behaviour, along with a genuine effort to become the person he would most likely prefer to be. But never lose sight when comparing the possibility of ending the relationship whilst engaged, to that of wanting to end it once in a marriage. – Chalk and Cheese.

Unacceptable behaviour!

When a male becomes verbally abusive to his partner, it could be a cry for help, and even though it's probably not, it's still considered unacceptable behaviour. In all likelihood he's just acting up, not unlike a spoilt child throwing a tantrum. However, under those circumstances it presents a genuine opportunity for you to attempt turning him around, particularly if his type of behaviour has only recently surfaced and hasn't got too out of hand - yet.

Unlike another type of abusive male, who again exhibits consistent escalated levels of anger when being abusive, making personal, derogatory, and spiteful remarks. It's during these types of episodes that only you can determine whether in fact you even want to resolve the matter. Perhaps ending the relationship is the most logical and safest thing you can do.

Let's not forget what we are talking about here. We are pushing ahead to prevent domestic abuse from ever entering your relationship. Therefore, waiting until you're married leaves it all far too late.

Ques: "I'm worried about him calling off the marriage if I say anything that upsets him, what is the best approach?"

Ans: "If you swallow your tongue, it may well prove to be difficult to digest, because by staying silent you may allow a situation you don't want to be in, to get so much worse."

— A marriage timeframe can be flexible, therefore conducted at anytime, anywhere. Whereas you cannot allow any flexibility when inappropriate behaviour is currently displayed; therefore, it must be remedied immediately. —

Confrontation

Again, there is a time and a place for everything, no more so than when we are discussing and dealing with confrontation, particularly during extreme unpredictable behaviour. But let's be practical here, it's essential to have that all important plan in place first, - which we will go into detail a little later. By first allowing him some time and space to cool off post-abuse, he may return to his normal rational self - assuming demeanor.

— Provide him with the time to reflect a little, as there's no doubt he will, then wait for the opportune time to approach him, - during a solemn moment—to discuss his indiscretions. —

This is where a woman can become a force to be reckoned with—by challenging, therefore showing him that she won't shy away from confronting issues that threaten her principles and values, and above all her safety.

— One day, many of those men may reflect by saying, 'It was my partner who straightened me out when I needed it the most'. —

Engagement

Ques: "How should a woman feel after finally finding the courage to confront her husband about his behaviour?

Ans: "Undoubtedly with mixed emotions, as you've taken a bold step in voicing your opinions, exposing your feelings, and that's something to be proud of. By continuingly speaking up, you've set in motion a series of positive changes that wouldn't have been possible had you stayed silent. But keep in mind, address these issues with extreme caution".

A woman should never feel she has to be afraid to make a man accountable for his indiscretions since there must be consequences, otherwise the entire exercise is a waste of time. He may even become a little remorseful—you won't know unless you try—perhaps becoming ashamed of his recent verbal outburst. This may well prove to work to your advantage, being the best outcome for any male under these circumstances, although further mentoring may be required.

Regardless of his reaction, you would do well not hold back. Make it clear to him he has broken the bond you both made earlier, to never allow domestic abuse to enter the relationship. Warn him that his behaviour is unacceptable, and if it continues the relationship will not last.

It could also be beneficial to identify whether his behaviour is to seek attention - a cry for help, by further explaining to him you are always there to help him with any personal challenges he faces. Particularly on issues that he wouldn't normally discuss with you. It may well be work-related, financial, even someone or something in the past that's causing him grief, that has a direct bearing on his recently changed behaviour.

—It may be, he feels the walls are closing in, as a pending marriage can have that affect-.

Remind him there's nothing the two of you can't resolve together, it's what couples do when they are in love and experiencing difficulties. Unfortunately, in many cases the male doesn't quite get it like a woman does, therefore he may need further convincing.

— Humans are prone to different levels of sensitivity and therefore there's a limit to what we can tolerate or are prepared to accept in a relationship, especially in terms of the way we expect to be spoken to. —

Living in the real world!

There are those women having reached this period of engagement that have already fallen victim to domestic abuse. If that's not bad enough many of whom have already adopted the mind set of continuing to get married. It's unfortunate when a woman thinks more about the status of marriage over her own individual well-being and long-term happiness.

Something that goes hand in hand with that previous statement is whether you are being brutally honest with yourself and living in the real world. By realising the extent of your true feelings towards your man, to that of understanding your man's nature and his true feelings towards you.

Ques: "Why do I feel a sense of apprehension?"

Ans: "Better to feel that way now than one day wishing you had. If there's nothing wrong, then you have nothing to worry about, but at least being a little apprehensive you're not resting on your laurels or remaining complacent, so continue to remain vigilant."

During the time of engagement, most women have their own financial independence, whereby in the event they consider severing ties with their partner, they could walk away that much easier. This is in stark contrast to the legal wrangling sometimes involved in dividing finances and assets during a broken marriage. Therefore, remain mindful: a marriage is the binding between two people, usually with everything you both possess.

Where do I really stand?

A woman who has marriage and children on her mind seldom thinks about other matters. Therefore, it's highly recommended you are aware of where you stand long before you enter into a committed relationship. Again, never lose sight of the position you are in, as many women feel obliged to follow through with getting married, simply because they are living with their fiancé, however that should never be the case. You are not obligated. In fact, you can end this relationship at any time. Walking away could result in the best decision you're likely to make in your entire life.

Ques: "Should I mention I want my own financial independence when we are married?"

Ans: "Yes of course, but have some type of strategy in place, never allow yourself to be caught unprepared, because he may already have different ideas to yours. This type of discussion can cause serious disagreements between couples, so remember there can be no compromise. You must have your own financial independence."

— There is arguably a significant psychological difference between how a male understands the way a woman conducts herself during the time of the engagement, to how he expects her to comply once in a marriage. —

> **CAUTION** – As mentioned there are males only too aware that until he receives his marriage certificate, his demands on his partner are limited. Including the relative ease of her freedom and her spending during the period of engagement, to that of what he could well expect of her once married. When that finally happens, situations can and will take on a completely new and sometimes disturbing dimension.

— Best to get it sorted out now —

Consequences of which can become unlike anything any unsuspecting woman could have ever envisaged during her engagement. The irony here is, how a male appears to be during the engagement then simply changes his tune once the marriage ceremony is over.

The dynamics!

The nature of men in relationships varies greatly. Some exhibit behaviours that deeply resonate with their partners, while others do not. Many women, however, follow along as if caught in some type of an intoxicating trance, without fully evaluating the reality of their situation.

For those who are fortunate enough to encounter a good-natured man, the difference is unmistakable. His genuine caring, understanding of the dynamics within a relationship and his awareness of a woman's needs stand out. He respects her personal space and the time she needs with her friends, along with her financial independence. In recognizing these expectations, he contributes to the long-term survival of the relationship while also enjoying the mutual benefit of his own private part-time space.

By making thoughtful comparisons, acknowledging each other's needs, and finding compromises, compatibility wins out.

Ques: "How often does a woman find a man like that?"

Ans: "That kind of man undoubtedly exists. Therefore, taking a non-committal step-by-step approach to dating, courting, and engagement is so important. It allows you to assess what you have, compare it to what you want, then make the necessary changes—well before stepping into a wedding dress."

If only I had a crystal ball

Whenever there is a sign of positivity in these types of circumstances, there can be a cruel twist. Such are the complexities of the human mind and behaviour. As an example, the seemingly decent honorable and respectful male can prove to conceal his dark side. By doing so he waits for marriage only to indulge in his new passion for domestic abuse.

This is completely new and totally unexpected, something his wife never saw coming, leaving her completely blindsided. Nor did she witness this type of behaviour at any other time during their relationship. But now she clearly does and is seriously concerned about what direction his new demeanour will take.

Therefore, since you are still in the relatively safe space of engagement, never assume your man won't become a domestic abuser once married. Whether it be emotional, verbal, physical, sexual, controlling, or financial, because any type of abuse can raise its ugly head at any time.

It may also be the case that he shows the epitome of everything good in a human being—a reflection of what a woman desires in a man—and that's why you are currently on this journey of discovery.

Engagement

-The love game can make fools of us all-

There will be many women perhaps reading this chapter that have already experienced that type of unexpected shock, having gone from a non-committal relationship to a committed one, only to discover her man had carried out a complete back flip on his agreement.

— That agreement was to never allow domestic abuse, to ever enter the relationship —

There are many women throughout the world who have been putting up with abuse in their marriage for far too long, without offering much in the way of showing objection. Instead, they believe they have little alternative but to come to terms with believing it's just part of being married. Having that mindset is not in line with modern day beliefs or expectations, because women are progressively finding their voice, becoming ever more aware of the law and the available support.

Fortunately, you are not in that situation—and hopefully never will be—because you are now far more attuned to the potential challenges that may arise once in a marriage. This period of engagement has given you a deeper understanding, making it your last opportunity to thoroughly evaluate your partner, as well as reflect on your own feelings and future expectations.

Yet it is truly astonishing how this common trend emerges among certain men who, upon entering marriage seemingly undergo a fraternity-like awakening. This misguided belief serves as their justification for reneging on previous promises opening the door to domestic abuse within the relationship—a troubling and unwarranted shift in human behaviour.

Ques: "How do I become more in tune about the way my relationship is progressing, even though I feel it's going ok?"

Ans: "And it may well be, however, read over your diary and reflect, identifying any entries of concerns you had but didn't act on. Talk to your family and friends and ask them for their honest opinions about your relationship. Be careful who you choose to confide in and remember, keep your emotions in check, and think rationally about any constructive criticism you receive."

These types of males provided their partners with a false sense of security from day one, playing their partners like fools the whole time. A trait you would do well to discover through various means of subtle investigation, again as recommended now and throughout the earlier chapters.

It's fair to assume that many deceased women had no former guidance or training, to either prevent and or end domestic abuse. Therefore, not knowing how to go about looking for those initial signs or to apply the skills and knowledge to maintain their safety. All of which you are now beginning to understand and develop, with the possibility of never needing to use once married.

I want to be a woman of substance!

You can be, and you will do well to build on that desire and exercise your equal status in life, particularly whilst in a relationship. Therefore, by putting any of those issues—you recently raised with your confidantes—into some type of order and priority, you can then raise with your partner and come to a mutual agreement.

Again, this must be carried out prior to a marriage, as this is twofold: first addressing and airing your concerns, and two, ensuring your issues are not just resolved but monitored over time, to ensure there is no relapse.

Ques: "Since I have some doubts that I can't quite put my finger on, I'm starting to wonder whether I'm overthinking, so do I need extra time?"

Ans: "Great thought, best to remain on top of your game mentally. Having doubts is a warning sign to determine whether you're making the right decision, particularly if you are to marry this man. If doubt persists, you must discover what those doubts are and get them resolved, one way or the other. Perhaps it's an intrinsic feeling you get, telling you that you aren't quite ready, maybe some intimidation associated with the tradition of marriage. Possibly even family pressures, religious beliefs, or believing you should be obedient, and doing what you're told—yes it happens.

If, in fact, you're feeling a slight touch of pessimism right now, then that's not a bad thing. That's because -from time to time- there are forces at work we don't understand, whereby we question ourselves as the type of decision we make.

Life holds different meanings for different people with some women in relationships that go through life with rose-coloured glasses on, unable to distinguish what really constitutes acceptable and unacceptable behaviour.

For others, they refuse to accept relationships as the be all and end all, wanting to experience other life's challenges and although they love their man and family, they also want to achieve personal goals. Rising above those traditional expectations and fulfilling their other dreams, all of which is both acceptable and achievable, but only when becoming a woman of substance.

There's a lot more to think about and accomplish now. Particularly as the clock winds down before the big day, the fairy tale beginning of your life together as a married couple. However, the reality for many will be quite different, as statistics show that fairytale life so many dreamed of, sadly proved to be wishful thinking.

Providing thought-provoking awareness, along with suggestions and recommendations to prevent domestic abuse, is the major component of this self-help book.

— Therefore, it must be said, domestic abuse is the manifestation for the continuing accumulation of unresolved matters. —

SUMMARY

- A time to reflect on the time you have had with your partner, through dating and courtship, to where you are now.
- Have his mannerisms changed; do you need to address any issues, what about the way he talks to you, is he a caring person who goes out of his way to do things for you? If so,

perhaps it's a true indicator of his respect for you once in a marriage.
- Do you love this man, have your feelings for him intensified, remained as they were, or have they shown signs of diminishing?
- How do you feel about your status? Are you given the equality you deserve, does he show genuine interest in your opinions?
- You can delay the wedding, or you can walk away. Don't feel you're cornered, as marriage is an enormous commitment.
- Continue to make entries into your diary as often as possible, which becomes priceless on reflection.
- Is your man, motivated, career minded, with reachable goals? If not, what type of security do you expect to have throughout your life?
- The fact remains we don't know what the future holds, so isn't it best knowing everything you possibly can about this man, and satisfying yourself one way or the other, before making the leap of faith?
- Consider reading the following chapters, particularly if you are currently engaged, as it will provide an insight into a committed relationship where domestic abuse already exists.
- As importantly, once married you will then transition from preventing domestic abuse to a completely different situation should domestic abuse begin in a committed marriage.
- Good luck.

PERPETRATOR

Engagement

Any man can get cold feet, no more so when having to deal with the realisation that the pending marriage comes with greater commitment and serious responsibility.

Having become verbally abusive, when you have previously shown genuine respect for your partner, the time has come to take yourself to one side and confront these issues.

As mentioned, throughout our lives we take paths we have thought little about the direction we are heading in, then having discovered we took the wrong turn, we get frustrated and angry. It's then we look for ways to vent that frustration. However, in your case you see your partner as an easy target, knowing how vulnerable she is, which is totally unacceptable.

This really is a cowardly act, when all that's needed is for you to keep a cool head, and to simply pause, reflect on the situation then engage by turning it into a positive. Try to understand that the best answer you will ever receive is to approach your wife with any concerns you have and by doing so you will resolve all your issues amicably. It's then you will discover that overwhelming sensation when shown encouragement by the one that loves and supports you the most- your wife/partner.

– If in fact that is something you cannot fully comprehend, then you best take a closer look as to why you were ever in this relationship to begin with. –

Were you ever really in love? Because there's a woman waiting and wanting to spend the rest of her life with you, to raise a family, which is something more rewarding than anything else, other than preferring to remain single.

Consider this: if you have strong feelings for your partner, then it may be a case of suffering the marriage jitters, which is understandable and completely normal.

On the other hand, you may well be expecting to take your partner into a marriage for your own selfish means, if so, then perhaps you're interested in why that's such a bad idea. Ask yourself, why would any male go to all the trouble of finding a partner, having completed different stages of a continued relationship, who's about to become married, knowing his heart and soul just isn't in it?

The type of rescue you need is from yourself, which you can do just as easily as when you decided to cross over to the dark side. Therefore, remind yourself that although there's both good and bad in most things we do in life, why not take this opportunity to look a little closer at what the good side of life has to offer? Especially now that you have already experienced the dark side, and now your conscience is telling you to cross back to where you belong.

It's time you understood; there's no substitute for equal standing between a man and a woman, therefore without equality, there's no genuine partnership, or any pleasure in a long-standing relationship. Either let this woman go, whereby she can rebuild her life, or you can stop and think a little harder about what you have and what you could lose.

By doing so, you may just discover that there is something inside of you that wants a wife and family for all the right reasons and always has been. This is perfect timing for you, to just give in, and experience all that good in life has to offer. Show your partner you want to share your life and raise a family together, making future plans, while communicating respectfully and compassionately as equals.

Give up on this false pretense and discover your true calling one way or the other.

MARRIAGE

Having covered 'Preventing domestic abuse', we will now turn to marriage—both pending and existing. In this chapter, the focus shifts to 'Ending domestic abuse'—since domestic abuse has now infiltrated the relationship—looking closely at the effects and finding the solutions.

– Have you taken a step too far by following through and getting married when you knew it wasn't in your best interest? –

Millions of women around the world continue to get married, again without ever giving themselves the time to truly discover all they could about their partner. Consequently, many are now destined to live their lives with regret and struggling to come to terms with the fact they married someone who wasn't suitable.

Regardless of the circumstances, women can now explore the following pages, reading through scenarios, identify and consider suggestions and recommendations. Discover the answers to something that has perhaps been weighing heavily on your mind or perhaps stumble upon your own revelation that comes as a complete surprise.

— Remembering our earlier discussions, for the need of a vastly different approach to resolving domestic abuse when in committed relationships, in particular 'marriage'. —

That said, it is again recommended that you read chapters 1–3 before continuing reading this chapter on marriage, if you haven't done so already. There you will gain a much better appreciation of the book's themes and intentions.

Ques: "My husband and I were only together for six-months before we were married, and that was over twenty-years ago, so how would the previous three chapters have helped us?"

Ans: "Assuming you're in a happy relationship, just as there are many other fortunate couples throughout the world in your circumstances, therefore earlier chapters don't apply to everyone. But let's remain mindful, there are those couples who won't be as lucky. As a result, that's where this book comes in, to reduce the rate of domestic abuse, regardless of personal circumstances or situations."

> **CAUTION** – Irrespective of personal thoughts and circumstances on the subject, we can't hide the fact that as many as thirty-plus percent of marriages end in divorce worldwide. With the greater portion due to young couples with little experience having spent inadequate time getting to know one another, even less understanding of the foundations for maintaining a successful marriage.

Relationship education

Would it not be wise to equip every child—at an appropriate age—with relationship education, empowering them to make conscious, informed decisions long before adulthood? Imagine the value of learning to navigate the emotional complexities of human connection and sustainability before stepping into the profound commitment of marriage.

Ques: "But relationships either work or they don't, with or without education, right?"

Ans: "That's a common belief but think of it this way, you wouldn't want someone delivering your child without proper training. In the same way, understanding the fundamentals of a relationship gives an individual a far greater chance of success."

While today's youth possess a natural aptitude for connections - shaped by evolving social platform awareness - they naturally lack the wisdom that only lived experience and emotional maturity can offer. This is where the authorities fail, by standing back and watching as young people enter partnerships with little preparation and even less support. The collapse of these marriages in their infancy continues without answers or any guidance from the authorities.

-The true breakdown stems from our institutions. For generations the education department has failed to integrate essential social education into the school curriculum. This absence isn't impartiality; it's institutional complicity through negligence-.

It is time for urgent reform. Relationship training must be treated not as optional, but as essential and embedded early, treated seriously, and delivered with the same weight we give to another tier one subjects. Because without it, we send generation after generation into adulthood ill-equipped for one of life's most crucial undertakings, expecting them to form healthy, respectful partnerships. And the cost of this inaction- a society weakened from within.

This type of training will have a profound effect on the minds of young adults, as they transition through adolescence to the early stages of their own relationship building. During this period, they could then fall back on that former learning, making exceedingly better-informed decisions, unlike today where the uninitiated continue to make mistake after mistake.

Introducing comprehensive relationship education into school curricula wouldn't just transform individual lives - it would reshape the very fabric of society. By equipping young people with emotional intelligence and the practical tools to build healthy relationships we could dramatically reduce the rate of divorce, incidences of domestic abuse, dysfunctional living, substance misuse, even criminal behaviour.

Research already shows that early intervention through respectful relationship education leads to measurable declines in bullying and sexual harassment among students. Now imagine the ripple effect: fewer court cases, reduced demand on social services, less strain on mental health systems, and a significant easing of pressure on law enforcement, hospitals, correctional facilities, and family services. Not forgetting the impact on creating well-adjusted young human beings from an early age who develop increased empathy and compassion.

This is not just a moral imperative—it's a strategic investment. One that promises a future where public resources are no longer consumed by preventable crises, but redirected toward growth, innovation, and wellbeing. A future where resilience is taught, respect is modelled, and relationships are built on understanding rather than survival. Once married, many couples make the mistake of falling into the mindset of having reached a milestone and generally think in terms of celebration. However, the time to celebrate is when couples have successfully reached a different milestone, that of many years having remained in love whilst keeping their marriage alive. Along with having maintained their respect and devotion to one another, raising a family and teaching the same values.

> **CAUTION** – Look at marriage as heading into a new dimension, simply because you are going from being single to becoming a part of a joint commitment, a partnership, especially for the need to become more aware of what you are getting yourself into.

That shared responsibility—raising a family, required income, managing finances and assets—all of which forms the stability of a partnership between husband and wife. Yet these pressures can also become the spark that ignites household tensions, sometimes escalating into various forms of domestic abuse. It is during these crucial moments that couples must recognise the seriousness of their situation and make a conscious effort to de-escalate, before verbal conflict spirals beyond control.

Ques: "My husband and I are always arguing over money, and just about everything else. Isn't that just all part of being married?"

Ans: "Is it? Wasn't getting married all about being in love, sharing your lives and perhaps raising a family together, to respect, care, and talk decently to one another? Most couples have their moments when arguing, with many having learnt early just how far to go, without becoming disrespectful."

The harsh reality for many couples is during and after an argument with the inability for either party to de-escalate the situation, preventing timely and amicable resolution.

Forgotten vows

Whilst couples need to remind each other of the commitment they made when they first became married, for some inexplicable reason, we are to all aware that many males fail to keep their side of the bargain. If it were a business partnership there would be instant ramifications from the get-go.

Ques: "I recently discovered a change in the way he speaks to me which I didn't appreciate, that happened almost immediately out of the blue after the wedding. I was shocked and explained to him that the relationship would end if he continued to talk to me in the same manner, and he knew I meant it?"

Ans: "That's the way to do it, never allow the situation to fester, be direct and decisive as it happens, and he should get the message. If only women would do the same, realizing these situations are much more than just a fleeting moment, instead a deliberate attempt to infiltrate and test your personal boundaries."

Upon hearing any form of verbal dissent a woman has every right to defend herself by again reminding her partner of the pact they made together—to never allow domestic abuse to enter their relationship. The last thing any newlywed ever wants to hear, or be forced to confront, is the painful realisation that her husband is disrespectful having suddenly become verbally abusive.

Have I been betrayed?

Whatever your understanding of the term 'abuse' is, the fact remains that once this kind of behaviour begins, it's like a cancer—silent, invasive, and progressively destructive. Another analogy of deep significance is that it marks the crux, the catalyst—*the embryonic stage*—for ongoing domestic abuse within a relationship.

– This is where domestic abuse begins, and where it must end. –

The sudden reality of verbal abuse in a marriage is a serious concern, since so many women have allowed it to continue throughout their entire life. These women who are still married, now wish they had taken a different approach, had they any inkling as to the type of relationship they were getting themselves into.

Once upon a time secondary schools offered young women the opportunity to learn 'home economics'. A school curriculum, teaching young female students how a woman is expected to run a household for when they become married. This memory is sure to raise some eyebrows from those women who still remember to this day.

Ironically, during that period the educational department touched very little on domestic abuse. That's because whilst it was known about, the authorities made it almost taboo, which in many sections of society, continues today. However, it's time for domestic abuse to come out from the shadows and into the open, to finally be understood, with the need for all males and females to become better educated.

Ques: "My marriage remains on track after fifty years, because unlike today, we took our relationship seriously and understood the importance of looking after and respecting one another, so why can't the couples of today adopt the same attitude?"

Ans: "While many marriages remain successful, humanity itself is marked by sharp differences, disparities, and subjectivity—making *us as awkward as we are intelligent. Though countless responses exist, often disguised as excuses, your explanation captures the essence: recognizing the importance of caring for one another long before a relationship begins to unravel".*

There are many reasons why people get married: financial gain, security, companionship, immigration, religion, family pressures, falling pregnant, and of course falling in love. The list goes on. Let's not be naïve, believing marriage is just all about love and raising a family, because it's not. Therefore, marriage for many women has proven, time and time again, to have been a poor decision. This was because they married for the wrong reasons, soon discovering they couldn't live together. It's a common scenario, usually at great emotional and financial cost, usually with long term consequences.

Again, there should be no doubt in any woman's mind that getting married is having realised long before accepting the marriage proposal, that yes, she does in fact love her man. Leaving no doubt, she also feels the love her man has for her—who respects and treats her well.

Abusive and unhappy households raise many young adolescents who unfortunately continue with these patterns of behaviour into adulthood. It's what they know, since they lack the necessary education and skills, to appreciate and understand acceptable social behaviour.

Worst still, where there's abuse, there's zero respect. This produces a state of mind, particularly for adolescents—that wrongdoing is seen as a normal part of life. An existence where underlying evil awaits, including becoming part of a dysfunctional and volatile family. Along with other types of related abuse, including physical, alcohol, drug, sexual, and crime, not limited to, all of which we will address in coming chapters.

Awareness – What an incredible contrast between how wonderful life can be for so many women who live in harmony, within a civilised, respectful, and mutually loving relationship, as opposed to the living hell many other women continue to live by.

Therefore, we all need to continuously remind ourselves just how unpredictable human nature can be, it's without warning, nor rhyme or reason.

This undeniable truth

If your man has become part of this unacceptable behaviour, you no doubt want it to end as soon as possible. It's shameful that a woman must step up and show her man how to behave. Fortunately, this is all achievable, or the alternatives are – to live a lifetime with abuse and unhappiness or end the relationship. Confronting a man comes with risk and therefore uncertainties, but under the right conditions it is a relatively small sacrifice in comparison to the life you could be otherwise subjected to, if you fail to do anything about it.

It is therefore advisable to acknowledge those many women over so many years who have sadly been in that exact scenario, having never contemplated the importance of early intervention. As a result, domestic abuse becomes deeply ingrained throughout their entire lives

Ques: "I'm one of those women who lives with a cantankerous husband, and has done for years, and would love to know how I can get him to talk to me decently, once and for all?"

Ans: Recognising that his behaviour concerns you is an important first step, but real change requires follow-through. Focusing on what might happen in the future rather than what you can address now is counterproductive, so aim to become proactive rather than reactive. As you continue reading, you'll find guidance that aligns with your circumstances. And if the answers don't appear immediately, trust that you've already activated the insight needed to uncover them yourself.

Once you have identified a scenario that resonates with you, we will then put a plan in place that hopefully aligns with your specific situation. Having done so, it's important you use your self-esteem and find the desire to keep yourself determined, it's all part of what you need to do in any situation in life. Along with finding strength, courage and commitment to follow through, after which time you will have also regained your self-respect. But for now, you only need to do one thing, and that is to be honest with yourself, and refrain from over thinking. Because, throughout this book it's a case of acknowledgement first then having the desire, commitment and the patience to take one day at a time.

These qualities are vital to shaping your mindset when approaching situations that demand more than a casual response. In such moments, it's important to present yourself with a more deliberate and composed demeanor—one that may take a little effort and discipline to embody- yet very achievable. The goal is for him to perceive you as someone not to be underestimated and commands respect, which we'll also explore a little later.

Embrace the idea of raising issues

If you have suddenly realised you misinterpreted his characteristics you won't be able to act as normal around him, which he will detect and could spell trouble. Furthermore, he will now feel the manipulation he had over you is waning. The mentality of some men is to use marriage as a springboard to primarily satisfy their own selfish needs, while showing only token interest in their wives and families with less purpose and intensity, as time goes on.

Ques: "Surely a woman would know her man's real intentions?"

Ans: "If only that were true! However, the numbers don't lie - divorce rates paint a different picture, one that often reveals a male's hidden motives. Not always driven by love, instead demonstrating the natural ability to be calculating and conniving, beyond most humans' imagination."

All too often true

Again, for the newly married couple, many women simply have not thought long and hard about the possible implications of a long-term marriage, instead remain caught up in some fairytale lifestyle. No one has a crystal ball; however, we can use the past and the present with a degree of certainty, to predict the future. Having noticed a slightly more condescending and patronising tone, acknowledge what's happening by confronting him. Or if worried about his reaction, write in your diary how you felt, what was said, the date, and the time. Continue to do so immediately after any new act of being disrespectful.

Although currently there's no suggestion of any further escalation to this type of abuse, it is, however, important to reference the matter in a timely fashion. However, emphasis on maintaining your safety is paramount, therefore we will address the planning and execution to resolve different issues and scenarios as we continue into this chapter.

Ques: "Once married, I learnt almost immediately, things weren't quite the same as before, so I confronted my husband over certain issues. But surely, I shouldn't have to keep this up my entire life?"

Ans: "Not at all, it depends on the severity of his behaviour, to the type of actions you take. However, in a case where you believe your man's behaviour borders on being abusive, then you will need to continue to chastise him. Only you know the extent of the abuse, and the level you are prepared to go to. Should you decide it's time to up the ante because you're not getting through, then ending the relationship must become a serious consideration."

> **CAUTION** – This is vitally important as it's the start of the creep, the escalation of abuse. This process happens without many women consciously connecting it to the possibility of a lifetime of pain and suffering. However, now that you have acknowledged his indiscretions in your marriage, it places you in a somewhat more informed position.

Hiding behind the curtains

Awareness of domestic abuse is fortunately on the rise at the time of writing. However, whilst family and friends along with the authorities show sympathy, they seldom want to get involved, similarly as do the neighbours peeking through the curtains. Unfortunately, and as mentioned, it's an issue looked upon by many throughout our society as just part of human nature, almost akin to having the attitude—there's nothing to see here.

That explains the misconception many women face in domestic abuse situations, where they believe someone else will come to their timely rescue. The reality is in more cases than not, they won't, certainly not in a timely fashion during a life and death struggle, however you will most likely receive help after the fact, when you're sadly deceased.

Ques: "It's one thing to read about what I already know—so why is it still so hard to fix my problems?"

Ans: "Because many women, perhaps like yourself, have felt isolated and that isolation can make your challenges feel even heavier. But you're not alone. Whatever you're facing, you can overcome it by embracing the guidance within these very pages."

That's what this self-help book is all about, challenging the status quo, this belief, this bygone era that remains instilled in the minds of so many women today. Where a woman's place is to stand by her man no matter what, can only be justified given he shows her the respect she deserves, by first earning his place beside his woman.

Is your man becoming a monster?

Many men have no answer when asked why they behave the way they do, nor do they understand or care how it affects anyone else. Does this behaviour come from our primate beginnings. Although it is inappropriate and completely unacceptable in a civilised society, we must nevertheless acknowledge that human beings are part of the animal kingdom. A species we know as warm-blooded mammals; therefore, humans have long inherited these traits associated with other wild species.

This type of behaviour can be remedied successfully through several options. Either he snaps out of it by his own accord, through your intervention, or by a professional.

> **Awareness** – Of course, and as mentioned, many women love their husbands and accept these outbursts as part of married life. If you fall into this category, then that's the path you have taken by your own choice and probably will continue to do so throughout your entire life.

Do you really prefer pretending to put up with this behaviour or would you prefer a man that talks to you decently? So, ask yourself, is it because you genuinely believe you handle these outbursts without fear or regret, or would you really like to do something, and put an end to it?

Or maybe the facts are quite different. You are in fact hopelessly confused, perhaps feeling trapped as you just don't know how to deal with this situation. Probably since it's been going on for so long, you remain numb and in denial, again believing it's just what comes with a marriage.

Listening, absorbing, analysing, and addressing?

As mentioned, it's all very well for someone to tell you how to handle your affairs by suggesting you should do this and do that. However, it's perfectly understandable for a variety of reasons, that many women can't bring themselves to do anything about it at all.

If this truly reflects your situation, then what really matters now is uncovering what's holding you back. When you tell yourself, "I can't," you close the door before you even begin. But if you choose to say, "I can," then we can work together to build a plan—exploring different scenarios applying practical solutions to overcome the challenges you may recognise yourself.

If you believe you are resolute in your decision not to say anything, then perhaps the reason is, you don't want to upset an already unhappy household any further. Perhaps you're worried about family and friends finding out. If that's the case, then look at the self-sacrifices you are making, which only exasperate the problems you face, all alone. So never compromise your own feelings because of someone else, particularly when that someone is clearly in the wrong. By doing so, your actions are making it almost impossible for any type of resolution.

Ques: "For some time now, I've been aware of the problems in my marriage, but I guess I thought it will just fix itself. Do people really understand what a married woman goes through?"

Ans: "Many do. In fact, there are millions of women just like you, who feel powerless. That is why there is now this ground movement you are hopefully apart of, whereby men become encouraged to call on their conscience. In return discover the rewards of virtue, seeking redemption, other than the path they are currently on."

— By admitting your relationship is now off track, is to have suddenly become true to yourself, and that's all you need to do for now. —

Building on that thought process and in doing so, watch your self-esteem and confidence grow. This process will go hand in hand with regaining your self-respect, as if by magic. All this happens naturally, as simple as instructing your mind to activate all those other possibly retardant bodily functions you seldom use or even think about, which we will also discuss further in greater detail in the following pages.

Making a pact with yourself shows not only your bravery and willingness to make significant changes, but also to continue keeping that promise you made to yourself, that you must now follow through with. By doing so, you will find and implement a permanent solution through proper training, planning, and continued resilience.

Show more interest!

This will surely be the greatest and most satisfying decision you are likely to make while in any relationship, perhaps in your entire life. Since you have finally come to terms with the magnitude of the situation.

You have answered the call, that's regardless of whether you're recently married, or perhaps it was something that's been haunting you for some time. Possibly because of many years of marriage, regardless, your life is about to change, but only with the on-going desire to allow it to happen, and by following through.

Preventing and Ending Domestic Abuse

For those of you who can't quite bring yourself to admit that you have a serious problem with your relationship, yet are still comfortable enough to read on, you may well change your mind. If that happens, it is a sign that you haven't given up altogether, which is a good start. A decision like that will most likely provide you with some solace, whereby you may well find the answers within this book. In doing so, you can approach your situation in your own way, at your own pace.

It's time to stop worrying, instead only think of positive outcomes, because by doing so it helps you to remain calm and rational when having to make those all-important decisions. Stay strong, stay brave, don't have second thoughts, and yes, this can be a somewhat complex and perplexing situation, but not insurmountable. That's because although we are dealing with complex human characteristics and personalities, along with a host of other issues, all of which can be addressed and resolved. Each one of them on their own merit, one by one, so whatever you do, don't throw your arms up in the air, as we are just getting started.

Ques: "I would like to do something, so where's the best place to start?"

Ans: "By keeping this decision to yourself, buying a diary and a highlighter, and highlight any words, sentences, even whole paragraphs you feel comfortable with, then make corresponding entries into your diary, complete with postdated, to do list."

Like everything we do in life whenever there's a problem, it needs to be resolved decisively, otherwise it's just a band aid fix. First, we must look in the right direction to settle this particular problem, therefore, careful planning is essential. In order to plan the best strategy suited to your circumstances you need to stay focused, as you can't allow yourself to drift off having any doubts or harbour any unnecessary distractions. Instead, remind yourself you picked up this book, so don't let this opportunity slip through your fingers by simply becoming or remaining another statistic.

Relationships are Partnerships

> **Awareness** – As pointed out it should act as a constant reminder, of the absolute necessity for documenting daily accounts of your life, from the time you picked this book up, whether it be to reference his behaviour, or for your own personal accounts, or both, it's highly recommended that you do.

It doesn't need to be long and drawn out, but it's important to keep dates and times as precise as possible. This process will ensure personal comfort from day one and can easily become a hobby, having discovered the pleasure in documenting your life. Therefore, focus on what was said and the outcome, and remember to record your personal feelings, especially those you harbour towards him, - good and bad-, for later reflection.

Because if you fail to document the accounts of your daily life, you will feel more deflated in the future, when you wished you had. Your memoirs must also remain completely secret and kept away from prying eyes.

– This is a serious matter, so take extra precautions and consider keeping your diary in a safe, well-hidden place. –

It can, of course, be extremely perplexing, not knowing exactly what to do or what direction to take, which is perfectly normal. For mums with children, it can be daunting as it takes planning, requiring energy, strength and courage. However, you are no ordinary woman, but someone with their own beliefs, values, and quiet resilience—someone who, even in the face of uncertainty, can find clarity by trusting her inner voice and remembering just how much she's already overcome. You may not have all the answers yet, but the fact that you're searching makes it that more likely you will.

Humans love gossip, so who can be trusted?

You may well feel having additional support will help you with the motivation that you need. Therefore, having someone like a trusted family member or confidante can be so beneficial, offering suggestions that may also provide you with better, safer solutions.

Preventing and Ending Domestic Abuse

As is the importance of remaining tightly lipped when in the company of people who don't need to know about your inner most personal and confidential secrets.

Remain open-minded but never carry out any type of confrontation with your man without thinking it through. Again, people have different opinions, reasons, and motivations for saying and doing what they do. Again, planning with caution for any type of intervention is key in maintaining your safety.

You must consider the guidance offered throughout these pages in terms of both theory and practice, because there is no single solution to marital problems. The theory being the thought-out plans, and the practice, being the safest tangible way to carry out the plan and achieve your aim. Both of which have an element of risk attached, however we will investigate both objectively giving you the best opportunity for success.

Ques: "I have spoken to my husband on frequent occasions regarding my dislike in the way he sometimes talks to me, and although it works for a while, he just resorts back to being verbally abusive when it suits him. Should I just ignore him?"

Ans: A common occurrence, but it's generally because a woman hasn't raised the bar so to speak, allowing the male to believe, "She's gotten over it already", again, it's the male mentality. The only way is to be a little ruthless by upping the ante until he has no choice but to concede and start to behave himself or end the relationship.

But for the time being, we are going to concentrate on something more important than the goal itself, and that is you. Being someone that has followed the path with genuine expectations for the perfect marriage, now coming to terms with the fact your man disrespects you.

Regardless of the type of problems we face in relationships, we usually take any conflict personally, which can create a type of standoff causing a delay in finding a resolution. However, there are some women who are overconfident and jump straight in, without considering their safety first.

Instead adopt your new mantra to – pause, reflect rationally, then to engage having considered both the consequences and your safety.

While for others who are less confident, it can have a profound effect on their mental health particularly when attempting to resolve hostilities in a timely manner. For these women, they feel further intimidation, being confined within the four walls that provides the male with additional security and therefore secrecy.

Having this type of dilemma in your life can have a negative impact. Therefore, unless you adopt the attitude that you're someone who is going to turn this problem into a positive with the purpose and vigor it requires, it will never get resolved. It is so important that every woman caught up in domestic abuse finally understands and accepts it for what it really is, as there can be no further tiptoeing around this type of situation. – It starts with you.

These next few paragraphs are of the utmost importance, as we discuss your actual involvement in this matter, in terms of your well-being, limitations and importantly your capabilities. Let's be honest, when we know we need to resolve matters, we would naturally prefer to have nothing to do with it. That said, when that time comes when a confrontation is inevitable, we need to be in sync with our mind, body, and soul. We will cover these matters in greater detail to ensure your mental and physical preparedness for handling any situation has been strengthened to its full capacity.

Having the Will and Desire

Can you honestly say you are feeling normal, or have you temporarily lost your way, becoming less interested in married life, and finding it difficult to get back to being the person you prefer to be. How are you coping emotionally? Are you maintaining your self-respect and dignity, together with keeping a moderate temperament and staying composed. Do you have the will and desire, all of which are imperative for reaching your goals, all being central and a part of facing adverse circumstances.

Preventing and Ending Domestic Abuse

Many women start out with making well intentioned interventions when domestic abuse has entered the household, by having conversations with their husbands. However, they can then be drawn into volatile situations, which can then escalate into raised voices, only for both parties losing control of the situation. By agitating one another further, to where the male can easily change his mood whereby losing control is commonplace. When all you wanted was a civilised discussion.

The verbal abuse didn't come as any great surprise, however, what did was when he grabbed your shoulders with both hands, applying pressure. Then looking you squarely in the eye, with his face close to yours, while ranting and raving. This is the time when you must realise you have been both verbally and physically abused. It's neither normal behaviour, nor just simply looked upon as something that happens occasionally in a marriage. Instead, it's a serious violation of your human rights and a criminal offence, therefore your life has now taken on a whole new level of risk including verbal, physical and emotional abuse.

Ques: "Although it hurts me when he becomes aggressive, - and all I want to do is get away from him-, he has a good side and he always apologises afterwards, so what should I do?"

Ans: "The token apology he offers is all too often about making himself feel better, because talk is cheap. Don't fall for that emotional, sociological persuasion, unless he proves overtime it was a one off. What is required are the type of consequences to end this type of behaviour once and for all".

This illustrates how effortlessly a husband can shift from being rational and composed one minute to exhibiting Jekyll-and-Hyde behaviour the next. Triggered by what appears to be an abrupt and inexplicable mental episode, resulting in verbal outbursts having now escalated to physical aggression.

— A time when too many women underestimate the significance of the matter, feeling they have little choice but to continue going about life as if nothing happened —

Many women find themselves in a desperately difficult position, where on one hand she may want out of the relationship, but understands the overwhelming odds and exiting factors she is up against. Are you in this type of situation being on tender hooks, not knowing from one day to the next what his behaviour will be like, or what you should do?

Before any thought of a confrontation takes place, the time has come to reinvent yourself, becoming someone who is less consumed by their relationship and that of their husband's sudden whims. Instead, become more engrossed in implementing your preferred self-styled form of living, the way you always wanted.

Thus, by allowing yourself to be more conscious of the need to maintain your own private space, gathering your thoughts and again regaining self-respect and self-esteem with increased fervour, with longing for more intensity in loving life- outside of marriage.

It's time to get out of the home on a more regular basis, to create even more personal space, by simply walking out the door. To exercise and clear the mind, then to begin a fresh thought process by taking on a new lease on life. This is just the start, training yourself mentally where you're no longer prepared to take any further abuse, whereby he discovers you're no longer going to just stand there and take it. – Time for change and time to get motivated.

Are you feeling it? If not, perhaps try a little harder.

By thinking positive, negative thoughts struggle to exist, so remind yourself of your principles and values you once had but probably have left on the back burner. Never allow age, disabilities, physical constraints to be a barrier, if you have the will, you will find the way. One of the biggest hurdles for many women is proving to their partners they are no longer house bound. When a woman comes home, it triggers the male mentality into believing he's got you where he wants you, but not anymore. That's because on occasion you now come home to change some clothing as you're on your way out again, without feeling the need to let on to him where you're going or when you're returning. His control over you at this point has just taken an unexpected turn.

Preventing and Ending Domestic Abuse

It's time to get back to where you belong, and embrace all those self-respecting thoughts, and don't keep them locked away anymore. Instead, start over by doing the ordinary things we generally take for granted, remembering—it's the simple things in life that can make all the difference.

Build on that self-esteem—by going back to basics and making yourself feel good. You can do this. Start by simply going for a walk, consciously breathing deep, becoming at peace with yourself. Try making eye contact with a stranger and offering up a smile. This one simple, unassuming gesture reminds you of your sense of kindness and belonging, along with that inner feeling of the pride you carry. Suddenly becoming more in tune with who you really are, guiding you toward a deeper sense of self-fulfillment and suddenly you're aware of what is more important to you in life.

Ques: "I'm just not motivated enough to go for walks or any other type of exercise, although I realise I need to help myself?"

Ans: "Reinventing yourself takes discipline, however we all have it. Walking, and breathing the air, gathering our thoughts takes little effort, as are the thousand and one other ideas you can put into practice. Once you discover the benefits, you will never go back to being someone's sound board. The less time you spend in the confines of the abuser, surrounded by four walls, the sooner you will find all your answers. It's hard to fathom anyone not wanting to end domestic abuse—yet the psychological effect it inflicts on many human beings in believing it's normal. Mental manipulation distorts rational thought, making it nearly impossible to recognize what a respectful, civilised relationship should really feel like."

By adopting and thinking about life from a different perspective away from your marriage will instinctively distance you away from domestic abuse. However, never lose sight of the eventual processes that you will need to undertake to resolve this matter, which we will soon do together.

Again acknowledgment, belief, desire, and both mental and physical well-being must come before attempting any type of confrontation. These fundamental elements brought about by your desire and supported by using your fortitude ensure that your intention is genuine and deeply rooted. Therefore, without a solid conviction, the effort and purpose required may lack the necessary drive to see it through, making the entire process less effective and potentially leading to failure and emotional disillusionment.

So, let's remind ourselves of what we touched on earlier, that of our fortitude, our inner strengths, that we can draw on anytime to help us accomplish our goals.

— People have heard about it, but how many know how to use and benefit from it? —

A chapter on the use of our fortitude is available in greater detail a little later in the book, which will provide you with the thought processes to empower you in achieving your goals. This is your opportunity since the time has come to embrace what you are reading and make a genuine concerted effort which is so important if you are going to change your life.

Ques: "I've never thought about fortitude before Is it really that important?"

Ans: "Yes, it's extremely important and most powerful, without it your entire life is hamstrung. Particularly now that you're preparing to resolve domestic abuse issues. There will be days when you feel mentally exhausted, when you doubt your abilities, and face setbacks. Despite these challenges, simply tap into your fortitude, and by doing so you're setting yourself up for success. Your perseverance, determination, and resilience will help you overcome obstacles, so stay focused on your goals, and complete the planning process. Using your fortitude enables you to endure hardships and achieve something significant through unwavering effort by simply using all the tools it provides."

Although you are a victim, be mindful not to portray yourself as the one who has grievances. Instead, address these matters so that your man fully understands it's about him being in the wrong, and it's his behaviour that's in question. You don't want him playing any reverse psychological mind games, whereby he will endeavour to control the situation. This is a common retaliatory tactic played out by men. Again, try not to give him the impression that you're the one with the problem, therefore remain strong, because he must be answerable to you, and not you having to answer to him.

It's time to immerse yourself in some examples of scenarios where you can identify the type of intervention that best suits your circumstances.

During this time, it's imperative you understand the likelihood of your man's reaction, ensuring your safety is always your number one priority. Particularly since he is about to be challenged in a way where you will soon discover what your man is made of, and indeed yourself.

— If you have never carried out any type of confrontation before, then once it's over, you will feel a sense of relief and accomplishment, the likes of which you have never experienced before. Then becoming empowered to stand up for yourself during any future confrontation-

Reminding yourself again that you have identified a different type of behaviour in your husband, whereby he has now shown physical aggression on top of talking to you in a more aggressive manner.

— Acknowledging a change in his behaviour is positive —

Therefore, having planned and assessed the risk, you believe you feel more confident and safer in your own home, you decide to confront him the very next time he talks to you using a tone you are not happy with. Then make your move by putting him on the spot and calmly saying to him, "Do you remember the pact we made with one another, about never allowing domestic abuse to enter our lives, ever", and wait for his reply.

If he falters in providing you with an answer, follow through with, "Why have you started speaking to me and man handling me the way you do", again wait for his response, if again no answer, then remind yourself of the adage—Silence speaks a thousand words—consider his silence an admission of guilt, because since he doesn't want to take ownership, finish by calmly telling him, "I never want to hear you talk disrespectfully or lay a hand on me again" and leave it at that. – For now.

This is significant, particularly since you conducted your confrontation safely, so again, simply walk away and refuse any further discussion that might lead to an argument, unless he's forthcoming and wants to talk rationally. Do not hold back, remembering to maintain your poise, your newly redefined demeanor whereby you will never allow yourself to sink to the same depths your man has currently descended into. Instead, always remain softly spoken without ever being tempted into raising your voice or making derogatory remarks. Doing so would only lower your standards whereby you will find yourself joining him in adverse behaviour, having further lost any remaining respect he has for you.

It cannot be over emphasized that remaining calm and dignified when discussing these matters will always serve you better other than adopting his tone and attitude, which would only strengthen his belief he's done nothing wrong.

Ques: "I have been wanting to find the courage to say something to him for such a long time and never seem to get around to it. Am I perhaps too scared, but not able to admit it?"

Ans: "Faced with difficult circumstances—even those people that come across as being capable and confident, all suffer from some type of anxiety, it's just our make-up. So don't worry about being a little scared, because it happens to us all. Your best defence however is to constantly remain in touch with your fortitude to assist you. Having done so, you will start to feel more confident and become more at ease, understanding what needs to be done. Once you achieve your goal you will be telling yourself- 'That wasn't so hard, why did I allow this problem to cause me so much stress'—having now realised what you're capable of and putting your mind to it."

Therefore, by allowing him to see you composed and in control with an air of authority, he may become a little overwhelmed and intimidated, suddenly questioning himself. This action further shows that by remaining rational during these difficult and sensitive moments, it demonstrates that there is an above average tendency to get a better result. In this case putting your man in his place, finding himself outside of his comfort zone, while you remain safe and comfortably composed.

There's no better time than to take full advantage than now, so if in fact he does open up with a remorseful tone, perhaps play the humility card- just alittle- however, remain dedicated to the cause. Explain to him again that he never spoke aggressively nor laid a hand on you in the past and you want to understand why he's behaving like he is now, so ask him to be honest with you, and to tell you what has made him behave this way.

This really is a defining moment in a relationship since you really need to get to the bottom of it, therefore if he doesn't offer a reply, prompt him by further by asking, "Is it me, have I done something to make you angry, is there something that has happened at work, have you fallen out of love with me". Most times it's none of the above, because in most cases men can't give a plausible reason for their behaviour, since they have no answer themselves. Instead, they remain quietly embarrassed, and if they provide an answer, they blurt out some type of meaningless excuse.

Or maybe it's a case of your man consciously or unconsciously reliving his childhood, having been raised in a dysfunctional family that you were unaware of. In which case he may be suffering from post-traumatic stress in silence, that's now showing itself and reshaping his behaviour.

> **Awareness** – If in fact that is the case, then women who genuinely love and support their partners should get the help their husband/partners need. This is an important reminder for all women out there to discover all they can about their potential long-life partner, long before committing to a relationship. This type of discovery is indeed a shock revelation that can sadly cause regrets, possibly having a profound impact on your future relationship.

Whatever the circumstances, let him know that you're there for him, explaining he doesn't have to become angry and frustrated with himself or take it out on you. However, take the opportunity to further explain to him, his domestic abuse will never be tolerated in your home.

I never thought I could do it and I have

This is a good start as you have shown both yourself and him just how capable of a woman you are in trying to keep a relationship intact, along with helping your husband with his personal problems. By continuing to show him you are a woman of substance, at the same time impressing upon him the need to change his behaviour, effectively putting the ball back into his court. Then continue to monitor him by remaining vigilant, whereby you will start to feel a proper sense of achievement, without having allowed the intervention to get out of hand.

This scenario shows the significance of making a thorough well thought out plan on such a vitally important and complex matter such as domestic abuse, and the impact it will have against any further escalation. A direct challenge to those males who have become accustomed to verbal abuse, having remained unchallenged—until now. The above sequence of events to confront types of abuse in the family applies to both recent and long-term marriages. However, the time frame is of little consequence, as you have found the courage to tell your husband exactly what he needs to be told.

Ques: "I remember having to find the nerve to confront my husband about his behaviour a long time ago, and when I did, I remember to this day the feeling of self-pride that overcame me afterwards. But sometimes I ask myself what my life would be like today had I remained silent?"

Ans: "Which is not only courageous but also an outstanding achievement. Since it sounds like you're still together, that provides you with as good an answer as you are likely to need. Some women remain in verbally abusive situations feeling confused and overwhelmed—not because they lack strength, but because their energy has been spent trying to maintain peace rather than confronting the problem directly. They may never have considered planning for change. That's why it's important to constantly remind yourself: this conversation is about shifting how you view life within domestic abuse, and exploring safe, practical steps toward a resolution. - as you have done"

Although you may be a little hesitant to admit, you have probably been sitting on your hands for far too long. So again, allow yourself to become inspired by what you read, and then become the woman you would like to be, without having to worry about someone else's feelings. As mentioned, women don't have the same type of make-up for a confrontation. That's because whilst one woman understands the level of risk another wont, and that's the reality of life when associated with something so diverse as the complexities of another human being.

Ques: "Why do I feel like I'm too old to try and change my husband, he'll never change, will he?"

Ans: "You're never too old, and it's never too late, so why allow yourself to become overwhelmed by the big picture? Instead, consider this as your greatest challenge in life, so simply think of just one change at a time, that you want him to make and concentrate all your efforts on that. Choose one remedy you come across in this book, implement, ensuring it works, then surprise yourself with what you can accomplish."

Returning to our scenario – This first intervention may not have been entirely the desired result you were looking for; however, you have now made a good start. This is a good outcome, because again you carried it out safely and he is now of the understanding he's under the spotlight. So, let's not forget how this first round encounter was first planned. Unlike perhaps other types of confrontations that have taken place, where there was no planning, and the risk remained far greater.

However, you remained calm and rational without raising your voice, and as importantly you have now settled those nerves you were earlier worried about. You have also gained confidence, having started a new self-styled transformation being so important, particularly since this is the first major hurdle you have ever faced against domestic abuse.

> **Awareness** – Did you recognise the tools that women used having called on her fortitude during that small but significant confrontation with her husband? Comprising of her self-esteem, strength, and courage along with having found her confidence whilst maintaining her self-respect. At a time when it was needed and mattered the most.

As mentioned, there may be an underlying reason -other than trauma- for which he doesn't want to discuss anything in relation to his recent behaviour. It may well be the reaction of someone who just can't bring themselves to say anything at all about the matter, or what's truly on their mind. – However, that's just not good enough.

Such as the male falling out of love, or having found someone new, or perhaps he may in fact be remorseful and embarrassed by his indiscretions, the list goes on. However, the upside is, now that you're proactive on the matter, you will find out. But only as long as you continue to go about your life maintaining a high standard of integrity, keeping high moral ground and keeping your dignity intact, along with monitoring his behaviour methodically. You cannot afford for this matter to just blow over with your man not becoming accountable and receiving some type of consequence. The two areas that women seem to easily disregard—which is guaranteed the male is relying on.

If your husband hasn't agreed to stop his abusive behaviour, you must decide whether to continue trying to resolve the situation or end the relationship. Should that be the latter, then only when you're ready, so best not to make any rash decisions at this stage. Instead stay put, unless you believe your safety is in jeopardy, or you have the capacity and the financial means to move on.

However, in this case, you love your man; therefore, you will do what you can to save your marriage. – within reason.

Ques: "I know in my heart if I say too much, he will take off, so what is a woman to do in these circumstances when her relationship is at stake?"

Ans: "A reality that is all too familiar for many women when presented with a situation fraught with fear and emotionally charged consequences. But ask yourself, are you really a better person in life pandering to a bully, all because you're feeling insecure and holding yourself to ransom. Because that is what you are doing, compromising and letting go of your principles and values, all because for some reason you can't envisage life as you want it to be. A life without his abuse, a life being happy, content, and being treated with respect—it's there if you really want it.".

— There will probably never be a more important time in your life than now, in coming to terms with the fact that your marriage should not be your gate keeper. Because nothing could be further from the truth. —

It may have been a widely held belief that men assume the dominant role—being the primary breadwinner—however times have changed. Women are as strong in the workforce as they are having to run a family household, so who is the dominant force? It's also true, the woman holds the key to the strength and stability of a relationship and keeping the marriage on track.

Again, without the diary having plausible and legible entries, you remain basically in no-man's-land in the event of a divorce, particularly if it comes down to your word against his in domestic abuse cases. Therefore, your diary will prove to be a powerful and historical account of your life during the time in your relationship.

— Never discount its relevance because without it, others will know very little about you, should you sadly become another statistic. —

'It won't get to that," I hear you say—and let's hope you're right. So, remain mindful of the women who have lost everything, their dignity, financial stability, and sometimes even their sanity who also once believed that very same thing.

— Regardless of what you may think about the legalities surrounding the entries you made in your diary becoming a source of evidence, there is an unwritten universal law that is acknowledged by any fair judicial system, the law of conscience. —

A scenario every abusive man should experience

So, imagine how he would feel if his employer spoke to him in such a fashion, by shouting at him in front of his work colleagues— "What have you been doing all day, not very much by the looks of things". It would be at this point whereby the male who is usually the one using abrasive language, now finds himself on the receiving end. Thereby instantly experiencing the consequences that come when feeling the hurt and the embarrassment. Along with that empty feeling when having to return to his place of work each day knowing his employer feels the way he does towards him. A feeling of not belonging, and the despair of being unappreciated, everything he is doing to his wife/partner.

Having received a feeling of encouragement during that first confrontation with your husband, you have now given some thought to continue with your intervention.

— However, always remain mindful, there's no greater uncertainty or unpredictability in life, than that of human beings becoming spontaneously volatile. —

No more so than in a relationship when we talk about a usually mild-mannered male who has now become belligerent, particularly when someone is turning the tables on him. This is a real travesty in life for any woman, now finding herself the subject of trying to resolve such a complex and uncertain matter. Particularly when all she ever wanted was a happy family life with a decent, loving, and caring man.

Ques: "I have only been married for six-months and recently I had to talk with my husband about the changes in him. Until then, I always felt a little reserved and intimated, but strangely I feel more invigorated than ever before. Is that normal?"

Ans: "It's the monkey off your back, that nagging irritant that puts so many women in such an uncomfortable position, without them *really understanding why. That's all changed now, because you have discovered what comes from speaking your mind, that feeling of inclusiveness and equal rights within a relationship".*

Now is the perfect time to fully indulge in your renewed passion for life, whilst constantly using your knew mantra to pause, reflect and engage. Along with your ever-present fortitude to revitalise your well-being and let marriage take a temporary back seat. You may even decide to open up to your closest friend, as this is an excellent form of release, by allowing someone to be aware of your situation.

Although you may believe you have turned the tables, you must contemplate the possibility of all your efforts having little effect on him, and therefore the relationship could well remain in turmoil and coming to an end.

– Should that be the case, how will you survive? –

Financial independence

Without him, do you have the means to provide and support yourself and perhaps that of your children, or find yourself having to survive without your husband's support? It's for this reason, patient planning is key, but again only as long as you remain safe in your home.

The conniving male knows only too well to the significance of this mind mindset, which he uses as leveraged intimidation, silently warning his wife against the thought of leaving him. That is why a woman should never, ever, become involved in a committed relationship to begin with, without prior rock-solid agreements. All of which are put in place to ensure she has her own ability to maintain her ongoing financial independence.

The days are gone when women should have to accept a mega allowance from their husband to cover groceries and other incidentals, having no access to a bank account. If you have found yourself in this situation then you are probably the victim of another type of abuse, coercion and control, which we will address at a later stage. But for now, regarding his verbal and physical abuse, it's highly recommended you start a cunning kick—slang for keeping cash hidden in reserve—in case you need to leave quickly.

Ques: "My husband keeps a tight rein on our finances, and although I haven't complained to him, I do miss not having my own money. However, I'm not sure how to really go about it, on top of his abuse?"

Ans: "Note the recommendations from recent discussions on proper planning, the location, when and where, and the potential consequences when contemplating a possible confrontation. If speaking to him feels uncomfortable then shift your focus inward—prioritise yourself rather than reacting to his attention-seeking behavior. This subtle shift draws attention to your strength and presence, which is exactly where it should be. Still, be prepared for any retaliatory remarks. If and when they come, remember to maintain your mantra-, by simply pausing, reflect on the matter at hand, before engaging".

– This perhaps represents the most effective psychological strategy a woman can employ to challenge a man's mindset in such circumstances—far more impactful than the often-fruitless path of verbal confrontation that all too often becomes a shouting match. –

Meanwhile start making early enquiries to get your own personal financial dependence, that all important means for survival.

It's now clear that after a relatively recent marriage, the husband in this scenario won't commit to remaining abuse free or even discuss financial matters, other than having carried out a complete reversal on his earlier agreements. Or perhaps it's a marriage of some standing where the male has for some time already demonstrated his verbal abuse and controlling manner. Therefore, by acting more distant and becoming less involved at home, you're making him notice that things have changed. – Remember actions speak louder than words.

It really sinks in when he sees you're no longer sharing a bed with him. This might seem like marital blackmail, but it's a necessary course of action, as it sets clear boundaries and forces him into a corner. As a result, he starts to feel increasingly isolated. The absence of affection weighs on him, the home no longer feels comfortable, and he begins to sense the walls closing in around him.

Should his demeanour remain as it is, this shows he has no intention of making any changes, - certainly not in the short term-, whereby he soon becomes entrenched in his own world of self-righteousness, stewing away, remaining stubborn. However, if he gets around sheepishly with an air of being less self-confident you have already made a big first impression.

Consequently, he won't know how to deal with it, certainly not immediately, unless he was waiting for this situation to come to a head so he could end the relationship. Should this be the case, he's attempting to make it easy for himself and providing less delay for you to get on with your life. Therefore, unless he can first admit to himself that he is in the wrong and tries to amend his behaviour by opening up and talking to you first, then you must continue holding firm, remaining unflappable.

Again, most men in this situation find themselves believing their wife will soon come around to their way of thinking, at the same time saying to themselves, 'she could be serious', and 'she might leave me'. This is all too familiar, where the male's selfishness hinders any immediate resolution, again believing the woman will simply give in and play into his hands. However, he has underestimated you, because you are no longer that easily manipulated person you may have been in the past, therefore...

— Under no circumstances can you allow this to happen —

While refusing to discuss his mistakes and remaining his own worst enemy, you, however, begin to feel empowered. You can feel good about the decisions you have made thus far and the journey you are now on. Therefore, it really comes down to an actual battle of wills, it's the innocent party that weathers the storm more comfortably knowing you are in the right. In contrast to the guilty party, who continue to wrestle with his own conscience whilst remaining in denial on issues he perfectly understands he is clearly wrong about.

Let's continue with this standoff, and again, you have now come to terms with going about your life paying less interest to your marriage, -other than

Marriage

your children if in the family way- and becoming more interested in you as a person.

— Never forget you're a woman of substance, a woman that's determined to make the necessary sacrifices to make the changes in her life to ensure she lives the life she has always wanted and so deserves. —

It's time to increase the pressure, so stop doing his cooking and washing, and while this strategy may seem harsh, it provides further consequences, producing the desired effect of making him accountable. Continue to force his hand, otherwise why bother to remain in this relationship under these circumstances, so just think about that for a while.

To accomplish your goals, there's another sharp tool within your fortitude arsenal—your resilience, that goes hand in hand with also being persistent. Both of which will ensure you will bounce back every time you appear to hit a roadblock. Because until he swallows his pride and man's up by genuinely acknowledging the errors of his way, you will need to show plenty of both.

Having continued to maintain your present demeanour— remaining composed, along with keeping your plan in place, let's assume he does finally attempt to discuss the matter. However, should that be the case, chances are he will sidestep the real issues, which men are very good at. So be aware, as this is your opportunity to say your peace, so continue remaining calm and composed, by simply remarking…

"I am happy to talk to you, so what would you like to say", with her husband replying, " well I'm not really sure", and that's because he has no answers, 'We need to pick up from where we left off regarding the way you have been treating me, which you know is wrong, and I won't be tolerating it anymore. If you don't stop, then I have made the decision to end our marriage, and I don't want to get into any arguments with you over this, because it won't do either of us any good do you understand me." With a faint reply of "yes" from her husband.

As mentioned, human beings dislike being chastised, even more so when a male is being reprimanded by a woman, with the man now believing he is being threatened. That's because a woman in these circumstances has little choice but to go to the extreme to ensure he feels the full impact, the magnitude of those immortal words - end our marriage - and although he may not be showing it, he will most definitely be feeling it. However, don't be surprised if he isn't further forthcoming as you would have hoped, it's what human beings do instinctively when they know they are backed into a tight corner and stubbornly preferring to offer token excuses.

So, the ball continues to remain in his court, and as mentioned, to get the best out of anyone simply talk rationally and calmly, which in return can pay big dividends. As was the case in this recent scenario, since the male eventually gave his wife reason to believe he wants to put an end to his behaviour and indeed the whole matter, although not having the courage to admit to his shortcomings.

Ques: "I found out long ago that respectful conversation with my husband was our salvation, which we are both so grateful for. I sometimes ask myself why couples can't or won't try doing the same, it's so easy, offering so many benefits?"

Ans: "Most people would agree with you, it's unfortunate that so many couples appear to prefer resentment rather than find a solution. Common sense logic isn't always as easy to embrace, especially when emotions run high and the habits of dysfunction take root. What seems like a straightforward procedure can become elusive and sadly for so many to remain out of reach. Everyone deserves a second chance in life, but it's that repeated message of hearing, 'it won't happen again', that so many women have heard time and time again. It's that pattern of behaviour, where women have allowed themselves to be browbeaten almost into submission, whilst at the same time continuing to struggle with their own emotions."

Therefore, on this occasion you can be certain your man didn't want you to leave him, and further proof your resilience played a pivotal role in gaining the upper hand. A good time to provide support for your man as only a woman can, as again he showed some remorse - in a roundabout way - although still no mention of his physical and verbal behaviour. Keeping in mind he will need to be reminded that this is the very last time you will ever defend him against any further domestic abuse.

-Her humility in this moment shows how deeply she cares, even when faced with his poor behaviour - something many men fail to appreciate. But the real shift is this, she also showed her assertiveness and authority, a strength he will always remember-.

This is a great outcome for those women who would not take a backward step on similar serious issue, and a profound reminder of what a woman can accomplish. Particularly in this case where a woman followed through with the difficult and quite daunting situation of living in an estranged household. As the facts show, there just aren't enough women standing up for themselves and following through during these types of matters.

That said, the necessity of monitoring and keeping him on the straight and narrow is paramount, as well as disciplining yourself against becoming complacent.

- Along with understanding the amount of time you are prepared to invest in this male-

This is such a key point, ensuring the male understands just how serious the situation really is, especially the high stakes in realising he could very well lose his wife if he doesn't change his ways.

That point needs to be pushed even further, because it shows the difference between a man who simply brushes off his wife's words as just complaining—and keeps mistreating her—and the man who suddenly realises his wife is extremely serious because she follows through on what she says.

— It's a profound reminder—don't play games or issue empty promises. If you're going to take a stand, mean it and follow through regardless —

Ques: "Now that I have finally made some inroads in turning my husband's behaviour around, I completely understand the benefits of standing up for myself. I question why so many couples are simply getting married and having children, with little knowledge of what is really required to maintain a stable relationship?"

Ans: "A courageous and positive move in your opposition towards your husband's behaviour. What a travesty it is when a woman not only discovers domestic abuse has infiltrated her space but then has to eradicate it, usually on her own. There are countless women who wish now they had been better educated and prepared having put in place domestic abuse preventative measures from the start of their relationship. In doing so avoiding the great pains they ultimately went through or continue to do so in order to save their marriage".

Remain mindful of how that outcome came about and the lessons learnt. Therefore, always go above and beyond with what would otherwise be necessary to resolve any type of domestic abuse issue. Then work backwards until the level of consequences matches the severity of the problem, in this case, his physical and verbal abuse. As you did, by making it clear, i.e. no more washing, cooking, or sleeping with him, which gets under every man's skin. So again, never underscore or become half-hearted about becoming judge and jury as you would be on other matters, otherwise he will know and he will do likewise, whereby you will soon be back to square one.

Maintain the pressure

But now we need to look at a not too dissimilar situation where the male who still hasn't opened up and talked about his unacceptable behaviour. Instead appears to just accept his wife's decision to live separately under the same roof.

Everyone has their limitations, particularly women who have endured being abused by her husband. Who now have provided their husbands with both an ultimatum and ample time to discuss and resolve the matter. However, the time has come for her to apply another strategy to save her marriage—by sending him a letter, since he appears to be waiting for this issue to simply disappear- which is not an option.

Marriage

This letter must not hold back and make sure you keep a copy, along with making continued entries into your diary—very important—as he needs to understand it's more than a letter, it's an ultimatum. Once again, you can't allow him to believe it's a trivial matter and that time heals everything, because in these circumstances, it doesn't—unless completely resolved. Therefore, the letter must specifically explain the situation is about him and not so much about you. So be very specific on that point, reminding him the letter is in response to domestic abuse and his refusal to talk openly with you on the matter.

Further reminding him, he broke his promise, by emphasising that he gave his word he would never allow domestic abuse to enter the relationship, fully expressing your refusal to live in a toxic environment. In this letter, mention what was described earlier by asking him how he would feel if his employer spoke to him in the same way he has been talking to you. Explain to him that's it's no different to the way he is making you think about possibly finding another man, a man that treats you with love and respect, so don't hold back.

Using different strategies is necessary, as it applies more leverage, giving you more options to get your point across. Particularly since the average male fails to comprehend the gravity of the problem, usually implying, "What's all the fuss about." Nor does he understand the hurt he is causing, or more alarming, that he doesn't understand why he is behaving the way he does in the first place.

In your letter, be fair but firm, and drive these points home, explaining that he is throwing away a lifetime of potential happiness without you, and that he will soon feel the impact of being divorced unless he is prepared to change his ways. Again, be very specific, as a letter of this nature can deliver him with profound psychological awareness, along with providing you with a sense of personal satisfaction.

The following is an example of a letter you may like to consider...

I hope you take a moment to read this letter with an open heart, as we have both been struggling with how to express our feelings, and I need to share what's been weighing heavily on my mind.

Preventing and Ending Domestic Abuse

Lately, the words you've spoken to me have cut deeper than you might realise. The verbal and physical abuse has left scars that aren't visible but are very real. It's not just the hurtful words themselves, but the way they make me feel, small, unworthy, and unloved. I know this isn't the man I fell in love with, and it breaks my heart to see you this way.

I want you to understand the impact your words have on the two of us. They create a distance between us, a barrier that keeps growing. I miss the days when we communicated with love and laughter, when we were each other's safe haven. I believe deep down that you don't want to hurt me. I believe in the good in you, the man who once promised to cherish and protect me.

This behaviour is not only hurting me but also changing you, it's turning you into someone I know you don't want to be. I want us to be partners, to support each other through thick and thin. I want us to be the best versions of ourselves, together.

I love you deeply, and it's because of this love that I'm reaching out to you. I want our marriage to survive, but we need to resolve this issue together.

Let's find a way to communicate without hurtful words and rebuild the trust and respect that was our foundation.

Please let's work on this together, let's seek help together if we need it, and let's remember why we fell in love and fight for that love.

With all my love.

There are times when no amount of talk can take the place of a heartfelt letter, which can do wonders about a couple's emotional well-being, but only if he is that way inclined. By going to these levels shows the passion and commitment a woman is prepared to go to, and not just to keep the relationship on track. It shows a man humility, empathy, and the expression of love for what it stands for.

These men may well believe they are a hard nut to crack, but on this occasion, he is very much mistaken. That's because the women who now follow these guidelines, have hopefully found the inspiration for defending themselves through skill and cunning, and for ever more.

It's time all women realised that men have had their own way for far too long in the family home, having remained unchallenged their entire lives. But now women are taking a new stand, with a fresh approach, and no longer prepared to just accept the status quo. They want their say without reprisal, without the threat of domestic abuse. Is that too much to ask of a husband, along with being spoken to respectfully and to be shown the love they both signed up for?

– If that means being without her man because of his refusal to resolve his problems regarding domestic abuse, then that's the way it must be. –

It could never be overstated the alarming number of women who have challenged their man for the very first time, then sadly relent only to give in. Men understand that possibility all too well. Sadly, this mindset provides escalation in further repercussions, being the male also realises the likelihood of any future attempt by their wives to interfere in their lives will end the same way- believing life will simply go back to how it was.

When these chauvinistic males discover through their wife's letter- threatening to dissolve the marriage- many soon develop second thoughts regarding their behaviour.

– Throwing down the gauntlet –

You have the tiger by the tail

He will then remind himself that you have already followed through with changes to the usual living arrangements. Whereby you now sleep alone and withdrawn from looking after him, where he now continues to feel ostracised. This man also realises that you're not sitting around the home but getting out and about, remaining happy and upbeat. Therefore, he must decide whether to continue with his childish and stubborn behaviour by standing his ground, and losing his wife, or come to his senses by taking a good hard look at himself.

– If he were smart, he would finally come to his senses and realize that his wife is protecting him from himself. Once the penny drops, he will hopefully come to terms with the fact his wife was right all along, by never allowing domestic abuse to come between them. –

As hard as it is to digest, we should remind ourselves of a common scenario, where there are many women along with their children who literally had no choice but to walk out the door. This is a far too common occurrence in our society with some abused women who can barely salvage what personal belongings they can, before exiting the home.

Because their safety was seriously jeopardized, with no money and nowhere to go, they threw themselves at the mercy of the authorities, family, and friends. This type of mindset must end, whereby women shouldn't need to feel they have to leave the home, unless, as mentioned, they are of course escaping violent and aggressive behaviour. Instead, women should remain secretive whilst seeking legal advice before making any rash decisions, in order to learn more about their rights.

Ques: "I'm beginning to realise that I have the drive to look into what my rights are as a woman living in an abusive relationship, because I agree, why should I have to be the one to just pack my bags and look for somewhere else to live?"

Ans: "Again, if the abuse is manageable, then looking into your legal rights without letting on to anybody—is a masterstroke—and more women should adopt the same attitude. By allowing yourself to be consumed within the confines of four walls where abuse is commonplace is unthinkable to those in society who experience love and respect."

Women of substance make their own way in life by looking into the law, which they can do themselves at no cost. By simply sourcing readily available material and information, seeking counselling, by engaging in legal aid, or by providing a professional to suit their budget. Whatever your preference is, you must start helping yourself, and when you do, you will suddenly learn quickly how you are reshaping your life, in so many other ways.

Be mindful, even if you have no money, there is a lot of information on women's rights, which is free, that you can easily access. Go to your local library, and discover a quiet sanctuary, where you can make further entries into your diary. Source text on legal matters involving domestic abuse, perhaps divorce—assisted by a librarian. A great opportunity to work on your fortitude, by leveraging your courage, self-discipline, and emotional resilience, instead of sitting back and watching the grass grow around your feet.

Face the facts, don't hide behind them

Should that letter continue to have little effect on him, then you know it's time to think about the future direction you need to take, probably without him. But sadly, this is when too many women cannot keep their emotions in check, and think negatively, then worry unnecessarily about things that most likely won't ever happen, and if it does, it will sort itself out, as life intended.

Although there will be a feeling of anxiety, you must remember you are being tested by the universe, as we all are from time to time. You need to stay focused, remain positive and be determined. All of which adds to your resilience being so important, and again everything will eventually turn out for the best. You must believe that, for your own peace of mind.

Ask yourself what's the rush in making any sudden decisions, if in fact he isn't responding the way you had hoped. So, remember you are now living as a single woman under the same roof as your now estranged husband. That's because, although you are perhaps raising children you can make your own decisions due to his inability to reconcile on such an important matter.

But first thing first, continue making entries on matters—as just mentioned—in your diary as this is a continuing, significant event, and remind yourself, unlike many women, you're not out on the street. Don't even contemplate leaving your home as you have every right to stay where you are, unless once again, you believe your safety is at risk.

When any type of physical abuse has entered the relationship, a woman should immediately call the police as violent behaviour is high risk, and no amount of standing your ground is worth losing your life over.

Followed closely by initiating the protection orders available to every woman and issued by the courts which are then served on him, so in the event he further misbehaves, the authorities remove him from the premises.

Ques: "I never wanted it to come to this. Why does it seem to be so difficult and soul destroying?

Ans: "Only if you allow it to be, therefore, take control of your life, as we have previously discussed and demonstrated in so many ways throughout this book. For further inspiration imagine a different type of circumstance where a mother will move both heaven and earth when she discovers her child has a serious medical condition. Your situation is potentially as serious, make no mistake about it."

As mentioned, don't make the mistake of just reading through the pages. Highlight anything that jumps out at you and follow through by making entries into your diary, then carefully consider the control measures you need to put into place and closely monitor.

Think wisely and contemplate filing for a court order to have him removed from the home and applying for a protection order keeping him as far away from you as possible. There are of course women preferring to stay in their home who have the option for specific terms attached to a court order that issues an apprehended violence order. Again, if he escalates his behaviour, the wife can have him arrested. However, this strategy is potentially at great personal risk to the woman.

The police can only do so much and cannot constantly watch over you. Therefore, if you do decide to run the gauntlet (again by facing the potential consequences of living under the same roof with your husband, then realise the personal high – risk situation you are taking.

Since you have decided to remain in the home with your husband/partner who hasn't become violent, it's important to maintain your new self-style image. By remaining calm and upbeat, reminding yourself you're not on planet earth to be intimidated by anyone. Especially by someone who once claimed their love for you but now makes a complete mockery out of what a respectful and loving relationship is truly all about.

As mentioned, although it will be difficult being under the same roof, it's the choice you have made, so try to imagine your estranged husband as being only a lodger. It's time to make subtle and suitable inroads into more serious adjustments in your life, as you are not about to wait around for him to behave like a responsible human being. Instead, think more on these realistic lines, if he wants you, he needs to earn you.

Whatever you do, don't make the mistake of allowing him to believe you are coming around and taking the foot off the brake, as it's almost guaranteed that's exactly what he is hoping for. As chances are his mindset will be, everything appears to be back to normal, almost as if nothing ever happened. Unless of course he has already made up his mind that the relationship is over. In that case, he won't attempt to save his marriage; and you would then have all the answers you need about your relationship- therefore time to take steps to end it.

– If in fact that's the case, then tread carefully and not do anything too drastic, like drawing unnecessary attention to an already sensitive situation. You can ill afford his behaviour to escalate, always remain mindful of that. –

However, it's more than likely he's not contemplating ending the marriage, instead maintaining a futile attempt along with continuous stubbornness, like a spoilt child. Therefore, the battle of the will continues, a type of psychological warfare, as he will probably be reading over your letter, wondering what his next move should be.

Meanwhile, now that you have hopefully become shrouded in your new aura of confidence and wellbeing, you want to be noticed for all the right reasons. Along with the appearance of someone feeling good about themselves since you are now heading in the right direction to take back control of your life.

Preventing and Ending Domestic Abuse

Ques: "Many years ago, shortly after our marriage, I did the exact same thing, by not pandering to my husband which I have no regrets. There was no way I was going to look after him in the home until he learned how to respect me, which he finally did, -Isn't that the only way to find out about a man's true feelings?"

Ans: Absolutely — provided his motives are genuine and enduring. Withholding attention, along with reducing the comforts and personal care he has come to expect at home, becomes a powerful form of tough love. Over time, it's remarkably effective, allowing you to create change without engaging in the confrontations that far too many women are drawn into.

These recommendations have real merit, offering safe resolute control measures, but only if there's a thought-out plan in place. By doing so, you are giving yourself the upper hand because of the way you have instigated this whole affair. This will have a significant outcome on your personal well-being and indeed reach your goal of finding future happiness.

-Your circumstances are unique to you, therefore anything you read that inspires you must be analysed in depth before exercising any action-.

For those of you with children, it's a matter for you to learn how to delegate - that's important - starting with your children, by ensuring they assist you with chores, naturally considering their age group, so take charge and stay in control, as it's an area a woman does best.

Now is an appropriate time to discuss a very serious matter particularly when children are involved - The worst situation a woman can ever possibly find herself in is when she confronts her man in the confines of the home and blurts out, "It's over, I've had enough. I'm taking the kids, and we are leaving for good." Those words may seem harmless enough to a woman, having finally found the courage to speak her mind, but the repercussions can be fatal. The male becomes suddenly shocked when hearing his wife is leaving him, but to also hear the children are leaving as well, is more than he can bear. It's at this very point that so many women are sadly killed, through their innocent enough actions of despair, but failing to understand the ramifications of what she has announced- releasing the monster that lurks inside the man.

Let this one piece of serious advice remain with every woman—young or old—and keep at the forefront of their mind. Likewise, whenever there's high intensity, simply align with your new mantra; to pause, reflect, before you engage - as a further control against making a potential grave mistake.

It's time for him to think things over!

It may be that your man isn't as brutal as some of those men who carry out this type of physical punishment on defenseless women, each and every day. However, you never want to find out.

Admittedly, it's a trying time, having to make decisions and arrangements in the absence of a caring and willing husband, while he contemplates what to do. During this time, it's so important to remain self-assured and you will accomplish all you set out to do. Call a family service councillor and meet up for a chat, it will do you wonders. Making that first move sets off a reaction you never thought possible, it can be life changing and is therefore highly recommended. Again, remain proactive, not reactive.

This is a highly recommended option, as these people have special skills to assist you, providing the type of expertise you were perhaps unaware of. It offers that all-important human touch that rekindles the belief that care and compassion in human nature still exists. It provides a reference to all important documentation you file to support you in the future, being a further reminder to make those entries into your diary.

If your husband doesn't provide you with any financial stability, you can learn how to apply for urgent financial assistance along with child support—again, documenting everything you can.

If you aren't working, then it's best you acknowledge this is the time to find a job. As difficult as that may be to acknowledge, perhaps only a casual position whereby you will receive some additional personal financial benefits.

In the event you haven't been in the workforce before you will discover the personal satisfaction that comes with being employed, meeting new people, and making new friends. Becoming more worldly, sustainable, independent, and more resilient. Not feeling you must be reliant on marriage as being your only source of survival. Remembering you are a woman of substance and not just someone that allows one other person to maintain a hold on you.

Ques: "My husband would just let things remain as they are, without thinking too much about the need for change, so what can I do?"

Ans: "There are so many options you can take in life, but only if you become motivated to follow them through. As for him not thinking about it, he has zero respect for you. However, continuing with the cold shoulder strategy gives you the time to make the necessary changes to your life."

We are discussing the importance of remaining one step ahead of this current situation that can realistically go either way, and although the relationship hasn't completely collapsed, it's in limbo or deadlocked.

— *It's okay to remain optimistic, hoping that he may come to his senses, it's equally notable to accept that he may not.* —

In your current situation living under the same roof together, you need to look for any further change in his behaviour as he could well become frustrated and further annoyed. Therefore, it is wise to review your safety and overall security during the night, such as having a lock put on a door.

The point here is many males in this situation don't take the matter seriously enough or want to understand the significance of the issues, telling himself that you belong to him—particularly when alcohol is involved, then the level of risk has just climbed even higher.

-It suddenly became clear what I needed to do.-

In an age where the cost of living prevents many women from moving away from their home, there's a lot of merit in women remaining in their own home and protecting themselves—under certain conditions. Therefore, women should look at these options regarding their safety and a lot more, by simply applying for a court order to challenge their husband's behaviour. As should other family members that suspect their loved ones are likely victims, again by becoming more familiar with the laws of the land that provide a level of protection.

Be mindful when applying for legal protection because there are women that fail to make the connection with the errors of their own ways in a relationship—perhaps it doesn't apply to you. When a male refuses to talk, again it's likely he is guilty and hoping the matter just goes away. It may also mean he has issues with you that you are unaware of. Therefore, in retrospect, women need to be completely honest and ask themselves whether their own behaviour is in any way connected to the source of his abuse.

— This is not to make any excuses for his behaviour —

Ques: "I have been married for many years and question myself over that possibility, and I will admit when we argue he sometimes brings out the worst in me, which I always regret afterwards, and wonder how to handle these situations better?"

Ans: "The most important thing to do now is to understand that although it may seem he brings out the worst in you, you must be accountable for your own actions. Though it may be difficult, approach any interaction with him calmly and rationally, following the recommendations, and you will find the peace you are looking for. - Stick to the script?"

However, by providing him with an opportunity to open up on this issue, he might make some surprising revelations about you that you weren't aware of. Or maybe he will open up another way, by offering excuses as a way out of the mess he first created. Either way you are drawing him out of himself, so maintain the pressure, and do not give up.

Preventing and Ending Domestic Abuse

It's time for a breather and to share a poem with all those females who may need a little -pick me up- and perhaps would like to read and share this poem with someone special in their life…

Remember the day when you said, "I love you."

And I felt the warmth of your embrace.

Remember the joy when you said, "I do."

And you saw the smile on my face.

Remember the times when we laughed together

And shared our hopes and dreams.

Remember the moments we cried side by side,

And comforted screams we could no longer hide.

Remember the love that once shone brightly,

A flame in our hearts that refuses to go lightly.

Remember the vows you solemnly made,

Promising love that would never fade.

Remember the energy, passion, and time,

You poured into love like reason and rhyme.

Remember commitment, respect, and truth,

The forgiveness we practiced from age into youth.

Love isn't magic that flickers one day,

It's something we nurture in work and in play.

It's not a fairytale made out of dreams,

But quiet contentment flows in between.

So, hold to the bond and give it your all,

Don't let our marriage stumble and fall.

Remember these things, don't walk away.

Let's fight for love, come what may.

Don't let divorce drive us apart,

Let's carry our vows back into our hearts.

Returning to our scenario…

So now you have decided to ring him, asking him to meet you at a coffee shop, in a further attempt to break the deadlock and find a solution. You reasoned that being in public, away from his comfort zone, he will hopefully be more inclined to listen and hopefully open up.

He will probably show up, because for him it's a case of curiosity, whereby you can come face to face with your husband and ask him if he has anything he wants to get off his chest about you. However, it's during this time that you discover he hasn't, although he confesses to reading your letter therefore providing you with the ice breaker you have been waiting for.

It could be argued, why would anyone chase after someone who appears to be so undeserving and that's understandable. Resolving matrimonial issues is deeply personal and therefore won't always align with all outside opinions. In this scenario this brave woman is attempting to save her marriage, other than just giving up. This is a woman who loves her man, believing he loves her, and despite his abusive behaviour she wants him to understand what he is doing, believing he is not the man he is currently portraying. – A bold move.

In no uncertain terms explain to him once again how you feel, and how hurt you are, particularly in the way he speaks and treats you. At this point, you want an answer from him so be extra assertive, as it's usually at this point that many women simply give in, being a big mistake. This is not to scare you, however you are now on the tilt and if you give in you will either walk away or spend the rest of your life under the spell of your abuser.

As any woman would understand when loving her man—since she is normally caring and compassionate—she can become highly emotional by this ordeal. Particularly after hearing him defend himself having been asked the question, "I need an answer from you before we leave this coffee shop, are you going to stop abusing me, and start to treat me with respect, when he tells you again "You have it all wrong", and "You're too sensitive" and "you're over-reacting". The battle of the wills continues, whereby he will most likely continue to make further excuses. So, unless you hold your ground and raise the stakes, you will have gained little traction, whereby he will only revert to his old antics.

Alternatively, he may just realise how foolish he has been and now wants to talk to you decently, because he doesn't want to lose you. Particularly since you have already made it very clear you are prepared to leave him. Either way, you have given him something profound to think about.

Safety in numbers

Remain patient, because although it may turn out that his explanation isn't exactly what you were hoping for, you may also be surprised.

However, on this occasion you believe he is starting to shift but you will still need to go that extra distance, by asking him, "If our marriage is to survive, we both need to respect, love, and talk to each other decently, isn't that what you want?" while waiting for an answer. Importantly, you must insist on eye contact because you need more than just an answer…

– You need to have looked into his soul, to see any genuine sincerity, or redemption –

Currently he feels the mounting pressure and looks you in the eye and answers 'yes', then there's no reason not to doubt him any further—at this time—because you have made yourself perfectly clear. In return for accepting his word, you will need to monitor him, thus allowing yourself to remain in the box seat, which he is now all too aware of.

You planned and carried out this meeting in a public place where there's safety in numbers, maximising the level of safety. You carried out your questioning with integrity, remaining calm and rational and to the point, never allowing yourself to be drawn into an argument. Achieving a reasonable outcome, given the circumstances, was significant enough. Especially considering the risk, had the meeting taken place elsewhere and unfolded differently.

Couples who pick up on each other's indiscretions and talk it over immediately are looking out for one another, maintaining a powerful level of unity and commitment. This is vitally important in every type of relationship, and although in this case the male was reluctant at first this woman never gave in nor is she about to give up. He now needs to be spoken to in a way he continues to understand what acceptable conversational etiquette is. Along with continuing to provide a little humility which can be framed as reconciliation rather than punishment.

Forward thinking is your contingency plan!

– Regardless of your present circumstances in a marriage, a woman should realise the importance of forward thinking, thereby always having a contingency plan in place. –

In complete contrast to the outcome of the above meeting at the coffee shop -where the male shows remorse-, in this next scenario the male won't give any ground or provide any rational explanation for his behaviour. All the while he kept his head down when you asked him questions. Then chances are you have completely misread this man from day one. Someone who suddenly and inexplicitly turned for the worse and perhaps now wants out of the marriage.

Whatever his motives, it's a desperately sad time, where you now must make some big decisions when moving forward. A woman, having until recently been supported by her husband, has now every reason to feel abandoned and alone. A feeling of despair along with the possibility of raising small children on her own, possibly with no job and little prospects. Regardless of what is going on in his head during this meeting, you can be sure you have taken this matter as far as you can- for now.

Preventing and Ending Domestic Abuse

Again, if no physical violence has occurred, you can decide whether you want to try to further resolve the matter or end it—but not a decision you should take lightly or indeed make straight away. There comes a time in all our lives when we need to make the type of decision we would rather not have to, but never during the time of frustration, anger, or when emotions are at their peak.

As mentioned, having a contingency plan makes perfect sense, particularly when faced with the type of complexities that are within a troubled marriage. However, these plans must be made early, in the event your preferred outcome goes awry, which provides you with alternative options you are ready to put into place. It's not ideal, but it's part of life we must accept, however having something else at the ready lessens the initial disappointment.

— It's only a setback, not the end of the world —

Reflecting on the weight placed on any young mother's shoulders, who has found herself in this difficult of situations with small children. Knowing it all too well, her husband can't look her in the eye and provide any explanation as to why he is abusive towards her. We can therefore assume he cannot commit to loving and respecting her, as he once confessed to. – How can this be? Is it now time for a court order?

Ques: "I suppose I am like many mothers that stress about doing this sort of thing, when living under the same roof as their estranged husband, worrying it might make things worse. Is this really the best solution'?"

Ans: "There is always an element of risk, but only if there's no physical violence and you can manage your mental health. If he lays a hand on you, call the police immediately, justice must be served. Women must be made to feel safe in their own home and never have to feel they have to be the ones to leave the home, he is at fault so let him be the one to leave. He must either realize the error of his ways, while you continue building your case against him, or put plans together to end the relationship.

Since you continue to believe in rehabilitating your man, the time has come to apply for that court order to ensure there will be consequences, but without him initially knowing about it. As mentioned, start thinking more independently by getting some degree of financial independence and plan for your possible future separation. He is aware that it's only a matter of time when the relationship completely dissolves itself—unless he acts. This action of a court order will again put the ball firmly back into his court, whereby he will be feeling further pressure, fully understanding he has also been given one very last chance. That being, to either follow his wife's lead and come to his senses, or live out the rest of his life knowingly, having lost his wife and family, by foolishly cutting his nose off to spite his face. – The choice is entirely his.

Is my head really in the clouds?

There are women of integrity and with high moral conviction who, despite their strength of character, remain unaware that their partners are narcissists or even sociopaths.

The type of personality disorder that allows the male to maintain his deception in front of their wife/partner—who easily becomes blindsided via his clever antics and subtle manipulation. Therefore, his behaviour remains unnoticed by those women who don't or can't read the signs, instead it's business as usual. Under these circumstances we should therefore assume that a perpetrator with personality disorders may well remain undiagnosed, for life. As a result, many women continue being a type of unwitting participant, while the male remains ignorant to his own condition and indeed his behaviour. It's a deeply troubling dynamic, marked by deep emotional confusion.

Under these types of constraints, the male is in a relationship under false pretenses, showing to be doing the right thing one minute, then becoming obstinate the next. Never able to truly understand what it means to commit to a relationship, let alone the responsibilities that come with marriage and raising a family.

Preventing and Ending Domestic Abuse

Ques: "But all humans display a degree of insensitivity and types of behaviour we don't always agree with. We just have to deal with it, isn't that, right?"

Ans: "Yes, that's true. Most of us have moments we would rather forget when we've acted thoughtlessly or hurt someone we care about. It's a vastly different situation to let off steam and being moody, it's another continuing to be verbally abusive towards the person you confessed your love for. The impact on women is lasting, made worse since the abuser then expects to maintain an intimate sexual relationship, as if nothing has happened. We should all remain aware, there are those—men—who don't show any remorse at all, not because they won't... but because they can't. It's ingrained in who they are, having a total lack of empathy and compassion. Something many women didn't recognise early on, that would have otherwise been the clearest warning sign, to leave well alone. As you say, we have to deal with it, and that's what we are doing."

As of now, this young woman knows more about relationship issues through the guidance given within these pages, along with having a renewed determination. She has now identified and understood the difference between what may have appeared earlier to be trivial was, in fact, extremely significant. That of her husband not being able to make eye contact with her or provide any answers regarding his abusive behaviour. All of which would have come naturally from a loving husband and father wanting to make amends.

You have decided to talk to a trusted confidant, and although listening to someone's point of view can also be refreshing, it may not be pleasantly rewarding. However, any objection to your decisions regarding your way forward should be held in high regard, since the views your confidante offers should not be emotionally motivated.

If you're not completely happy or convinced about the discussions you had with your confidante, and remain somewhat confused, then seriously consider making an appointment with a marriage counsellor. By doing so, again as mentioned, - you will receive professional advice, which will provide you with more clarification of how your mindset reacts to your set of circumstances.

— Unless he wants to start a rational conversation —

Instead, remain civil towards him and give him no reason to believe anything is untoward, other than his understanding that you will no longer sleep with him, or do his cooking and cleaning. However, in all probability he continues to believe you will come around to his way of thinking, so promise yourself that won't be happening. Unfortunately, there's no silver lining even with a protection court order, and while it's a good start the earlier facts regarding the lack of timely personalised protection by the authorities remain.

As mentioned, the police cannot constantly guard your home, nor are they able to prevent anyone with secret, premeditated, and sinister motives from committing heinous crimes. Sadly, you are alone. That said, be extra sure that you find out exactly the date and time the court order is to be handed to him, so that you can be in a safe house at the time it is executed. Do not take the chance of being with him alone in your home after he receives the news. Instead, you have previously planned, amongst other things your temporary escape—remember that contingency plan? Again, keeping yourself one step ahead of being in harm's way.

This is where you will stay put for the time being, until the time comes when if you believe you can return home safely—if that's your decision. Should you make that decision to return home at a later date, then ensure you have spoken to him or having met with him in a public place, making it very clear, and in no uncertain terms, that it will only take one phone call for him to be arrested if he continues to show any signs of domestic abuse.

Let's be very clear, we are talking about the rest of your life, so why would you be in any hurry to return home. Particularly since he has just been issued court orders, or unless you are completely satisfied, he is rational and calm, perhaps genuinely expressing his feelings about missing you and the children. A truly complex and emotional rollercoaster, however a woman is fortunately equipped to handle these situations better than most men, but only when controlling her emotions.

All the while he gathers his thoughts, wondering what he should do, remaining acutely aware of the protection orders along with having to look after himself when at home. With only two options, by remaining stubborn and losing his wife and family or two—relents by refraining from any further abusive behaviour, being acutely aware of dire consequences he now finds himself in.

Again, there are those men who choose for whatever reason to be their own worst enemy and remain pigheaded, but a woman inherently understands how to remain true to herself, her cause and her children.

This is where a woman should provide her man with some home truths by explaining to him, he loses control of himself, that his better judgement becomes temporarily impaired. Further explaining his need to pause, reflect before he engages, i.e. says or does anything, helping him to suppress any urges he has for abusive behaviour.

Discuss it and bring it out into the open, addressing the elephant in the room, a subject that can be as astonishing to the male as it is to you. Having the courage to raise these issues can lift the weight of an entire nation from the shoulders of the male. Particularly since he couldn't muster the strength to face up to his own indiscretions without your help. Should the day come, when the male in this scenario wants to finally discuss his shortcomings, he will know it was all made possible by his wife, through her courage, her determination, and her resilience.

On this occasion this stubborn male did in fact come to his senses, but not before this wife had again used her powers of persuasion. She made it known to him in no uncertain terms that he would need to earn his place alongside her and the children. Then having reflected on her diary entries and becoming completely satisfied he has become a changed man whilst remaining away for a calculated amount of time before returning to the home.

That statement will cause controversy since many would say leave him for good. But keeping in mind, every situation is different, however a considerable amount of time apart will seem of little consequence compared to a lifetime of uncertainty. It provides enough time for him to show himself, so he will provide for his wife and children, will he share the load picking up the kids from school, will he shower his wife with genuine love and affection. It's surprising how a male with react to the uncertainty of losing his family. But frustratingly only once his wife has gone to these extraordinary lengths will she discover whether her man has finally woken up to himself and stop his abuse – for good.

A type of discipline that every woman deserves enormous respect for, however the mistake far too many women make is falling at the last hurdle, by failing to ensure the entire procedure is followed through in its entirety.

And yes, there's no guarantee he will behave once the family resumes living together, but rest assure, he will know in the future you are not a woman to be trifled with. That's because she has now made her position perfectly clear, becoming firmly entrenched as a woman of status and substance.

Whenever we feel we are making good progress in life, there are times when the universe inexplicitly reacts differently. Consequently, although the outcome we have just discussed in this scenario produced a good outcome, it could have well turned out so differently. There is no other situation in life that is more unpredictably dangerous when resting on your laurels in these circumstances.

> **CAUTION** - As an example, when a woman is notified by the police explaining they have removed the perpetrator from the home she fails to understand or pre-empts his mindset. Whilst these women start putting their lives back together the ex-partner can turn resentment into revenge that he cleverly disguises with desperate calls to come over to talk. This coward who wouldn't talk previously now calls around and pretends to want to make amends, working on her emotions when his true motivation is to take her life. – Isn't it time you became a forward thinker?

The chapters you've just read don't claim to offer a guaranteed formula or a step-by-step solution for resolving marital or social issues. Instead, they offer a profound thought process for guidance and suggestions—tools that you're invited to explore and apply in a way that feels right for you. With your own insight, strengths, and life experiences, you can draw from what resonates with you, shaping a future that suits your unique circumstances.

SUMMARY

- Have you ever asked yourself why you think you want to get married, or why you want to stay in your marriage?
- If you haven't yet become married, why not read chapters 1-3, and discover if you feel the same way towards making that decision?
- You should only marry after you have resolved all doubts about your partner, yourself, your compatibility, and your genuine love for each other.
- Marriage is a committed relationship not unlike a business partnership where both parties need certain protection.
- Marriage also requires constant vigilance on many levels, in order to keep love fresh and alive, which can only come with ongoing imagination and maintenance.
- Never allow any type of relationship to keep you from being who you really are, and from being who you really want to be.
- Pay particular attention to any early behavioural changes, irrespective of the nature that he displays, whether you're in a new or established marriage, and address as recommended.
- If his behavioural changes bother you, write simple legible entries into your diary, make copies and recordings, using correct dates and times, and don't be afraid to do so.
- Defense mechanism—find and understand your fortitude, it's there waiting to be used whenever you need it. Continue to believe and aim towards your principles and values as this will keep you inspired, where you will achieve your goals.

- It's imperative you have an exit strategy, even if the thought makes you feel uncomfortable, of which your safety, that of your children and your financial independence is top of the list.
- Have you been in a long-term marriage where domestic abuse has entered your space, then are you ready now to start by simply acknowledging the time has come to be that woman of substance.
- If you feel safe and confident about remaining in the home, then start your personal transformation from the inside out, and reinvent yourself. Change your way of thinking and living, remain upbeat, have a contingency plan, and you will succeed.

PERPETRATOR

You need to hear this plainly. When you yell at your wife, when you put her down, when you raise your hand against her, you're not just hurting her — you're tearing apart the very family you promised to protect. If you're a young husband, just starting out, those early years should be about building trust with joy. Instead, your anger is poisoning the marriage before it even has a chance to grow. If you're a husband with young children, every word and every blow is teaching your kids that cruelty is normal. Or whether you're an older man having made a life of hell for your wife then the time has come for you both to listen up.

You might not realise you cause harm- but you are -, maybe you were never taught how to deal with frustration or how to talk rationally, instead feeling you must raise your voice, become heavy-handed, feeling the need to be in control. Regardless of your belief, your behaviour is unacceptable and you're now under the spotlight. Not by these words alone, but because your wife / partner is about to help you become more civilised or you will face the possibility of losing her and your family forever.

So, before you allow that mentality of yours to instantly reject any notion you're somehow at fault in any way, take this opportunity to listen for a change, and understand the real strength in being a man.

Real strength comes to terms with identifying and accepting your problems and doing something about them. It's in understanding equality by giving but also accepting advice. It comes from owning up to your mistakes and making the effort to change them. It's in treating your partner as an equal, not as someone beneath you. It's in showing patience with your kids, even when you're tired or frustrated. It's about controlling your temper instead of letting it control you. It's in asking for help when you can't manage alone and not seeing that as weakness. It's about building trust with honesty, not breaking it with lies or violence. It's in protecting your family with love, not fear. It's about being remembered for kindness, not for cruelty. It's in proving your worth through respect, not through intimidation. It's protecting your family with love, not fear. It's proving your worth through respect, not intimidation. It's leaving a legacy of kindness and compassion, having felt that emotional inner feeling when showing empathy

Before you go, try to imagine having reached your twilight years, feeling lonely and struggling with regret, knowing you have little time left. How would you respond to the question, 'If you could, would you change your past?' Fortunately, you have that opportunity now - unless you have allowed too much time to lapse- since you're not living in the future, you're still in the present, possibly along with having your family and your whole life ahead of you.

So why not now, at this very point in time, just think hard about what was just said, and you can end your current behaviour and discover family life as was intended? With a wife and family eager to love and learn from you, to hear you laugh, and to be encouraged by you. Isn't that what family life is all about?

Marriage

When you choose this path, you'll become the husband your wife hoped for, the father your children deserve, and the man you yourself can finally be proud of.

In which case when your day finally comes, it will be with a smile on your face, looking back on what you have accomplished. Having raised your family to become decent caring human beings, knowing they loved you, as they too felt the love you gave them. The feeling you felt inside knowing you treated your wife with the respect she deserved, whilst you both remained in love, through to the very end.

More importantly, you can further reflect, knowing you became the man with no regrets, having found peace within himself.

DIVORCE

The mere mention of divorce can cause the most self-assured person in a marriage to question their vulnerability with mixed emotions. Whether you're on the side of getting divorced or not, someone will suffer emotionally, either sadness, happiness, failure, anxiety, relief, even resentment. Therefore, we can also reasonably assume that many women experience some form of domestic abuse during a divorce.

So how did it come to this, what ever happened to those earlier golden moments when couples would acknowledge and confess their love for one another, making plans to build a new life and raise a family together. So, how can it be that so many couples appear to adopt a desire for divorce particularly after a relatively short-term marriage.

— Extremely disappointing, considering human beings have evolved over thousands of years being renowned for problem solving and moving forward successfully on almost any issue they come up against. —

It's because rather than attempting to resolve any suggestions on divorce and keeping emotions in check, humans who find themselves in this situation inexplicitly become resentful and stubborn. Worse still, become involved in bitter feuds and soon double down, allowing bitterness to consume them. This usually throws any notion of reconciliation out the window. Not stopping there, becoming verbally aggressive at one another, to satisfy one's belief of being self-righteous, yet failing to realise its further escalation in domestic abuse, now being exercised.

Children

One area seldom discussed is the pain and suffering children go through, at the age of having realised their parents are possibly separating for good.

As a result, children suffer emotionally and beyond measure, because many feel abandoned and overlooked, becoming caught up in the conflict and witnessing feuding parents. This inadvertently causes division, with some young children consciously challenged believing they should take sides, causing them further stress, anxiety, even emotional blackmail.

It doesn't stop there, because while mature adults in many cases are primed to handle serious altercations (even though some become mentally scared), children are not. It becomes another type of tragedy altogether, since children not only become traumatised, but in many instances are destined to become dysfunctional.

This failure to protect children under these circumstances results from husband's and wife's own self-interests, with little or no thought of the impact divorce would have on the little people they brought into the world.

Ques: "I remember when my parents would argue going through their divorce, my younger sister and I would hide in our bedroom, and I would try to listen. Eventually our father brought us up because my mother left home and never came back. My sister has never recovered growing up without our mum becoming almost introverted. But since we are both mothers ourselves, we understand how devastating for everyone the whole affair is. Why can't married couples sort their problems out for the sake of their children and stop the selfishness that destroys so many people's lives?"

Ans: "We like to think of human beings as being intelligent and caring creatures, and to a large degree, they are. That's usually when life is good and rolling along smoothly. The problem is, we have never learnt how to cope properly when disappointment comes along. When it does, we can easily become upset and angry—usually at ourselves—along with a tendency to lay the blame elsewhere, usually at the expense of our own demise".

I'm better than this, aren't I?

Unfortunately, humans are prone to playing the victim to get attention, especially when their struggles are caused by their own decisions. For example, rushing into divorce without thinking things through often reflects how today's culture appears to encourage impulsiveness, self-interest and a sense of self-entitlement.

— Couples should be forgiven for thinking that getting a divorce is some type of natural progression-a type of relationship etiquette-allowing them to simply move on and start over. Again, this mentality persists because the authorities lack the vision to provide early social skill education, inclusive of a learning module based on 'Sustaining Social relationships-

Ques: "Having become teenage soulmates we fell madly in love and were married and divorced within just two years. Something which I desperately regret to this day, as I suspect he does. We were young with a son, and it just fell apart. My ex-husband remarried, while I remain single, however, to this day, I ask myself, "Why couldn't we have patched things up the right way?"

Ans: "A sad reality, but the tragedy here is so much more than just two former love birds falling apart. It's also the reality of a young boy having to grow up without his parents being together, showering him with love. Your marriage was likely dissolved due to immaturity, and the lack of respect for one another—even though you confess your loved one another. However, the overriding reason was the fact the two of you had no education in such a crucial area. This would have provided you both with the social skills so necessary in controlling and understanding your responsibilities, instead of being overwhelmed by intense emotion. An all too familiar situation that continues to weigh heavy on countless couples throughout the world today."

— If divorce were both discouraged and frowned upon in greater terms, humans would soon adopt a much higher cultural driven level of understanding and respect for their relationship, giving way to making better informed decisions for those emotionally charged, defining moments. —

Despite the widespread belief that troubled marriages are destined to end in divorce, there are often far more compelling reasons in persevering in the relationship than to walk away. It's disheartening along with short-sightedness— particularly after all the effort that was invested in building the relationship to begin with. The foundation of which was laid through possibly months, even years of commitment, deserves more than a premature token surrender.

Instead, it should be the very last consideration for any couple to make, other than for extreme circumstances, such as a male's unwavering abusive behaviour. In many cases, getting a divorce is looked upon as a failure, particularly in terms of what a marriage should truly represent and stand for. Or once did. Because as mentioned earlier, it's the most important, recognised and celebrated family orientated institution on earth. Throughout the earlier chapters of this book, we looked at what is involved in finding a compatible partner, particularly in terms of having patience in finding Mr right. Again, isn't it time married couples heading for divorce reflected on the earlier mountains they climbed together before agreeing to the relative ease of severing their relationship.

A sad reality

Having made the argument and repeated call for early education for our younger generations in becoming better prepared when looking for a relationship, I can almost hear people musing and saying, 'They will learn soon enough', yet whilst on the surface that may appear to be a fair comment, it's also an irresponsible one. Since we don't allow untrained people to perform duties that require a high degree of care, respect and responsibility, do we?

Divorcees often seek help from one government agency to another in a revolving-door scenario, which in many cases lacks accountability simply allowing couples in failed marriages to repeat the process. The ease of getting remarried, having more children, and moving forward with minimal learning perpetuates the cycle. As a result, this situation leaves little room for meaningful change, with little or no thought to address previous commitment misgivings, or the most precious of all attributes. – The children.

> **Awareness** – Better educated couples would likely demonstrate a higher level of both personal and partnership accountability by taking a harder line and seeking a resolution rather than having the immediate mindset to get a divorce. Again, this shift in thought process would encourage more couples to manage their relationships with greater care and commitment, ultimately contributing to a continuous reduction in both domestic abuse, divorce rates, and a greater decline in child neglect.

The sooner the authorities look at the bigger picture within this proposal—and throughout this entire book—for early education, the sooner younger couples can support one another on a grander scale than at any time previously.

Again, this current ideology, this culture, and this pattern of behaviour, suggests couples can fall out of love simply because divorce has become such an easily accessible escape. It's a tragedy, as many couples simply don't realise that the very idea of divorce can take on a life of its own—like a self-fulfilling prophecy. The moment it is introduced, it can influence subtle thinking, almost like a kind of psychological spell, leading couples to believe it's the only solution, the only path forward, the only way out. – What does this line of thinking really achieve?

When the truth is quite different and can be told by those couples who, despite having their share of relationship difficulties, endured, finding a solution other than surrendering to the belief of divorce. A reminder that every couple finding difficulties should embrace the culture of not looking for retribution. Marriage and raising a family are sacred acts, a relationship that demands moral responsibility and respect. Treated with the purest intent, not discarded in favour of personal beliefs rooted in self-centered entitlement.

Ques: "I divorced my first two husbands many years ago, and now into my third marriage, and I believe men are all the same, why does it appear there's no getting away from it?"

Ans: "As you say, 'It appears', and if that's your opinion, it's your prerogative. As individuals, we become better people within ourselves when we try to correct the wrongs. It's what sets us apart. Again, if you truly want to believe there's no getting away from the source of your unhappiness, then that's the way it will be for you. However, you now have this opportunity to retract that thought process and steer yourself in a completely new direction, starting now. The choice is entirely yours."

Why on earth would any female allow herself to live with domestic abuse? What possible reasoning could there be for it, when it can be defeated without necessarily believing divorce is the one and only option, - because it's not? Unless, as mentioned she is the type of woman that somehow tolerates this type of behaviour. Perhaps she has extraordinary resolve, or maybe there's another underlying reason as mentioned—believing men are simply all the same. While it may seem like a cynical outlook, it's important to recognize that such views often stem from deep personal experiences.

Still, it's not always the full picture, and we shouldn't accept it for what it only appears to be.

Pathway to empowerment

While divorce is a possible outcome in every marriage, it's not something couples should dwell on. However, when the signs of an impending separation become clearer, especially those due to domestic abuse, it's crucial to take proactive steps, sooner than later. Concentrate on putting an exit strategy in place with major emphasis on your safety first, consisting of financial independence and a safe house, if needed. As discussed earlier every woman in rocky marriage should know what her entitlements are along with her capabilities.

Not unlike any other type of partnership that protected it's interests when both parties signed on the bottom line.

There are women who now acknowledge they have allowed their husband's abusive behaviour to go unchallenged for too long. Despite all reconciliation attempts failing, a significant last remaining option remains which will reveal her husband's true character. As mentioned, there are many husbands who believe they have their spouses exactly where they want them. However, unlike those previous unsuccessful attempts—including documented discussions, letters, and protection orders—nothing impacts a man more than when he is served with divorce papers. – Shock horror.

However, in some countries the law states there must be a twelve-month separation period before a divorce application can be lodged. Therefore, when a woman decides to separate due to domestic abuse, she must make completely different arrangements to those women that aren't subjected to abuse. Although the twelve months separation is designed for couples to reassess their marriage, it is highly recommended to seek initial professional guidance, this cannot be over emphasised. Particularly where domestic abuse exists, and a woman is prepared to remain in the home with her abuser, she needs to fully understand the precarious position she is putting herself in.

Divorce

Make no mistake: whilst a woman has every right to remain living independently on her own when a relationship is heading for divorce, her safety is paramount. Attempting to change an abusive man—who is all too aware of the separation and pending divorce—may seem logical to a woman trying to salvage her relationship. Yet expecting a male to remain stable under these circumstances while resentment builds, can be her undoing. That resentment may unleash the animal within, directed at the one he now blames for his pending downfall. It is a sad indictment on the term civilised human being, a man who once confessed his love to the woman who only ever wanted to love him, ultimately taking her life.

Therefore, if a woman cannot have her spouse removed or he won't leave the home then being concerned about her safety, moving away from him is by far the safest option. By doing so unfortunately creates other issues, and that is why the on-going mention of maintaining diaries and filing copies of statements is as important as any document you are ever likely to have in your possession.

Take the woman who moved out of her home with her two children because of systemic mental and physical abuse. Having moved heaven and earth to re-establish herself, she failed to let the authorities know of her situation, or keep any records associated with the abuse she endured. Consequently, she could never prove any injustices were carried out, because hearsay assumptions, gossip and suspicions are just not enough. In this instance the man remained in the home, never having any thoughts of providing for his wife and children. The wife and her children continue to struggle as she never attempted to fight for what was hers. Instead, like so many other young mothers, she remains totally unfamiliar with the judiciary system on separation. Had judgement been made against the male in this matter, her circumstances could well have been completely different, yet sadly the reality for many is- 'you can't get blood out of a stone'

Discover how you can become both inspired and enlightened in so many ways when you express yourself, penning your diary. A feeling of great release, and enjoyment, becoming unburdened whilst experiencing a great sense of relief. Then to find clarity in only the way your diary can provide, when on self-reflection you suddenly discover the right course of action to take.

Always hold onto this adage –'*You only get out of life, what you put in*'.-

Ques: "Do I really need to consider doing something so drastic to get his attention?"

Ans: "Unfortunately, yes, you do, as it will force his hand. Now is the time to stop thinking about his feelings, instead of concentrating on yours. It's the 'coup de grace', the final blow. After all, you have given this man enough chances, so now is the time to watch the final events unfold."

True colours

This is the irony many women face, having experienced his once charming and respectful demeanour, realising now he suppressed his authoritative and abusive nature the entire time—until now. Once married, his level of authority implicitly increased, solidifying his dominance within the relationship. Over time, he finally wore his wife down to a level where she is almost broken and now has little left to offer. This was all his own undoing, possibly never really understanding what was happening around him, as difficult as that may be to comprehend. Although strangely enough whilst he believes divorce will be his escape, what he doesn't understand is, —escaping from what?

Such is the mindset of many people, since there is a profound ignorance of what marriage truly represents, and an alarming readiness to pursue divorce without genuinely trying to reconcile. We are often stunned by behaviour that contradicts the very essence of what marriage is meant to uphold — yet it is real, it exists, and it remains an unfortunate part of human nature.

– In this case, you can rest assured he has done you the biggest service, despite the possible hurt you are going through and the love you have or had for him. Because any man who walks away from his marriage under these circumstances, instead of doing everything in his power to reconcile, is a man not worthy. –

Therefore, without expressing contradiction, if on the other hand you have exhausted all avenues and want a divorce, or to discover what your man is really made of, you should seriously consider proceeding with making enquiries into a formal separation, being a pending divorce. Whether you are sitting on the fence at this stage or completely convinced you want to end this relationship, then this type of intervention will force his hand, and provide the definitive outcome, whatever that may be. – As long as you follow through.

Majority of the time, men are renowned for believing their spouse won't go through on certain matters—believing they are idle threats—and therefore will attempt to call her bluff. If that day comes when he receives divorce papers, you can ill afford for him to believe you're not going through with it. Even if divorce is not your true intention at this stage and you remain hopeful for reconciliation, this action of separation is pushing against the outer boundaries of a male's domain.

Ques: "Why did I take so long to wake up to what was really happening in my marriage, before I went through a stressful divorce? I lost eight years living with a man who treated me appallingly?"

Ans: "In retrospect hindsight is a wonderful thing, at least in the context of looking back at the alternatives and options you had, and less on the scarring. There's no simple answer, other than hoping every single female reading this self-help book now takes your question seriously. By first acknowledging that they will never let the same thing happen to them. You remained with him, having a sense of commitment and loyalty, and possibly for love. It's what decent human beings do, and although you probably have regrets, you moved on, hopefully having become a wiser and happier person."

Because of the unpredictability of the male, and the overwhelming significance of being served divorce papers, as mentioned throughout similar situations, it's best not to be at home when he takes possession. Instead, allow him time to digest what the possible ramifications are, while you remain acutely aware of the timeline for the divorce papers to be delivered, being extremely important.

What's he really made of—anyway?

You will soon discover what his intentions are, either he will say 'Ok let's get a divorce', or he will be shaken up. In which case, you know with the latter, whether you believe there is potential to turn this male around. That's because nothing affects a male more than the threat of potential divorce itself when in writing—particularly if he loves his wife.

– Although you could be forgiven—in this scenario—by questioning if that love he has for you, really exists at all. –

Don't be surprised if the male, who initially agreed to a separation, doesn't do an almighty back flip, particularly having given his own predicament plenty of thought. Men quickly understand—when they want to—as to the gravity of the situation, particularly when the circumstances have taken on a sudden legal aspect, where again, potential pending divorce papers can set a terrifying precedent. It's your decision, and yours alone, as to the direction you decide to go from here, just as it is his.

While the possibility of divorce continues to hang over his head, you can continue to be proactive in saving your marriage or you can follow through with getting a divorce after the separation period. Either way let him stew for a while.

Again, you will discover what your man is made of now that he has met with the ultimate challenge, where he too, must decide one way or another, if he wants to save his marriage. He may well decide to carry out counselling and rehabilitate himself, eventually showing his new congenial behaviour on a continuous and genuine basis. Then again, he may not.

A difficult dilemma to be in, and one that requires careful consideration, but above all, a permanent resolution. A period where a woman should consider letting the separation paperwork talk on her behalf. That's because too many women again fall victim to the male's charm and excuses, allowing themselves to become emotionally drawn into a game of psychological warfare.

Divorce

If the male appears to be visibly shaken by the possibility of further divorce proceedings and is genuinely remorseful, you will know your ploy is working. However, humans are cunning creatures, so don't be surprised if he's attempting to play his hand in another way.

Ques: "It's such an ugly process, with no guarantees. I realise that, but is this really the best option? If he changes his behaviour and ends his abuse, I fear he will always hold resentment against me, for what I have done, I know he will."

Ans: "Perhaps he will, but if he genuinely loves you, any resentment he holds won't last for long, because he will have been put in his place, as well as knowing you won't stand for any of his abuse. If only more women used the power they possess. On the other hand if he doesn't make any attempt to reconcile, then best prepare to follow through by parting ways."

Whenever there's a serious matter and the male is under the spotlight, he will usually attempt to deviate away from its true significance. As was in this case by treating the divorce papers with sheer contempt, while making further attempts to lay the blame elsewhere. A diversion, making false accusations and unsubstantiated claims, particularly when it becomes clear this time round, that time is running out - for him.

Every woman that becomes involved in divorce proceedings particularly because of domestic abuse, either willingly, or through necessity, needs to gather every bit of evidence that's available to her. That's whether she believes it will in fact be of help or not. Therefore, those diary entries, we continue to highlight and discuss—with copies of statements, records, and documents are priceless. Obtaining this information as early as possible is essential, ensuring you always remain one step ahead, long before divorce raises his head.

In this scenario, the male, like so many others, finally relents, that's because his wife was given no choice but to fight tooth and nail if she wanted to try and keep her marriage alive. However, the percentage of women who are prepared to go to these lengths remains low. A fight worth winning to live in peace and harmony whilst remaining in love—that every woman can accomplish with the many types of options opened to her. An awkward yet true analogy of the adage - love hate relationship. By issuing divorce papers on the surface appears to be the extreme, yet there's no denying of its significance, as it cuts to the chase, puts an end to tip-toeing around issues that could otherwise last for all eternity.

— Be mindful of the potential consequences when divorcing, if one day considering starting all over again in a new relationship, only to discover that domestic abuse hasn't travelled far. Worse still, there are new, even more irritating human surprises, and yes, it suddenly hits you, you miss your first wife/husband, and you would do anything to turn back the clock, and change everything for the better, as you miss the one you love. Such is life. —

As stated previously, if couples who talk about divorce were to apply the same amount of genuine intensity and energy, they used on each other when first falling in love, the rate of divorce would and remain significantly lower.

SUMMARY

- Women who discuss divorce, either with a confidante or with their husband, should understand the actual need to reflect on what they have gained and what they could lose.
- Your diary will offer you insights, giving you the courage and determination to either try and save your marriage, or it will provide you with reasons to end it.
- Plan well, as we previously discussed in the various scenarios, ensuring your safety continues to be at the forefront.
- Build on your financial and emotional independence. You need both, regardless of your circumstances.
- Saving your marriage is by far the most courageous and admirable role you are ever likely to undertake. Therefore, consider both his and your true feelings towards each other, before deciding on which direction to move in.

- Controlling your emotions is by far one of the most challenging yet rewarding skills to develop. It allows you to communicate more confidently and effectively, having less personal attachment.
- Educate yourself by connecting with your fortitude, a unique inner strength and quality that's completely personalised to suit your circumstances, with genuine powers to transform you into becoming the person you want to be.
- Never make the mistake of telling a man face to face you want a divorce, when domestic abuse is on the table, it could become a life-threatening situation.
- Consider this experience as the basis in becoming much more in tune with who you are, and who you want to become. Remind yourself of another adage, while one door closes, another one opens.
- Finally-never allow tit for tat exchanges, stubbornness or selfishness prevent a reconciliation.

PERPETRATOR

You may be interested in reading the previous chapter on marriage to put your behaviour into better perspective and then continue reading from here.

So, you have become all too aware that your wife wants a separation with a pending divorce—the result of your inability to address your verbal and physical abusive behaviour. Is getting divorced really what you want or is this just a cumulation of events you didn't see coming? Now you're unsure of what to do... Have you fallen out of love with your wife or is it a case of having trouble swallowing your pride. Can you admit to being responsible

Preventing and Ending Domestic Abuse

for domestic abuse, or has anger and stubbornness also gotten the better of you?

Let's assume you love your wife and your children, but you just can't bring yourself to talk to your wife decently or restrain yourself, not knowing why you do it. The reason for this is you have lost respect for yourself and your wife, the worst possible direction you could have taken. Therefore, isn't it high time you accepted the fact you need to ragain control of your life and become the leader who cares about his wife and family? – It really is that simple.

Being a male, there are times when we all do things we wished we hadn't, of which I am sure I could write an entire chapter on, perhaps even another book. However, what you're doing isn't an isolated case, you are being challenged like we all are, except you're not meeting that challenge instead you have succumbed without a fight. There are so many more positive reasons to climb out of this hole you fell into other than remaining in this dark place you're currently in, knowing everyone around you frowns upon you.

When you're at work, do you speak to your boss, your employees, or your mates the way you speak to — or physically handle — your wife and family? Of course you don't; if you did, you wouldn't have a job. So why direct that behaviour toward the people who matter most? It makes no sense, and deep down you know that. Confront those inner demons with the same determination you would show if your family were threatened — because this time that threat is real, and that threat is you.

Just take a minute to absorb what you just read. No man ever gets any satisfaction from domestic abuse—particularly against their own family, ever. So again, just think about that for a minute—what value is there in doing it, a big fat zero? You have already experienced that empty feeling, - assuming you love your family- knowing you're on the path to living your life without your wife and children, a feeling of desperation and loneliness – doesn't that hurt just thinking about it?

Assuming you love your family, this situation you find yourself in will hit you even harder when the divorce is over, and you come home knowing

Divorce

your wife and children are no longer around. It's at this exact time that every male feels their entire world has been taken away from them and now wishing and praying they could tell their family how much they love them.

Fortunately for you, that hasn't taken place—yet, but just hold that thought for a minute, to fully appreciate just how deep the intensity of despair, desperation and anxiety really is, being without your family. This is the reality for men all over the world who suddenly come to their senses, again after the fact, and realising how foolish they have been, while their wife remains strong and determined.

Again, would you allow anyone to be physically and verbally abusive towards your family? Of course you wouldn't, so why are you doing it, then expect your wife and family to want to be anywhere near you. It's sheer madness. You don't need to agree to getting divorced. What you need instead is to wake up to yourself, find contentment, then swap abuse with respectful and rational behaviour. – How difficult can it be?

If you give in and get divorced over such matters you have failed yourself, along with your wife and family, but even more maddening, possibly to do it all over again with another woman. Where's the logic in that, saying and doing all the right things at the beginning of a new relationship, having more children, only to resume with your abusive behaviour? Then to continue where you left off from your previous marriage. Once again, causing even more emotional stress and heartache on so many other lives—when you had it all to begin with.

Now that you have experienced firsthand repercussions from the effects of having received the news that your wife wants a separation, a pending divorce, then for your sake, you have hopefully received a lightbulb moment. An awakening, unlike anything you have ever experienced before, almost like shock treatment, now realising just how foolish you have been. Now you want your family more than anything else in this world, which of course was all made possible by one person who showed their individual strength and courage—your wife. A woman who never gave up on you, something you should remain proud of and by telling her so.

Preventing and Ending Domestic Abuse

As for the wife who has taken a different approach and wants a divorce, it may be that she has fallen out of love with you. Should that be the case, it's best to either accept her decision and come to terms with it, since it's probably for the best, or make a plan of your own to win her back.

Which you can do by keeping those thoughts of losing your wife and family with you, and you can move mountains. So don't hold back, with the hope she still holds a candle for you, as the thought of receiving divorce papers had a disturbing effect on you, whereby you have received one big wake up call. That said, divorce papers are just that, pieces of paper, although significant. However, you now plan to win your wife back having now realised just how deep your love for your wife and family really is.

If you truly believe your wife has a spark somewhere, then start behaving as you know you should, by first explaining to her what has happened, that you have had a real awakening—but only if you're genuine.

Then discover what happens to you when you treat your wife and family with respect. It's a feeling only the person themselves can experience and describe someone like yourself. This is the way forward because when the penny drops, men show a type of desperation unlike any other experience they ever had. That's because the male is now fully aware to the dire consequences of the situation in terms of his potential loss and wants to exercise that desperation to reconcile with his family as urgently and as fast as he can.

However, you need a plan, and although it's understandable, you just want to blurt it all out, you could easily make things worse. Put a plan together, a real one, and start showing your wife and family the change in you. Because unless you haven't heard that all too familiar adage…

-Your behaviour tells the real story-

LIVING ALONE

Living alone may not fit with some people's idea of what domestic abuse represents, however, every woman that lives alone should realise her independence carries a certain risk. Women who live alone are just as susceptible to the same safety concerns - we identify as domestic abuse- whether in a relationship or not.

Although living alone can provide a sense of personal satisfaction, it can lead to a false sense of security, so don't think for one minute you haven't been or won't become noticed, because you have. Not a comfortable thought, is it? However, you can empower yourself to stay safe, by simply coming to terms and fully understanding your potential vulnerability and putting safety control measures in place. – Acknowledgement comes first.

It's a completely normal part of everyday-to-day life whereby the male instinctively notices and observes the fairer sex, as that's the world we live in. Therefore, for every woman to feel safe she needs to stay alert and maintain steady awareness of her surroundings.

Living and commuting alone takes on a much higher level of vulnerability and therefore risk, which undermines the notion of 'Safety in numbers'. However, when having your family, friends and loved ones around, your senses allow you to relax, and for good reason. When you're on your own, you simply must heighten and maintain a reasonable level of conscience awareness. If you're the type that has the attitude, 'what will be will be', then hopefully you will reevaluate your line of thinking as we continue throughout this chapter.

> **CAUTION** - Ask yourself, "Am I better off to prevent something adversely happening to me in the first place, or do I wait and try to resolve issues after they happen?" Having the latter attitude places you at higher risk, and should a situation arise, you will wish you had thought much earlier about making better decisions with clearer choices regarding your safety.

Your safety is in your hands

When having any doubts or thoughts about your safety, it's your cognitive powers alerting you to take another look or reconsider what you're planning to do. That's before you act, so to help you along, adopt the mantra—to pause, reflect—before you engage to do anything.

As an example, have you crossed the road only to get stuck precariously in the middle and waiting for a break in the traffic, to make your escape? Then you end up cursing yourself once you're on the other side, realising you hadn't first thought about what you were going to do—with your safety in mind. We are all easily distracted by having other things on our mind, particularly when we are carrying out repetitious activity, allowing ourselves to become complacent, putting ourselves in potential danger. Living alone escalates your vulnerability because unfortunately you are simply an easier target to that of a couple, or part of a family, therefore it's imperative that you make your life as secure for yourself as practically possible.

Take a closer look at the area you live in, the surroundings and the residence you have inhabited or about to move to. What does it tell you? Does the area have a good or bad reputation? Are the police constant presence? Is there a reputation of drug and alcohol abuse? What is the level of crime? These are just a few questions you need to find answers to when living alone. By making these types of discoveries early, it allows you to make better informed decisions, increasing your overall level of security.

Ques: "I live alone in a troubled location; I can't afford to live anywhere else, what else can I do?"

Ans: Consider your options, can you rent a room out to free up some costs and save to relocate to a safer area? This is the type of consideration you need to consider. Perhaps find ways to make or save that extra money, of which there are many. Cut back on the expenses you know you can do without. Upskill and apply for higher remuneration. By doing so, the day will come when you then look back on the times you lived in a troubled unsafe area. Having now achieved your goals and living in a safer neighbourhood, with a sense of pride in overcoming those earlier challenges."

For the older women, again positivity is the key, so don't shrug off the notion you can't reinvent yourself because you can. Regardless of your past, never allow your circumstances to deter you from becoming the person you really want to be. Become pro-active and experience where your life takes you.

— A secure and safe residence must be your number one goal —

Ensure there's security screens and new keyed deadlocks on windows and doors, install a peephole and a chain on your front door, and never open your door to a stranger. It's an excellent investment to install a proper security screen door, so you have that added protection between yourself and a stranger/visitor.

Be mindful, home invasions are commonplace, so again never feel inclined to open your front door like so many people feel intimidated to do. Remember to instruct your friends and family to ring you first if they intend to make a visit. Having a pet dog is a sensible type of security that can alert you at different times, when you may be oblivious to your surroundings.

If you drive a vehicle, then living amongst a gated community with a garage that leads directly into your residence provides you with extra layer of protection. Women who don't drive a vehicle should make strong consideration by living closer to public transport i.e buses, trains and trams.

Ques: "Being an older woman and living alone, I try to pay attention to what I am doing, along with where and when I go out. When things don't go according to plan, I try to make changes when necessary. Changes that suit my best interest, so why do I still feel apprehensive from time to time, particularly after hours?"

Ans: "It's perfectly normal to feel that way, if the anxiety remains at a minimum. It's your presence of mind that remains on standby, that alerts your senses, when you least expect it. When it happens, review what you're doing and try to determine why you became anxious, then decide if you should consider a new course of control. Don't just dismiss it."

A perfect example of the sociological impact is how it exposes our instinct for safety in numbers — and the unease that follows when that safety disappears. Consider a woman travelling on public transport late at night, staying consciously aware of her surroundings, relying on her senses and intuition to feel secure. When she reaches her stop, she faces the walk home alone, suddenly aware that the comfort of the crowd is gone. It's a moment that demands continued vigilance.– Keep your antenna on.

This is far from being ideal, particularly in an area with a bad reputation, and although you might say, "but I work late", and I "couldn't get a cab", and that may be true. However, when it comes to your safety there should be no excuse other than to ensure you make better pre-arrangments arrangements at a time when transport and communication have never been easier. - in most cases.

Vulnerability

Another all-too-common mistake that many women fall victim to is having become separated from friends or their date late at night, then deciding to go home alone, never to be seen again.

This is a bad decision and plays in the hands of any perpetrator—of which there are many—who are willing to prey on a woman's vulnerability. Men are extremely cunning and seldom approach a single woman during the daytime, yet become brazen enough to do so at night, in many cases for the want of sex. Throwing caution to the wind is not an adage any woman should want to rely on when out at night and all alone.

Females go missing regularly, and for various reasons a large number are sadly never seen again. Disappearances are more common than you think, with over thirty thousand cases per year just in Australia alone. The majority of which results from females failing to have a plan, as easily as contacting family and friends, before deciding to go somewhere. It only takes a few seconds to report your location and the decisions you have made, along with vehicle registration number plate details- if possible.

– It's more difficult for the police to apprehend a perpetrator that has no family connection when investigating a missing person, and the perpetrator is all too aware of that fact. –

Your safety comes in a variety of measures such as feeling safe when parking your car in the basement of a building during daylight hours, where again there's that feeling of safety in numbers. But what about when it's late at night? Do you now wish you had thought more about your safety before deciding to park your car down in the back street or in a car park basement in the first place?

Preventing and Ending Domestic Abuse

Ques: What must every woman know about her right to personal safety, and how should she act when that safety is threatened—particularly while living independently or traveling alone?"

Ans: "First and foremost, unless it's of her own choosing, a woman should never feel either uncomfortable or unsafe, and if that's the case, she must reconsider her present circumstances. She can easily accomplish this by understanding the potential risks she faces and making the necessary changes - as mentioned above - to feel and remain safe. Furthermore, no woman should ever believe she is exempt from being looked after by the authorities, because it's simply not true. If, in fact, she feels that way, then she has possibly detached herself from reality. What every single woman needs to ask herself, does she have appropriate safety measures in place, again with having made prior phone calls."

Remember we are all primates, some of whom act more like wild animals, therefore, we don't live in a perfect or safe world—far from it. So, while the police have a 'serve and protect' motto, they have an uphill battle, since society comprises of a diverse range of people. All with different agendas and motives for what and why they do the things they do, many of whom by their very nature are out there looking for trouble.

SUMMARY

— Make the following - your new affirmation —

- Awareness is the key to safety.
- Pause-Reflect- Engage is your new mantra.
- Confidence is your armour; vigilance is your shield.
- Be prepared, stay secure, live empowerment.
- Trust your instincts - they are your strongest ally.
- A secure home nurtures a fearless heart.
- Knowledge is power, safety is freedom.

Living Alone

- Always remain being that woman of substance.
- Trust no one.

CONTROL AND COERCION

In this chapter—at the time of writing—we will look at a relatively new acknowledgment, at least by the authorities, however less understood now that control and coercion is formally recognised as domestic abuse within relationships.

These types of behaviour are nothing new; originating from a time when humans first began relationships, whereby these traits often share similar characteristics. Whilst controlling behaviour precedes coercion, we must differentiate between them, understanding the intended context of their delivery when discussing domestic abuse. We should also acknowledge that ambiguity exists, whilst one person acknowledges a certain tone and dialect as being acceptable, another doesn't, and here lies the dilemma, since context, perception, and emotional impact are not universally shared.

Below are definitions of control and coercion…

Control and Coercion

Control – In the early stages of a relationship one partner may begin with subtle influence to dictate the other's choices—such as deciding who they can see or where they can go. This control may initially appear to be framed as being caring, yet beneath the surface, it could well signal an emerging imbalance of power.

Coercion – Over time, this control can escalate—the controlling partner might start using coercive measures to ensure he receives compliance—through threats, emotional manipulation, or ultimatums—forcing their partner to act against their own will or desires. In this progression, control establishes the foundation of dominance, while coercion becomes the mechanism to enforce it.

– This is where both confusion and deceit can disguise actual intentions, since the conniving male can insist, he's only being caring, when the truth can be quite different. –

Born to choose, not to obey

There is an underlying trait where some men have adopted the belief they need to break a woman's spirit, both mentally and sometimes physically.

– It could be argued; humans sometimes engage in coercive control through their innate power of persuasion—often unintentionally—therefore inadvertently believing ourselves to be blameless in our efforts to achieve our objective. –

Ques: "The way I see it, controlling and coercive behaviour is just part of everyday life in a relationship, so what's the problem?"

Ans: "Presumably it's not a problem for you, if it exists. However, it could be of good debate whether control and coercion in a relationship are based on individual assessment, i.e feeling, impact, and belief.

The troubling factor here is the rate of growth and the scale of both control and coercion within a relationship. That being, to be successful at this behaviour, the cunning male must be equally good at calculating as to how far he can go at any given time. His reasoning for this is to never push beyond the boundaries of limitations. In other words, how he perceives what is an acceptable level of control without pushing her completely over the edge. With that mindset he believes he has you exactly where he wants you.

Humans are complex to the extreme, and as cunning and conniving we all can be, we are nevertheless at the same time both naïve and gullible. It's in all of us, as again, we all too often allow our emotions to get out of control, therefore it's time to take that emotional control back during this type of behaviour.

Control and coercion are often deeply ingrained in the perpetrator's mindset, reflected in their unique, self-fashioned method of manipulation and entrapment. These tactics are not insurmountable. By harnessing your inner strength, you can dismantle the hold such behaviour has on you. A vital component in this process is gaining insight into the structure and workings of the journey your mind set takes, which we will delve further into when we look into the chapter on fortitude. This will empower you to reconstruct your perspectives on control and coercion, shifting the balance back to your advantage.

A disturbing factor is that for many women, they have long since held the view to never question their partners, instead believing they have little choice other than to accept his wishes, sadly accepting their fate.

It's also quite possible you have misunderstood him, since he may well be unaware his actions are both unacceptable, along with remaining unchallenged. – All too common due to a lack of deep communication.

Interpretations

> **Awareness**-The very second your partner makes some type of gesture toward you- whether through conversation, a physical touch or leaves you a note, you should instantly understand the context. Do you believe he is being reasonable, or in the event you feel uncomfortable, do you see it as a sign of his controlling and coercive behaviour.

– The first gesture may not speak loudly, but the repeated rhythm tells the truth. –

As mentioned, humans are unique creatures with natural powers of observation. Therefore, a male, through his understanding of his partner's moods, her sensitivity and behaviour, can carry out a random act of assertion and intimidation that suits his timing.

— Under the banner of controlling and coercive behaviour —

This type of action displays the domineering behaviour of the male, leaving no doubt what he expects from her.

Humans, typically the male are naturally aware of their physical attributes and indeed their abilities, therefore he realises he is far more superior in that domain than a female—most times. Consequently, he isn't about to meet any problematic opposition in terms of physical confrontation. He therefore can confidently continue to assert his control and coercion through inadvertent physical fear alone.

So how do you handle being told, what you're going to do, how and when you're going to do it- be it in a subtle tone? Would it be your normal reaction to become completely submissive, perhaps let it go in one ear and out the other, or do you make it clear you won't accept his type of rhetoric?

Ques: "I have adapted to my husband's tone, his suggestions, or instructions, even when it may seem slightly controlling. Why does it seem so difficult for other women to understand their partner's true intent?"

Ans: "That so called 'true intent' as you put it is precisely the question, as there are some women with a more sensitive nature, who need tailored advice, empathetic guidance, and stronger frameworks to help them feel empowered, safe and respected in these challenging situations. They can do this and get off to a good start by following the recommendations and suggestions within this chapter. But one thing is clear, whilst you may have conditioned yourself to your man's tone and intent, there are others that are suffering in silence."

Are controlling men insecure?

— The ten-million-dollar question —

It's disappointing to witness those men who initially engaged in open and equal dialogue with their wife and partner, who now by way of their rhetoric, display controlling overtones, appearing to have become so blatantly insecure. It is therefore counterproductive for a woman to accept her man's behaviour simply because she does not want to hurt his feelings or because she believes it's all part of being in a relationship.

> **CAUTION** – Anyone in a partnership who fails to recognize the profound benefits of relinquishing their need for control and embracing a shared, balanced life with their equally deserving partner, is exhibiting irrational, unfair, and again insecure behaviour.

So how deeply concerning is his behaviour and do you think there's perhaps an underlying problem where he feels both a little insecure, perhaps even jealous. Or is he a man who likes his own way, and expects you to remain loyal no matter what, by remaining at his side and behaving as though there's nothing wrong? Under the latter, how is a woman made to feel sharing a bed when he possibly controls indulgent sexual escapades.

– We will soon look closer at a confrontation between the wife and her husband on this topic of control and coercive behaviour, whereby the woman can ask her husband questions and gauge his reaction. –

Let's look at some examples of the male's controlling behaviour in simple terms, which is basically when the male attempts to manipulate a woman using a variety of measures. Typical controlling behaviour by the male, whereby he raises issues along with restrictions. Such as, where she can and can't go, who she can and can't see, what she should and shouldn't wear, how much she can spend, even the time he wants her home. He may be blunt, getting straight to the point with his instructions, or he may go for the physiological approach, believing charm and the subtlety of his words will win her over. Not revealing his true feelings or intentions.

Whereas being coercive is more on the lines of attempting to apply pressure, making threats, emotional intimidation, and harassment. However, both control and coercion co-exist and reinforce one another.

It could also be argued that this type of behaviour is somewhat easier to remedy being in a non-committal relationship. Because generally there's less emotional, legal and social entanglements involved, whereby a woman should find it easier to walk away. To that of a committed relationship, where a woman has usually invested all she has, her love, finances, emotionally and maternally making the decision to leave more complex. We are all unique in our own special way, therefore whilst we see and hear, we all understand differently.

– In the concept of this topic, it's not just what someone says— it's how we choose to interpret their words and the underlying effect it has on us afterwards. By making our own distinctions and coming to our own conclusions because of how we feel, rather than the relevance of what was said. Therefore, a man may talk to his wife or partner in a tone using a dialect that she accepts, whilst a close friend in ear shot may not—that's the world we live in.-

Fortunately, life can also provide honourable good and decent men, who genuinely treat their wife/partner with the love and respect she deserves. In return, he undoubtedly receives one of life's greatest personal pleasures, that feeling that provides a sense of being fair and well balanced.

That's in direct contrast to the male who controls his wife/partner, because he failed to control himself and lost his way in life, a consequence of his own lack of self-respect, and again insecurities.

– Males who find themselves in this position are often suffering from a sense of self-righteousness—although delusional—to justify their controlling behaviour. In doing so, they manipulate and orchestrate an unwitting accomplice, who unfortunately is you. –

Unlike the actions and conversations of the rational male that reverberates in all directions, giving off inspiration, showing integrity, producing positive vibes and energy. Which further compounds creating endless opportunities, making friends easily, being loved and admired by many, experiencing all the good that life has to offer.

How well do I really know him?

As we have continued to do throughout this book, we need to remain mindful of those people who were or perhaps remain subjected to some form of abuse during their childhood. Perhaps within a dysfunctional family, who now consequently suffer from an undiagnosed level of trauma, believing their need to show a level of assertive control. Therefore, how well do you really know him and more importantly how well does he truly know himself?

Although easily said, try not to get confused between what you believe to be acceptable behaviour and what's not. That's because women by nature, are more caring and therefore are more sympathetic. With this mindset, most women can't do enough for their man, regardless of how they perceive to be treated. By doing so, provides their husbands or partners with further justification to continue with their unchallenged and unacceptable behaviour.- Stand firm.

Ques: "I live with a man who is quite direct with me, and although he probably does control and coerce me from time to time, I believe he loves me, so I wouldn't want to make a bigger issue out of it. Isn't it best I just keep things the way they are?"

Ans: "Imagine how surprised you could both be, discovering he was never aware of how he was being misinterpreted. So, isn't it time for that little chat together otherwise you are prone to suffer in silence? There is no justification for this prolonged behaviour or the possible self-contempt you may be placing on yourself.

That being the case, you may well be in an extremely intimidating position, whereby you falsely assume you are content in your relationship. Having survived up to this point, by adopting that far too convenient adage, "It is, what it is", when clearly it is not, and never will be, as you are living with a man who currently has you, exactly where he wants you. -The moment has arrived!

Having perhaps received a sudden lightbulb moment makes you realise a problem exists in your relationship. It's also fair to assume that you have been acutely aware of this for some time.

— This is your moment in time to look for whatever resonates with you throughout this chapter and beyond. You owe it to yourself. You cannot afford to miss this chance, the opportunity to have your respect and your freedom returned, putting your life back in order. —

Don't slip back into this degrading lifestyle, being submissive and obliging, while all along pretending and continuing to be a normal partner when you're not. Instead, cultivate a fresh attitude, and say to yourself…

— "I will see this through and become more independent" —

Set aside those obstacles for now and instead focus on the accomplishment and relief you'll feel once you've reached your goal. Your mind, body, and soul have been persistently urging you to recognize that continuing in this relationship as it stands prevents you from achieving true self-worth and as importantly—peace of mind. It denies you the fulfillment of being whole and remaining the authentic woman you strive to be. Someone who simply desires to love and to be loved, yet all the while remaining in the grips of a controlling and coercive partner.

It's all very well for those who would say "Just leave", however as mentioned the realities in life are so very different, as should those people who make those remarks understand. Since there will always be women who are strong enough to deal with these types of situations, there will always be those women who unfortunately don't have the capacity to do so.

This book has repeatedly stressed that transforming your life requires a determined approach that must be taken seriously. Therefore, going about these types of matters without understanding the holistic approach required for good planning including taking the necessary precautions, can and will result in the worst type of repercussions.

Never underestimate the power of the controlling male who may well be exercising restraint when using control and coercion—as difficult as they may be to understand. Reason being they are relatively low forms of abuse compared to his immense physical capabilities that are potentially dormant waiting to be unleashed. If that happens, it's a clear indication the male has lost complete control, then descends upon his wife/partner carrying out the most brutal attack imaginable that all too often results in the woman losing her life.

If you feel apprehensive, uncertain, or fearful about the possibility of his behaviour escalating during a confrontation, take some reassurance. From this point forward, you are the one setting the terms. You are no longer the one being summoned like a schoolboy to a schoolmaster — he is.

Everything we do in life carries some degree of risk, yet our instincts often help us recognise the situation at hand, therefore we must navigate those risks wisely. Just as importantly, we can draw on our own fortitude — a personal arsenal of inner strength — that equips us with the tools we need to face and overcome life's challenges.

— I know I have the confidence to do this -

There shouldn't be any more indecision on "Will I or won't I" and there shouldn't be any turning back, only the belief in yourself and the thoughts for your future peace of mind. From this time forward you will never compromise on your principles and values, your ambitions, beliefs and happiness ever again. Therefore, there is no reason for you to be controlled and coerced by anyone any longer.

This type of revelation is truly profound, simply because no one can ever take it away from you - it's yours alone. It's this type of thought process that will lead the march forward and defeat anyone or anything that stands between you and what you truly believe in.

This realisation you've reached by confronting him may be one of the most significant decisions you will ever make in this relationship. But let's be clear: you don't need to make a sudden or immediate decision. This is about you — rebuilding your self-esteem, reclaiming your strength, and gathering the determination to see this through. In time, he will come to understand that his behaviour must change, or you will begin taking the steps necessary to end the relationship.

Ques: "I have frequently protested to my husband's ongoing controlling nature, and he just laughs it off. What else can I do?"

Ans: *"Acknowledging and voicing your objections is an important first step. However, it's essential to go beyond expressing your protests and focus on setting and enforcing clear boundaries. Start by adopting the notion of 'actions to speak louder than words.' Become defiant on the lessor instructions he gives out to gauge his reaction. This will clearly communicate to him that you have started to take a stand, against his controlling behaviour."*

We must all deal with unsavoury matters from time to time, with our natural demeanour influencing how we go about it, particularly by how we carry ourselves during those moments. It's worth thinking about, because as mentioned if you allow yourself to get angry and become upset, you might only inflame the entire process. Instead, remain calm and dignified, whereby he will see you in a different light. When a controlling man senses a less than confident woman, he immediately seizes the moment realizing how easily she can be further manipulated and continues with his usual repertoire.

Although it's best to keep the decision for a confrontation to yourself for the time being, share it with your diary, or maybe with someone trustworthy, a friend, or family member. However, all too often, it's someone you believe you can trust who fails you by masquerading as a loyal friend and becoming a turncoat.

– The reason for this is that you only assume that the person you want to share your information with agrees with you, whereas their beliefs and loyalties may lie elsewhere. –

As mentioned, it's imperative you have a full understanding of your partner's likely behaviour once he discovers you're seeking to make a stand against him. Women who are victims in a controlling and coercive environment are generally in a safer position whereby her man has shown no previous physical abuse. However, there's always the first time, so understand that possibility.

In contrast to those women who are currently in a toxic relationship, enduring physical, threatening, and intimidating behaviour. However, the situation requires a not-to-similar approach in how it's handled, again due to the sheer unpredictability of human nature.

Preparation

> **Awareness** – The very first step is for you to come to terms with your present feelings towards this person, and not to be confused with how anyone else – including him- expects you to feel. Whatever you do, don't make the mistake of allowing your emotions to take control without good reason. If you're unsure of your feelings, it is best to exercise caution and take time out until you do.

If you believe you live with a controlling husband/partner, and you are with the mindset that you just don't want to do anything about your situation, then that is your choice. That said, the following passages within this book may well inspire you to rethink and possibly have a change of heart.

Regardless of the outcome, it will always be because you went to such courageous lengths attempting to straighten out your relationship, and you were the one who didn't give in like so many women do. Along with giving your partner the opportunity to mend his ways and live a normal, happy life - if he sees the errors in his ways.

– This is when those males who knowingly are in the wrong allow their emotions to work adversely by becoming angry and stubborn. It's only when a woman exercises her further resilience by showing her man humility, that provides him with the soft landing he so desperately needs. –

Although it's fair to say he may never truly understand what he has done wrong or comprehend what you have gone through in attempting to save the relationship. A monumental challenge and once you succeed, it will always remain one of your greatest accomplishments.

Although believing your husband will not become violent, you however prefer to write him a letter – a smart choice -, outlining your grievances and demands that will hopefully have the desired effect. With good reason, since a male who receives a dear John style letter whilst being on his own, can take out any immediate frustrations, away from you. Furthermore, he will probably become enticed to read over the letter a few times, a lasting influence while hopefully remaining calm.

An example of your letter: "I've taken some time to reflect on our relationship, and I need to express my feelings openly and honestly, therefore it's essential for us both to understand where we stand. Your controlling and coercive behaviour has deeply affected me. You're always giving me instructions, and you seem to monitor what I do, asking me so many questions when I get home. Then you try to stop me from seeing my friends by telling me I could do better and further commenting on what I should wear. You also control the finances, this is not how I see a husband caring for his wife.

I deserve respect, trust, and financial safety. I cannot continue to tolerate this type of behaviour that undermines my well-being. Therefore, I want to make it very clear that unless you make immediate changes, by ending your domineering ways, you leave me little choice other than to end our relationship.

I hope we can address these issues together. However, it requires your commitment to change. I urge you to either stop now, or seek professional help, whether through counselling or therapy, to work on your controlling and coercive behaviour.

Please understand that I did not make this decision lightly, and although I love you, I value myself and my emotional health more. Let's take this opportunity to communicate openly and find a path forward—one that either leads to positive change or allows us to part ways amicably."

Ques: "Several years ago, when my husband was much younger, I wrote him a long letter on this very topic, and he didn't think too much about it at the time. But he did when he discovered I was no longer around, trying everything he could to get me back, but I stayed put, having moved in with a girlfriend. My question is, or rather a statement—young males have little idea about relationships, so it's a shame us females have to go to these lengths to make our men understand. I don't regret it, as I did go back to him because I knew deep down, he loved me, and for years now he has always respected me, and has never tried to be controlling or coercive again. Amazingly now, he encourages me to do the things I like to do with or without him."

Ans: "I hope the women who have read your story become inspired, as it shows what's possible when you stand up for yourself. In your case you also discovered the true extent of your feelings toward your man, and that of his feelings towards you."

Using your own words when writing your letter will also provide you with a sense of emotional fulfillment, since this type of communication normally comes from the heart. This will also provide you with the confidence you need to reach your goal.

An appropriate addition to your diary, for which it cannot be overlooked or over emphasised enough, to its importance. With your first diary entry, be sure to reference that you have finally acknowledged the fact you are being controlled and coerced by your partner/husband and have decided to do something about it.

As a further example, you could write in your diary:

For quite some time now, I believe my husband/partner has ordered me around and I have been made to do things I didn't want to do. I have had concerns as to my feelings towards him on this matter for quite some time, and have written him a letter expressing my views, which I gave to him and kept a copy.

By writing that one small paragraph (naturally it's an example only), in a diary, adds significantly while keeping hold of documents and statements. It's the very essence of allowing yourself to feel a sense of release and expression like never before. A time to recall and reflect, remembering what happened at a certain time and place, along with identifying any pattern of behaviour.

Again, it's also a very important legal document for the authorities to act on—if in fact you should ever need to use in divorce proceedings. Because in most cases it provides so much more than hearsay, it's that all-important tangible evidence resulting in a decision that can produce a favourable outcome.

— Many women become mortified with the decisions that are made by the legal process when understanding the importance of having kept written references in their diaries. -

As mentioned, the attitude amongst many is 'you made your bed, you sleep in it', and that is why only you can right the wrong.

Give your husband/partner some time to take in the contents of the letter in your absence, don't be surprised if he doesn't comment, other than wanting it to just disappear, being generally the case.

— Having given him that all important cooling-off period, it hopefully opens up for rational discussions, but again, your composure and maintaining your safety is key. —

But don't allow him to control the conversation, instead remind him he is the one who needs to answer - to you. Address the grievances in your letter and don't let him coerce you any further into losing track or forgetting the intervention's purpose and meaning.

Wife – "Did you read my letter?"

Husband – "Yes, I did, and I have to say; I don't control you; I only look out for you."

Arguably a fair comment, however, one that was predictable alongside his failure to show any empathy or compassion for your feelings. This is where so many males come up short. Remember, it's not whether he believes he is controlling or coercive, it's not about him. It's all about how you interpret what he says and does, and how that makes you feel and what you believe.

Wife – "Was there anything in my letter you wish to discuss with me?"

Husband – "As I said, I don't understand what you're talking about."

Again, the type of response expected from this type of male, who has no courage to address the matter, preferring to be allusive on the subject, whilst remaining in denial, and hoping it just goes away.

Wife – "I realise you have no intention of trying to understand what I am going through, you're either playing games with me or you're oblivious to what I'm talking about. Therefore, I'm not prepared to stay in this relationship any longer unless you start taking me seriously.

Husband – "Alright, what is it you want me to do?"

Finally, a positive reaction, since the male has woken up to the dreaded realisation that the wife/partner is not only on to him but might be serious about leaving him. As previously mentioned, never assume a male is naturally aware of his behaviour, because he may not understand what is unacceptable in a relationship.

Wife – "Although I appreciate you looking out for me, the point I'm making to you is how you go about making decisions on my behalf, without asking me. You must understand, I am completely capable of making my own decisions. Why can't you relax, and stop being insecure, because that's how you are behaving, even if you don't want to believe it. You're pushing me further and further away, as your domineering behaviour is having the opposite effect to what you think you are achieving. Can't you see what you're doing, to our relationship?

Husband – "I've never really thought about it."

Wife – "Well, for the sake of our relationship, it's time you did."

In which case, any male who truly loves his wife/partner will listen and process both what he's being told and analysing wants really behind the rhetoric and tone he uses. It may be a defining moment, where the penny drops. Thankfully, it turns out he was the type of male who has never been questioned or challenged about his controlling and coercive behaviour—until now.

As a result, the thought of losing his wife/partner weighed heavily on his mind, being the catalyst for his desire to change his ways.

This woman was brave enough to express her feelings rationally and calmly, whilst using the leverage of threat to leave her man. Desperate measures for desperate times, because there's no point in any half-hearted measures, the approach must be tough love, remember that adage, 'To be cruel to be kind.'

Control and Coercion

However, in a case where the male digs in, there are basically only two options. You can continue in your attempts to turn his behaviour around, or you can end the relationship on your terms, which he is now aware of. Because the thought of a third option, living with someone who continues to have it his way by controlling you- is out of the question.

But since you have tried to salvage your relationship, it's now a wait and see, as you have clearly given him something profound to think about. That said, you now need to give yourself a realistic timeframe with an end date, to follow through with this intervention while secretly making enquiries to end the relationship in the event he won't change.

As difficult as it may first appear, learn to ignore him; don't be coerced into conversation when he becomes verbally controlling. Instead, go about your business as if he weren't there. Finding yourself needing to comment, use terms such as, "Don't tell me what I'm going to do, ask me what I would like to do".

— The risk here is the situation becoming unintentionally inflamed with the male's frustration boiling over and escalating to another higher level of abuse. —

Try not to be alarmed, instead remain aware of your end goal. Should you ever become too concerned about your safety, then move out immediately, as inconvenient as it is? As mentioned, a woman's personal safety in any type of domestic abuse situation should always remain your number one priority.

Ques: "I am in a similar situation myself, but I can't help thinking it's just too difficult, why is that?"

Ans: "Then stop thinking that way, instead think positively. You can build on your confidence, finding your strength and courage, by simply reaching out to your fortitude. Constantly be aware of the actions you need to fulfill, which will provide you with a clear sense of direction. Understand that change takes time, so remain patient and honest with yourself regarding the on-going process"?

Regularly remain in contact with your diary, reflect on your progress and adjust your approach as needed, by giving yourself tasks, remaining flexible and willing to adapt to new circumstances. Remember, it's okay to have some doubt, because without doubt you will never discover problems or find solutions. The key is to remain focused on the outcome you want to achieve, and take small manageable steps, then ask yourself: Would you put up with any other overbearing person - on a daily basis? Of course you wouldn't. So why should he be any different?

Remaining steadfast

There's little doubt about the challenge you both face, since he refuses to open up, remaining in denial, however it's your belief that you can change him. Your reasoning is, you love him, and you believe he loves you, knowing he has better qualities and needs direction. That said, monitor his behaviour, in particular note any signs of a change in his style of conversation, particularly whether he has shown any decline in his level of control.

Now that you have made it perfectly clear as to your intentions to leave him should he not comply, remain steadfast, and he will sit up and take notice, as he knows all too well of the consequences. In the event he doesn't, then you have your answer, being, he just doesn't respect or love you as he maintains or as you had hoped. A devastating blow, however, you have successfully forced this matter into its conclusion, for that you should be proud, although it comes at a price.

Whenever humans experience such disappointment, their emotions take over, as it's a type of shock to the body that requires time to heal. However, the human body has extraordinary powers to recover, helped along again by our fortitude and remaining positive—one of many essential attributes—during these complex circumstances.

In conclusion, never lose sight of the fact that whether a man recognises his own controlling or coercive behaviour is not the central issue. What matters the most is the male understanding his wife or partner's innermost feelings by showing empathy and compassion. Therefore, any male that fails in this area is a male that simply does not understand women.

SUMMARY

- First coming to terms with being controlled/coerced, is a profound moment.
- Understand your perception of controlling/coercive behaviour, may differ to him, find common ground.
- Gauge to what extent this behaviour has in you and write down your most personal feelings into your diary, so you can reflect on it at any time.
- Ensure you leave no stone unturned when explaining to your man how his behaviour affects you.
- Confrontation is necessary, plan how to safely direct your grievances at him.
- Your plan should be decisive, with no room for inconsistencies, or small talk, only thorough conclusive remedies – so important.
- Time to be honest with yourself on your true feelings towards your man, as it is, to refocus on his feelings towards you.
- Continue to use your senses when he addresses you and analyse without bias, both the content and the context, and come to a conclusion you are comfortable with.
- Remain calm and stay in control, and never become unhinged, by doing so further reduces the respect you need and deserve.
- Once a man finally realises he may lose his wife/partner, it's astounding the ratio of those men who miraculously have a change of heart. But only if you follow through.

- If you choose to try and save your marriage, then regardless of the outcome you will have discovered what you're capable of.

PERPETRATOR

Whether or not you believe you're controlling, it's recommended you read the previous chapter. This may give you a different perspective and insight into the effects that this type of behaviour has on a woman. Along with learning something about it and indeed yourself.

Consider questioning whether your behaviour may be controlling or coercive, it's important to pause and reflect before you speak. Start by considering the words you intend to use, picturing the conversation as though it has already taken place. Having done so try to understand a woman's point of view as to whether your tone and message come across as being controlling and / or coercive. From that perspective, you may now begin to understand how your wife or partner feels emotionally when she listens to you.

Humans are sensitive—including that of your wife/partner—as I suspect you are, therefore remain mindful of the effect you have on others. Instead, ensure your type of rhetoric is relatable in a measured caring, thoughtful, and compassionate way, and more importantly refrain from disguising dominance for care. You might want to give that some additional thought.

– Ask yourself, *if you used your type of rhetoric in the workplace, would you be seen as a workplace bully?* –

If you feel you're being misunderstood, the first and most effective step is to speak openly with the one person who can help you understand how you're coming across — your wife or partner. Changing the way you speak matters. Shifting your dialect, softening your tone, and expressing a point rather than issuing a demand can completely transform how your message is received. The way couples speak to one another has a profound impact on respect, calmness, and the long-term health of the relationship.

In the event you have been raised in childhood with this type of behaviour, having difficulty in either talking about, or coming to terms with, simply explain to your wife/partner, she will understand. But don't use this as an excuse, as she will know that you are now becoming deceitful as well as controlling. Just come clean, even if there are underlying reasons you think you can't open up with, she will help you. So, again, it's probably high time you came to terms with addressing these problems, recalibrating your life for the better.

Human beings are always amazed when proved wrong on matters they held steadfast beliefs in. Only then do they feel an inexplicable sense of relief shared with overwhelming joy, having realised their behaviour was all in vain. As in this situation, where you will discover there was never any need or any point to being either controlling or coercive to begin with, it was all in your mind.

It's time to forget about your insecurities and allow your wife/partner to be the woman she wants to be, who will appreciate and love you that much more. Listen to what your wife/partner is telling you and make simple adjustments to how you first talk to her in the future. Stop being possessive, and that's all you need to do.

Leaving something in reserve—by doing so provides others with a sense of curiosity, intrigue, fascination and perhaps even admiration for you. Particularly for the most important person in your life, your wife/partner.

By adopting this attitude relaxes your anxiety, giving your wife/partner the autonomy she wants, needs, and deserves. In return, you will receive the sign that controlling and coercive behaviour is a complete waste of time. If you believe your wife/partner is continuing to be wayward in the broader sense, and believing it's the cause for your controlling ways, then you may have to consider whether this relationship is for you. Regardless of the circumstances, control and coercion attack the very foundation of a relationship, including the control it has over you. – Relax a little!

SEXUAL ABUSE

This chapter on sexual abuse makes for a powerful headline and so it should, since for many people it evokes debate over definitions, accountability, and the silence that allows such harm to persist. Generally showing the highest levels to be, the worst overarching and degrading violation that could be perpetrated against another human being. Non-consensual sexual abuse, especially the sodomization of adolescents, surpasses all other forms of abuse in its depravity. Victims are the only ones who can truly account for these horrific crimes. It doesn't stop there, repercussions of which cause potential long-term mental and physical scarring.

For the perpetrator, it's less confronting, having little effect on their conscience, instead they seek future self-gratification and continue to carry out their abuses and atrocities. Worse still, without challenge, feeling comfortable with their thought process of never being caught. In family homes, the worrying statistics show one in three women is subject to some type of sexual abuse, that in many cases remains a secret for a variety of reasons. Of which isolation, insecurities, threats and intimation are at the forefront.

This behaviour crosses many boundaries including the well-being of the perpetrator's own partners and offspring, all behind closed doors, under the presumption of a normal functioning family environment. Statistics also show, the act of penetration carried out on a young adolescent females are twice the ratio to that of a male. Many victims go through life with the added burden of guilt, feeling worthless, and suffering self-loathing. These traits are challenging to remedy either by the victim themselves, carers or with professional help.

A young female, having been sexually abused before her time, may very well carry another type of guilt, that of never having had her rightful opportunity in life of perhaps having given herself to that someone special. A process no female should ever be denied, and all because some degenerate has forever stolen her most precious virtue—her innocence.

As mentioned, these types of abuse fall into the lowest depths of human depravity, suffering and degradation, which can also destroy the mind, body and soul. Whilst one coward engages in this style of self-gratification, one innocent adult and child's life is being tortured and ruined. It's the type of abuse we all prefer not to know or even talk about, because of the sheer level of horror and anger it creates in the human mind.

-There are young children most likely at school right now sitting in their classroom, unable to remain attentive, since they are distracted by what potentially awaits them when they get home, with no one likely to come to their rescue-.

When we hear or think about domestic abuse, we don't generally think about sexual abuse, instead we imagine only what we perceive to be happening, usually commonplace acts such as verbal arguments.

Therefore, how easy is it to become blindsided in life, to the real depths of the horror that infiltrates some homes, and indeed throughout society?

Instead, we prefer to consume only what we want to hear and what we want to believe—but only then if it doesn't affect us. Humans by nature struggle with the process of complex issues, sometimes unwilling to face the realities of life. Instead, we choose to leave it to someone else, preferring to believe it's not our problem.

How should this be addressed

As noted, for many, the pain is so overwhelming that even thinking about it becomes unbearable, let alone taking any action. As a result, some may believe it is easier to suppress the truth and pretend it doesn't exist. However, it does exist, and we should and must acknowledge it. Then confront it, taking decisive action to intervene, and work to put an end to this type of abuse on a continuing basis. It's the responsibility of all compassionate, caring and considerate civilised human beings—are you one of those people?

– Out of sight, out of mind –

Many countries around the world have neighbourhood watch, a community initiative to look out for one another and report any suspicious behaviour or activity. However, most sexual abuse atrocities lie hidden behind closed doors, out of sight, out of mind.

It's troubling when we hear the authorities break down the front door of a home to arrest a suspected drug dealer, yet a child experiencing sexual assault at that same premises will not be thought about. Isn't it a simple matter to introduce legislation to protect every child's well-being, particularly from sexual abuse, mandating a welfare check on children in any home during a police visit. Although authorities will investigate- if they learn of this abuse-, it will only remain a talking point unless ordinary people provide crucial information. That's why sexual abuse against children continues on the scale it does throughout the world, because it's a behaviour that most perpetrators see as a risk worth taking. That feeling of remaining anonymous and the almost concealed transgression that delivers privacy and secrecy surrounding these sickening events. A crime that receives minimal public attention, gains little awareness, therefore invites even less discussion.

As a result, adolescents remain confused, while unaware of the psychological effects it's about to have on them now and later in life. Each human being is uniquely different; therefore, every individual's recovery is complex, and it could never be suggested there is a one size that fits all diagnoses and therapy sessions. This is nothing short of devastation, since these young adolescents were only wanting to be filled with childhood dreams, finding their way in life whilst being free-spirited, instead of having their innocence taken away.

As mentioned, we should all realise that the authorities have zero information to act on, unless the victim comes forward or the ordinary people in this world—open their hearts and minds and use their voices whenever they become suspicious.

– Imagine for a second if you were aware of sexual abuse but remained quiet. What if you were the abused victim? How would you feel, knowing that someone knew what you were going through, yet they didn't come forward, to end your intolerable suffering? –

This type of behaviour perpetrated by low life sexual predators on very young victims, can only be stopped through intervention, again by ordinary people. Although your suspicions may be circumstantial, you may well save the life of someone who would have otherwise continued to suffer in silence.

People like you could help end the misery of a hopelessly trapped, sexually abused adolescent perhaps unable to speak up or seek help for themselves. For those of you who lack the courage to come forward, then although that's nothing to be ashamed of, why allow a child to continue to suffer? There are other ways and means to solve these types of problems without you ever having to be exposed or ever having to come forward- use your imagination.

Are you someone that's willing to help

It pays to be mindful, there's people in your circle who may need help, or in contrast, may need to be arrested. Therefore, don't for a second believe you are just some insignificant busy body, far from it. Rather, you can become the very essence of what good over evil represents, by exercising your rights, and contacting the authorities.

If you are a strong advocate- being a confident person- you may take it upon yourself to be upfront and openly find out what is going on, without fearing retribution. However, as mentioned, if you want to stay safe and remain anonymous, walk into any police station and make a confidential statement.

You could also send an anonymous letter to the department of family services stating you have concerns for the safety of e.g. Jane Doe in relation to possible sexual or other abuse. Sending a copy to someone of good community standing that will have the matter investigated.

— Spread the word —

Your intervention and contribution make you a real-life hero, regardless of how you feel about that. It doesn't end there, as something quite profound will also take place, whereby you will experience an overwhelming feeling of profound achievement, that of knowing you have perhaps saved a human life.

Contacting the authorities

It's remarkable that whilst there are people who ring the emergency hotline with trivial information, those who genuinely need police assistance have chosen the extraordinary decision not to.

— How many people have allowed their pride to obstruct their better judgement? Never allow this to happen, it's fraught with internal and lasting regret. Instead, immediately call the police, even if it turns out to be a false alarm. Isn't it time we all took ownership of what we see and hear, particularly when we suspect sexual abuse is taking place. -

When recognizing conversations that carry subtle hints or insinuations of sexual abuse, humans have the ability to hone in. These instinctive traits trigger heightened alerts and awareness, prompting humans to listen more closely encouraging further intervention. A cause so important, you may now want it to remain as part of your everyday psyche, to remain alert, always being inquisitive, a noble cause for now and for all time.

What does it take to conduct this type of initial impartial analysis, other than to use our senses, and perhaps a little cunning, particularly on such an important matter of discovering and reporting sexual abuse.

Are you a sibling worried about the safety of one or more of your brothers or sisters, especially late at night—but too afraid to speak up? Or do you want to be brave and reach out, yet feel uncertain about who you can trust? If so, this is completely understandable, and you are not alone. Like all complex challenges, there is both a right way and a wrong way to approach them. The greatest obstacle for many is believing the issue belongs in the 'too-hard basket,' and as a result, doing nothing about it.

– How will that help those people who are suffering unimaginable horror? –

Getting evidence requires honesty, discretion and to keep your emotions in place if you're not sure about your suspicions. Therefore, you don't want to make either assumptions or accusations that are proven to be false, particularly when you're living under the same roof as the person you believe could be the perpetrator.

– Don't become despondent –

Let's assume you have suspicions that concern another family member. Wait for an appropriate time when no one is within earshot, asking that person you suspect is being abused if they want to talk to you about anything they're not happy about. Wait for their reaction by looking into their eyes to gauge their response. Does their head drop, do they look ashamed, are they forthcoming with an answer, if so, then assume for the time being your suspicions are correct? However, tread carefully, because at this crucial stage some victims can become too scared to open up, or tell the truth. Often, perpetrators warn their victims to remain silent, along with making threats towards them.

– It's a time for extra sensitivity, especially when discussing such issues requiring tactful and truthful transparency, particularly when heavily burdened by a child's age for their comprehension and perception of events. –

Comfort them, explaining there's nothing to be scared about, as you are there to help them—remaining mindful of the extreme necessity in fulfilling that promise. Confirming your suspicions is all you want at this point, so be mindful that the best way forward from hereon is to allow for a professional to handle the matter.

So again, it's imperative a professional handle this type of situation, as they are trained to read the signs, which many of us don't see. As an example, a child might appear calm when being questioned, however, that response could be a consequence of being under duress. In some cases, a child may unintentionally give the impression that sexual abuse has occurred when it hasn't.

Again, should your suspicions be confirmed, then reassure the victim they are not in any trouble, and you are going to do everything you can to make it stop.

Ques: "Now in my fifties, I have always carried the painful knowledge that my sister was being abused by our father as we shared the same bedroom, and I remember how terrified I was to speak up. My sister took her own life in her early twenties, and even now, I still ask myself why we never told anyone?"

Ans: The heartbreaking reality of what goes on behind closed doors continues as the perpetrators use intimidation to silence their victims. Their fear tactics keep those in the household both scared and trapped. Losing your sister is tragic and serves as a powerful reminder of the urgency for intervention no matter how difficult it may seem. Speaking out can break the cycle and protect others from enduring the same suffering. Your sister would probably have known you were both too scared to speak up. Although it's a tragedy that your sister ended her life, she wouldn't want you to carry any burden of guilt knowing how scared you both were, instead remember her for the way you both loved one-another."

Recorded statistics show that family members commit over forty percent of sexual assaults, while fewer than twenty percent resulted in charges and only fifteen percent result in convictions. Proving how difficult successful prosecutions are, giving perpetrators a larger safety net.

— A sad indictment, and a blight on the term civilised. —

Once authorities learn of possible sexual abuse, they should immediately investigate—one would hope. Sadly, a stigma persists, creating a troubling hesitation around intervening in family matters both from the authorities, family members and ordinary citizens.

— An attitude the perpetrator is often all too aware of and happy to exploit, which further reflects the difficulties the authorities have in obtaining proof. —

Inquisitive, not intrusive

It must be repeated, whilst remaining vigilant and sometimes suspicious against sexual abuse, we become alerted via our gut feeling, being our own alarm system, that triggers and drives our inquisitiveness into action. This is where humans should instinctively take a closer look at whether a person of interest is a victim or in fact a perpetrator, without raising suspicion. This is not being intrusive, instead it provides an opportunity to observe their character and their personality more closely. Discovering their past, asking loaded questions without appearing to be probing, noticing any change in their demeanour that may just provide you with some pertinent information. Best of all let them talk and should they open up, explain they have done the right thing, and offer support. You may have saved one or more people from being further sexually abused, and indeed the perpetrator himself.

— There's nothing wrong or unnatural about being suspicious, it's another part of our human defense mechanism. It reminds us to remain safe, not only for ourselves but towards others. —

Perpetrators are both cunning and calculating, therefore, it's best to try and think as they do- in a manner of speaking. Doing so may well provide a would-be super sleuth, even any ordinary-thinking person for that matter, with a better understanding of how, why, and when to take advantage of opportune moments in furthering their suspicions.

Preventing and Ending Domestic Abuse

Doctors are in the unique position of discovering whether a child is a victim of sexual abuse, not unlike teachers, child and family services, and care workers. All of whom have a duty of care to remain mindful and suspicious by reading any mental and physical signs along with identifying any behavioural changes.

Through a precise set of protocols and criteria, both a general practitioner and a teacher can have a one on one with most students, and in private. Although it's a delicate and difficult situation, however, where there's suspicion there's an opportunity that's not to be missed or overlooked when the opportunity presents itself.

Like all other decent and caring people, teachers -in particular- have a moral responsibility in introducing safeguards to protect our children. Covering many aspects of their growth through their initial early learning stages all the way through to when they become senior students. How relevant are these safeguard teachings for students to learn the potential dangers that may be lurking within the confined spaces of their own home. - yet seldom mentioned.

-This type of sensitive education would act as a deterrent that would bring about greater change and awareness ensuring a decline in the incidence of sexual abuse in the family home-

Suspicions are one thing, but unless we look deeper into a particular situation, only then will we learn to the extent of the truth. In many such instances, it's revealed that mothers and guardians knew the children in their care were being sexually abused but were under severe duress—while others had the courage yet remained complicit through deliberate negligence and indifference.

Ques: "I was aware of what my husband was doing all those years ago, and I am ashamed to say it. But in those days, it was so different to how it is now. Back then, my husband was abusive, angry and sometimes violent, and we never knew what to do. I regret it so much and would ask every mother, 'Would they know what to do, having heard my story?"

Ans: "As we should all recognise, where one person has the courage to confront complex and dangerous situations, another person can't. Despite the seriousness of the matter, it's never in anyone's interest to point the finger or broadcast personal opinions. Therefore, it's in your best interest to make peace with yourself because life moves on for those harbouring regrets. To the point of your question, women today are hopefully more aware of the growing movement against domestic abuse, and in this case— to find the courage to report any sexual abuse."

As earlier recommended, the best way to ensure your safety or that of someone you suspect is a victim of sexual abuse is to either ring the police or walk straight into a police station and provide a statement. Keep in mind when questioned by the police, making absolutely sure you tell the truth, because it's a serious matter. Making false allegations against someone is not only a crime, but a situation that can also ruin a person's reputation and indeed their life. A consequence that can deliver long term severe mental trauma for any innocent person wrongly accused. However, don't be deterred and just tell the truth, and the police will know how to investigate.

The police are not miracle workers and may have other urgent matters to deal with. Matters they may well believe are more important than yours, as difficult as that may be to comprehend. Again, it's the world we live in, but perhaps one that needs review, that further highlight types of domestic abuse.

Let your conscience guide you!

Perpetrators often operate under the assumption that their victims are neither believed, won't come forward, nor able to find someone willing to help. Therefore, as mentioned, proving perpetrators wrong adds another layer toward the need for the continuous fight against sexual abuse.

Being a victim, you don't need to be alone, as there are genuine caring professional people who want to help you, but they can't if they remain unaware of your situation. It's important that you report any behaviour you find offensive or not happy with. Never suffer in silence, otherwise your situation may never improve, let your conscience guide you.

This is where another type of tragedy often occurs—during interviews. Sexually abused victims can develop sympathy for the perpetrator. A serious mistake, although understandable when intimidation, threats, even emotions are heightened. Failure to follow through and make a report against this heinous act tells the perpetrator he's not accountable, allowing him to further believe he's unlikely to suffer any consequences for his behaviour.

Silence for self-preservation

Also remain aware of some family members and friends that may pressure the victim to retract their statement and remain silent. Prioritizing their own reputation and personal interests over that of the victim's well-being. Their actions are despicable, showing a disturbing lack of compassion and empathy, expressing a willingness to interfere in a way showing total disregard for a loved one's suffering. This highlights the lengths some individuals will go with protecting themselves where self-entitlement masquerades as self-preservation, driven by greed, despite the gravity of the crimes committed.

As a victim, embracing courage and finding inner strength during this time will greatly assist in shaping the course of your life. Knowing you stood up for yourself, ensuring that good prevailed over evil and reinforced the distinction between right and wrong—marks a defining moment. Had you surrendered, the perpetrator would have remained free to continue their abuse, harming both you and others.

Throughout this book, we've emphasized that humans can use natural means to overcome many kinds of challenges. Understandably, this depends on age; therefore, we should specifically help younger people who have not yet developed cognitive skills to protect themselves.

As a mother, even if you're not directly involved in this unthinkable behaviour, you should realise the seriousness of your situation. You are being exploited in the same way as the victims themselves. To a lesser degree granted, however, if you are within the same four walls and aware of these atrocities that are taking place, and not reporting it, you are both an accomplice and therefore complicit. Maybe you are subjected to other forms of domestic abuse, controlled and coerced, suffering emotional abuse, and living a traumatic lifestyle few are aware of. Nevertheless, find a way to make a report and free yourself.

In which case the perpetrator is aware of his complete control over you, understanding you know exactly what is happening in the family home. His brazen act will continue unchecked and unchallenged, destined to remain a secret to the outside world. Unless you start to understand the severity of what is happening in your world. Take a minute to think about those you know who are suffering sexual abuse and mental torture, and who desperately need your help.

Ques: "I was a teenager when my father came into my room and made me do things I never wanted to do. Now that I am a mother myself, I protect my children as much as I can. I finished seeing my father many years ago and always ask myself why any father would cross the line, knowing it would cause a lifetime of hurt and regret?"

Ans: "It is deeply painful to live without a relationship with your father, yet in your circumstances, entirely understandable. People can behave in ways that fall far outside what is acceptable for many complex reasons, but none of those reasons excuse harming a child. While human behaviour can be influenced by powerful impulses, every person has the capacity—and the responsibility—to exercise self-control, restraint, and moral judgment. Choosing to commit such a violation is an abuse of power, not an inevitability. For that reason, there is little room for sympathy toward someone who inflicts such profound and lasting harm."

— There would be people thinking, 'how can it be possible that a mother or a guardian of children could ever remain silent, knowing that one or more of their children in their care, is being sexually abused' —

There are many perpetrators with no idea or understanding as to why they are in this position or how they first became a sexual abuser. Nor do they have any understanding of the type of destruction they cause on the mind, body and soul of their victims.

Coming to terms with the truth

Assuming the path you're on in your relationship is not your intended one, then your situation likely stems from just one source, the male you chose as your partner. Any male that orchestrates a scare campaign with everyone around him, taking liberties to the extreme including sexual assault, is a male that requires being immediately arrested.

Ask yourself what the benefits could possibly be for remaining the way you are, with a criminal for which there's no logical explanation. What on earth happened to your self-respect to ever allow this to happen, or to those dreams and aspirations along with that zest for love and life you once had. Instead, you now live a life of misery, covering up for a criminal, while pretending to be happy, when you know you're consumed by guilt and sadness.

What would you prefer, to show courage with a clear conscience, surrounded by decent people that put that smile back on your face, or remain in the shadow of a cold, calculating sexual deviant.

The easiest way to start that all important resurrection process is to turn your mind back to the time before you met your partner and reflect on the person you once were. Perhaps someone that had dreams of living a life with a decent man, raising a family in happiness. But somewhere along the line, you became derailed, now finding yourself in the abyss of evil, and hopefully looking for a way out. Well, now you can reach out and become that very person you always wanted to be.

Having the desire, you set off a chain reaction, when almost by magic, your self-respect is restored followed by your self-esteem and gaining self-confidence. Then you discover that your strength and courage have also returned, sparking a long overdue feeling of well-being. It's there—trust yourself on that. You weren't born to be the person you have become; you simply made poor decisions and choices. Therefore, you can just as easily become the person you want to be.

If it's your child that's being sexually abused, then say nothing to anyone and take your child immediately to your family doctor and explain the full details and don't hold back. As difficult as that may appear to be, any negative thoughts are only on the surface. The simple answer is twofold- what matters most concerns the welfare of that child and for you to return to being the person you know you want to be.

Ques: "My mother knew my father was abusing me when I was young and I now realise how scared she was of my father as we all were. Both my parents are deceased, having divorced many years earlier. My mother went far too early, and I have always believed it was caused by the guilt she carried with her. I live with that belief, knowing the abuse I suffered was small compared to what my mother went through. She was a good person who found herself trapped by this man, believing she had no escape. Therefore, I continue to wonder how many other women there are out there suffering from the same torment my mother did?"

Ans: "Acknowledging what your mother went through and using that as leverage to maintain a normal civilised life is wonderful therapy and would make your mother proud. We must remember the importance of understanding how different we all are. It's so easy just to assume a woman should have done this or that when we stand on the sideline. However, it just doesn't work that way, we should therefore never make assumptions, unless we know the true facts."

Having gone to the authorities and provided your child with the professional medical help needed, you can return to living your life without the intensity of guilt. As importantly, you are returning to your maternal instinct, a decision you will never regret.

There will be initial consequences, however the repercussions you may face in contrast to those of what a sexually abused child would have continued to endure, are inconsequential. There will be many questions to answer, so just be honest with the authorities and yourself and don't hold back, letting it all out. Don't have any thoughts about your partner's reaction, worry not, this isn't about him—not now, not anymore. It's so much more than that, it's about saving a child's life, and for your future wellbeing.

Again, human nature is as complex as it can be disturbing. So much so, it's hard to imagine there are people that are presumably loved within their own family who are also conspired against. Relatives that carry out unimaginable sexual abuse on their own flesh and blood which continues to remain almost taboo due to a continuing attached stigma and lack of education.

As to your further involvement with this person, only you can gauge the situation as to whether you love him enough to remain with him, assisting him with the help he needs. A brave woman indeed, who would stick by her man under these circumstances- though many would say foolish.

While human beings are capable of vivid imaginations mixing fantasy with sexual gratification, it could be argued it's unlikely pedophilia will ever go away. Therefore, human beings should carry constant reminders of potential sexual abusive behaviour in both families and throughout our communities.

When the relationship appears to be on course and the male has been showing the respect that every woman wants and deserves, he inexplicably becomes filled with a sense of self-entitlement when wanting sex. Let's be clear, there are many men of all ages that have the desire to lie, cheat, charm, con and scam their way into having their way sexually, it's the type of behaviour that continues to exist. A male can become physically demanding when he realises his sexual needs and advances are not being met. This is particularly true when he's influenced by the lack of self-discipline, and or by drugs and alcohol.

That's not to stereo type men by saying men don't know how to treat a woman with respect, because they do. However, women should remind themselves of the male's prowess and the potential danger that lurks within the mind of that male. Whether he has good intentions or not, most younger men will instinctively have sex on their mind at one time or another. That's not the problem. It's whether he has trouble containing those feelings instead of crossing the line, allowing himself to become a sexual predator.

Statistics show that women across the world continue to face attacks, rape, and sexual abuse—both within and outside of relationships. These violations occur in the family home as well as in public spaces and can be perpetrated by someone known to the victim or by a stranger.

> **Awareness** – Defining sexual abuse continues to be a highly contested debate, amongst therapists, the authorities and both men and women, differing from all sides. Ask the average person to distinguish between sexual abuse and sexual harassment, and you're likely to receive a range of different answers, opinions, and interpretations. Similarly, asking a group to define sexual flirtation versus sexual advances will yield varied responses, although each term carries distinct meanings. However, one could also argue that flirtatious behaviour—while often perceived as harmless—can, in some cases serve as a subtle precursor to the more assertive pursuit of sexual entitlement. Hence the need for education!

Is traditional behaviour under threat?

In recent times, it's fair to say, men have become more consciously aware of how they should behave when in female company—at least in some circles. Since the term 'inappropriate behaviour' has become more prevalent in our vocabulary, like some type of buzzword.

Should women then analyse every interaction, particularly the physical elements between a male and female, on a case-by-case basis? Whilst every woman deserves to be treated respectfully, there has become a growing controversial trend. Whereby well-intentioned men have become somewhat less reluctant to engage in pleasantries when in the company of women. Brought about by fear of rejection or failing some type of interactional etiquette test. Therefore, women should realise that without experiencing that feeling of being touched around the shoulders or receiving the occasional kiss on the cheek, they miss out on those unforgettable old-world charms, as well as potential missed opportunities of finding a partner.

Whilst this belief would provide some females with being more respected, for others, it delivers both bemusement and disappointment. The potential drawback here is for those women who once accepted and appreciated the occasional suave and chivalrous antics of the male, will one day be wondering, what ever happened to all that attention they once received.

— Why disenfranchise men who know how to treat a woman, simply because of some new minority broadcasting their overzealous beliefs that stereotype most males? —

Therefore, there will be women who see through this for what it is, a futile attempt—again by some new age minority—putting women up on a pedestal where they don't want to be. Instead, women should consider becoming desensitised to this narrow-minded belief and continue receiving the same type of attention the male has been displaying since time itself.

Ques: "If society respected women, men wouldn't feel the need to touch another female other than by their partners. I always question a male's actual intent if I find myself on the receiving end of an unwanted kiss or an embrace, so why would a male think about being familiar with me in the first place?"

Ans: "Contrary to your belief, it's human nature—being opposite sexes—to engage with one another, nothing on earth could be more natural. To show respect and to make a woman feel good, and if there's the opportunity to have some fun flirting, then shouldn't that be considered innocent enough? Again, we are only human, especially in the competitive world of seeking a partner. If a male is being overzealous, then a woman has every right to put him in his place. On the other hand, a woman may not consider those actions inappropriate and enjoy the attention. Is there any reason to take this mindset any further, denying couples the chance to discover one another by remaining distant and feeling incredulous. Think in terms of the Aussie idiom — 'you can't blame a bloke for trying.'"

In a professional setting, any physical interaction or flirtatious behaviour is generally considered inappropriate, as there's no appropriate time and place for such interactions inside the workplace. Companies establish these workplace boundaries to ensure a respectable environment, with clear protocols, boundaries and policies in place. These guidelines help safeguard a woman's personal space, - and indeed the male- reinforcing the importance of professionalism and mutual respect among colleagues.

Just as a woman in the home should ensure her partner is under no illusion, for respecting and understanding her sexual beliefs, including her body clock, preferences and desires—as she with him. Although sexual compatibility is an important factor and held in high regard, it's equally important to reject any form of self-entitlement, other than what is reciprocal.

High testosterone levels cause many young men to believe they are entitled to sex, leading them to overlook their sexual behaviour is causing their partner serious concern. Therefore, knowing he is aware of your objection, and he continues to coerce you into having sex, then it's time you had that all important discussion with him.

– Otherwise, he may never become aware or understand what acceptable sexual behaviour must be between consenting couples. So don't be too concerned about hurting his feelings, as your feelings are more important than his under these circumstances. –

The sooner you talk to him, the quicker a considerate male will understand your feelings, having learnt an important lesson not to control or coerce you, using intimidation to have sex. More women should adopt this mindset, implementing controls from the outset, with the male being under no illusion.

Be careful not to become the type of women that feels as though they must somehow make amends after direct discussions on such sensitive issues with their partners, even though she has little to feel guilty about. It's based on her maternal inclinations that women should show humility and calm the waters. She believes it's the rational thing to do, sparing the male from possibly having to endure his own guilt and perhaps hiding his embarrassment. A selfless act by woman under these circumstances, and sadly one that usually remains unappreciated.

Does familiarity breed contempt?

The realisation that the male in these circumstances has come to his senses is profound on many levels. Unlike the unknown numbers of males, reflecting on what they had, now that it's gone. Wishing they too had been more understanding, while now having to start all over again with someone new. Encourage yourself to become inspired by expressing yourself openly with your partner and continue with the sex education, if you believe his behaviour borders on inappropriate behaviour. He most likely had no concept of where he was going wrong. – Hence the need for earlier education.

At what point should a woman question what is or isn't acceptable and reasonable sexual behaviour—answer being, anytime she likes, which may sound selfish? As an example of when she experiences her partner not attempting any foreplay, instead, fulfilling his own sexual desires that falls into self-entitlement regardless of whether it's consensual or not.

– Non-consensual sexual behaviour is sexual abuse –

The law now recognises marital rape as a criminal offence, treating non-consensual sexual acts within a relationship the same as any other form of sexual assault. However, these cases can be difficult to prove, as they often occur in private, rely heavily on personal testimony, and involve complex questions about consent, coercion, and power dynamics. As a result, investigators and courts may face significant challenges in determining whether a man's behaviour within a relationship was consensual or sexual abuse.

It is an extremely difficult situation to prove either way. Any woman who has experienced this situation through the court system, having now moved on with her life, would in all likelihood have preferred avoiding litigation. The demoralizing questioning is an experience many women would rather want to forget about with many remaining ashamed. Hopefully, this is why you are reading this book—to either prevent or end this type of behaviour.

The key is to gather evidence, so use your imagination along with modern day technology. It's never been easier to capture audio and visual footage- discreetly, so give that some serious thought, without compromising your safety. Perhaps something as easy as your phone recorder activated prior to when you believe he is about to take liberties. A watershed moment in any woman's life under such personal circumstances. Any male who can't accept his partner's wishes on such a sensitive issue is not worthy of the relationship.

Ques: "Before we were recently married, my then fiancé wanted sex frequently, and I always tried to keep him happy, by letting him have his way. I tried to explain to him the importance of considering my feelings, but he never took me seriously. Now that we are married, I fear he has lost all respect for me and is demanding more sex all the time. Do I talk to him again, or what is the best approach?"

Ans: "It's a serious concern, and one that all women must deal with decisively. The reason he continues with his disrespectful behaviour is because he simply gets away with it. If you oppose his sexual advances, and you're not giving your consent, he is raping you. A disturbing reality, and one you are best to understand is criminal behaviour rather than a marital one. Your first consideration must be your emotional and mental wellbeing, along with some soul searching. Discover the many options throughout this book, one of which comes to mind, is to send him a heartfelt letter. Should that fail, then professional counselling, because it tells you so much more about your man other than the problem at hand."

If you have any concerns about your safety, consider leaving home with the children and staying with relatives or friends. Make it clear in your letter that he only gets one chance to understand your feelings. Should he fail, it's time to make a case against him; by ensuring you keep a copy of the letter and continue to make entries into your diary. As mentioned, there are many practical solutions throughout this book to help you, but again, don't make the mistake of allowing it to continue- instead follow through.

Unless he is made to understand, he is unlikely to think about any type of consequence in terms of whether he is committing sexual abuse.

The facts are, it's just how many men are. That is why this book spells out in the earlier chapters of the utmost importance for women to scrutinise potential partners including receiving sexual respect. Again, making those all-important discoveries over a sensible time frame that satisfies your curiosity and aligns with your principles and values. Long before considering marriage.

Am I a mere object of desire

For those who have advanced years in a relationship and are experiencing sexual abuse, isn't it time you made a concerted effect to put an end to this behaviour. One major problem some couples have is failing to take the time to have an actual heart to heart with one another. With many women believing, 'nothing will come of it', and 'it's all too late', which couldn't be further from the truth, unless you continue to do nothing about it.

Are you someone that endures sex with quiet strength, knowing your man shows little else in the way of romance and intimacy, having sex for the sake of having sex. Then consider changing his attitude. He needs to understand that having sex isn't just about spontaneity, it should be considered more in terms of being deserving and fulfilling for both.

The relationship, along with his respect, has perhaps gone a little stale, if so, then he needs a refresher course to remind him of valuing each other's boundaries, feelings, and individuality. Together with open and honest communication, with equality and partnership, affection and appreciation. Show your man the benefits and rewards of these processes that lends itself to wanting one another with purpose and desire.

> **Awareness** – Remain slightly illusive whilst educating your man to earn you, by doing so more respect will follow. Relationships must be about compromise if they are to survive, therefore the sooner he understands the more likely he will start looking at sex, not as a right but a privilege.

Some couples prefer a de facto relationship. It's because for many, it fosters a more relaxed and questionably respectful, non-committed mindset. Since this type of relationship was never set in stone, it often carries a sense of emotional freedom and fewer perceived constraints. Nevertheless, it provides for the same intense passion for one another, as in a committed relationship.

While personal preferences differ, a consummated marriage often deepens a couple's sense of responsibility and commitment, creating a stronger, more respectful bond. This is an understanding every man in a relationship should not only grasp but genuinely accept and feel at ease with.

Ques: "I remember how my father treated my mother when I was young, and my mother going into detail and telling me to be careful when I get older. Those words remain with me today, and thankfully I made the right choice of marrying a kind and considerate man, which has made my life so fulfilling. I am so grateful for my mother sharing her troubles and explaining to me what she went through, 'Why can't everyone encourage young women the way my mother did?'"

Ans: "And they can. But only through people like yourself, and those mothers like your mother who only want the best for the children they raised. You may agree that without the stories and encouragement you received from your mother, you could be expressing a different tone with less pleasurable thoughts altogether".

Should you ever question yourself about your relationship, now is a good time to maintain your diary, as mentioned on previous occasions. Doing so allows you to look at life from a different perspective, make new discoveries and remember it's never too late in life to make a new start, with or without your current partner.

And that is why there are literally millions of women throughout the world this very second, who are now living with a less than suitable partner. All because they themselves never had the initial thought process or were provided with any guidance, denying them the skills to have made better choices- if in fact they were given one.

Accountability and the consequences

Although we touched on assisting those young people who may be suffering from sexual abuse, this section is directly dedicated to those young people who are at that tender age, and who need additional guidance.

Are you someone who is young and looking for some type of help, not knowing where to start, wanting answers but are too afraid to ask questions or to do anything. If your answer is yes then you're not alone and there is help available for you so you can better understand, so make sure you continue to read, and above all, try to understand.

-For those of you who are older and aware of a young person unable to read, then perhaps you can continue with the earlier recommendations in helping someone you suspect needs help, by explaining the following. A personal achievement you are unlikely to ever surpass in your lifetime-.

When you're young, life can sometimes be confusing, but that's ok, because you will grow fast and become so much stronger and smarter. It just takes a little time, but it will happen and while you are growing you will discover and understand more about what is right, and what is wrong.

Do you know it's wrong when someone touches you on your body in places where you don't want to be touched? If this happens you might think you shouldn't complain or say anything, but that's not true, you must speak up as loud as you can and say… "DON'T TOUCH ME THERE", then do whatever you can to get away from that person, as fast as you can.

But it's very important you know the difference between being touched accidentally and being touched on purpose. When your mum or dad helps to dry you with a towel after a shower or bath and touches you in your private places, you need to understand whether it's an accident. But when someone touches you in those same places on your body at other times, then you will know when it's wrong and they shouldn't do it.

If you have being touched more than once and at different times after saying to that same person to stop and they keep doing it, then it's wrong, so it's best to talk to your schoolteacher. You can also tell your bigger brother and sister or someone else in your family who doesn't live with you, someone that you're not afraid of. But remember, you must talk to someone you think you can trust and explain to them what is happening and make sure you tell the truth.

Ques: "I am only eleven and my aunt sometimes sits on my bed helping me to get undressed when I go for a shower, and although she doesn't touch me, she makes me nervous and uncomfortable. I say nothing because she is my mum's sister and I don't want to upset my aunt or my mum. Should I say something to my aunt?"

Ans: "Yes, you can, and you should, even though it's understandable you possibly feel scared, ashamed and frightened, but don't be. So, the next time your aunt or anyone else enters your bedroom when you want privacy, tell her you're busy and lock yourself in. Your aunt may not have meant anything and may well be innocent, but feeling prying eyes on you is unsettling as it is embarrassing, which can start at a very young age. Stand your ground early in your life, and make your principles and values known to everyone. Being a young person, when someone is so much bigger than you, can be intimidating, but never let it be. If anyone touches you or makes you touch them in places on their body that you know is wrong, tell them to stop and run away to find help. Understand that the person forcing you to do those things is bad and must be stopped. If this person tells you not to say anything, or threatens you, try to be brave, and just say "yes, ok". If that bad person asks if you understand, then say, "yes, I understand". You need to stay safe, so it's ok to tell a little white lie this time. When you get away from that person who is doing bad things to you, you must again find help and explain what that person has been doing. If you can, ring the police, or talk to your teacher, and again remember it's best to talk to people you can trust".

For those of you who believe in providing sexual abuse guidance to young people on such matters as being inappropriate or too controversial, then consider this. Would you have wished you had been better educated from an early age with the knowledge to protect yourself when someone tried to sexually abuse you? Of course, you would, so isn't it high time children were given the right to read this type of guidance themselves?

– While we understand we can't protect everyone, educating individuals about early sexual abuse prevention can foster greater awareness. Ensuring those who could become potential victims are equipped with a better understanding of what is happening to them, along with what they need to do to survive. –

Need further convincing, imagine yourself as that abused child while in bed all alone at night, scared, not knowing what to do. You're frightened because you anticipate that at any moment the door will quietly open and the same person who has been coming into your bedroom will walk through your door and make you do things you know are bad.

SUMMARY

- Acknowledging the severity of this deeply troubling behaviour is the first step toward accepting its existence. In doing so, we gain a clearer understanding that, while we strive to believe in the goodness of humanity, there remains a hidden undercurrent of betrayal and hurt.
- Becoming more aware of what we need to do and how to address situations, to first prevent and finally stop perpetrators from continuing with their soul-destroying sexual abuse, is our challenge.
- We must remember whether a victim, a whistleblower, even a perpetrator, or by remaining silent won't achieve anything.

By speaking up loud and clear, we will draw attention to the authorities.
- If you are young and being touched by someone, talk to your teacher at school, never be afraid to walk into a police station to explain what is happening to you at home.
- If you know a victim of sexual abuse act immediately, call an ambulance. Victims are helpless without someone like you. They are suffering unimaginable pain and torture.
- There is no greater feeling of achievement in life having stood up against and exposed the perpetrator for what he is, someone who has been going about his despicable behaviour unchallenged, until now.
- Remain a beacon of light by allowing your natural inquisitiveness to guide you, and when a warning sign flashes before you, investigate further, but don't allow yourself to become misled or be in danger.
- Be prepared to receive some type of backlash or opposition, particularly from direct family members when you raise either your concerns, suspicions or having made direct accusations. That is why it's so imperative to get your facts straight, and more importantly, never talk directly alone with a suspected perpetrator unless you are absolutely sure you are not in harm's way yourself.
- Remember that strength and courage are just a small part of the tools you can use at any time. Whatever we humans think about, we need our fortitude to accomplish our goals. Without it, we remain as zombies.
- By failing to use these tools, you become stuck in the present, almost becoming dormant, preventing you from becoming knowledgeable, and worldly.

- Being a mother and a wife can be stressful at times but never allow a male's dominance to prevent you from making the right decisions for the sake of that child. By allowing a child to be sexually abused without intervention and reporting to the authorities has significant ramifications for both you and the victim in later life.
- If you're feeling a change is in the air, then do something about it, and read through the pages again. Highlight, take notes, make entries into your diary, and get excited about reinventing yourself.
- Start thinking more about other people and discover the effect it will have on you. With that knew found love for displaying empathy, you will want to pay more attention to anyone you suspect is a victim of sexual abuse, and less on the criminal abuser who has kept you imprisoned.

RAPE

(SUB-HEADING)

Rape is another degrading and demeaning act where the abuse is usually in its most savage form. It is both terrifying as it is the lowest form of deprivation perpetrated towards a defenseless person by a coward. In many cases victims are subjected to extreme physical violence, mental anguish, and the indignity of a substandard creature penetrating them. Horrific in nature, because of the sudden and overwhelming violent impact on the unsuspecting victim, with many rape victims who survive having their own horrific stories. Unlike the many victims during their ordeal who met their untimely death.

If that's not unimaginable enough, the legal system usually shows the perpetrator—if caught and charged-, compassion of sorts, including legal aid, minor sentencing, opportunity for appeals, accommodation, meals, wages, and early parole for good behaviour.

- *How should it be possible for a criminal to receive good behaviour when serving a sentence for bad behaviour ?*

Does that not offer a certain level of acceptable risk in the mind of a perpetrator, realising that perhaps getting caught and being sentenced is a risk worth taking? Therefore, where consequences are concerned there is no inner fear preventing males from committing rape, no thoughts of ever having to break rocks in the hot sun. Instead, once sentenced homelessness along with financial issues are of little or no concern. Instead, receiving comfort and moderate living standards, better than many people currently struggling on the outside who remain on the breadline.

That may sound cynical, but shouldn't every survivor of sexual violence have confidence that our justiciary system would ensure the punishment is proportionate to the crime? Wouldn't such certainty serve as a more effective deterrent against rape and other crimes? After all, if first offenders with a conviction for rape carried a mandatory fifteen-year sentence without parole, it's fair to assume offenders would be thinking a lot more about the consequences before committing a rape offence.

In times gone by strict sentencing and tough conditions were commonplace, again having shifted towards leniency and sympathy. As a result, repeat offenders often find themselves in a legal system that functions more like a revolving door. If that wasn't bad enough many of these offenders continue to show contempt for the judiciary system.

Ques: "I was raped and made to feel I was partially responsible after reporting that a male forced himself on me without my consent. He was never charged, and I now live with shame and guilt. Why should I have to feel like I'm the one who is at fault?"

Ans: "Living with feelings of guilt, shame, anger, or helplessness is incredibly painful, but you're not alone. Healing is possible, and there are people who want to help and support you. Therapists, advocacy groups, and survivor resources can help you process these emotions and reclaim your sense of self-worth. You deserve compassion and justice, therefore as hard as it may be, try to understand the value of doing that for yourself. You know you have nothing to feel responsible for or feel guilty about, so start building on that fact and worry less about what anyone else wants to believe. Find your strength and courage, and you will become empowered to focus on the positives in life and leave negativity far behind."

Being a rape victim affects woman differently, with some wanting to have their day in court, yet for others just grateful to be alive and want no part of being exposed. That's a tragedy within itself, since men hedge their bets on women not wanting to prosecute, since they know all too well of the emotional and financial cost involved. That's along with the stigma attached and the pressure women feel when under cross examination. Due to this outdated process, many women become re-traumatised whilst publicly humiliated and made to feel like second-class citizens—a blight on society and the justice system.

-No alleged rape victim should ever be put on public display-

I'll take my chances in the courtroom said the rapist

This is the reality a woman faces with the legal system, when an alleged rapist defense team portrays the defendant as the victim which can and does happen. This psychological tactic often leaves women feeling betrayed by the system—having to prove that the assault occurred, while in contrast the defendant merely sits in the courtroom exuding confidence knowing the burden of proof rests entirely on the prosecution.

Remember what we discussed earlier about the virtues surrounding the interpretation of sexual behaviour? Rape is no exception, since whilst one juror finds the rapist guilty, another juror might point the finger at the victim. Again, this is the world we live in, and women of all ages need to understand never to allow themselves to be in a sexually compromising position to start with- if possible. Make no mistake, in most situations - particularly when out socializing - the male wants sex first and foremost, it's the nature of the beast.

In the courtroom there will be constant accusations and denials which can be soul destroying. Such as, "Isn't it true you wanted sex that night", and "That's why you went back to his house, in the first place, isn't it". Even if you object loudly, there will always be doubt, because mud sticks. All because you admitted having had some drinks earlier that night. Hence the murkiness of the entire situation, whilst the accused retains the presumption of innocence.

Ques: "Why does it appear there's a gross underestimation of the mental and physical impact sexual violence has on victims. Together with the grief endured by families and friends who have lost a loved one to a violent rapist. Why do these lenient sentences give the impression that the inflicted harm is minimized or ignored?"

Ans: "As mentioned, there's a tendency for the authorities to show compassion, leniency, and sympathy for the accused, regardless of the circumstances. Yet sadly they fail to offer the same type of compassion to victims. The reason for this is humans don't cope as well with the uncomfortable truths that force them to face difficulty when making decisions. As a result, it becomes a failure to fully understand the emotional toll sexual violence can have on survivors. The trauma is not just immediate; it lingers, shaping thoughts, emotions, relationships, and affects long term health. Lenient sentences make it feel as if the depth of harm experienced is dismissed or undervalued. So, until there's some type of seismic shift in attitude, with mandatory early educational programs and harsher penalties, the mindset of the perpetrator will remain as it is—driven by compulsion."

Advocacy plays a powerful role in pushing for stronger protection, fairer sentencing, and survivor-centered justice. Raising awareness about the lifelong impact of sexual violence can help shift laws, policies, and societal attitudes. If this is something you feel passionate about, then contact the many organizations in your neighbourhood that can provide resources for survivors and those advocating for justice. You deserve to have your pain heard, acknowledged, and healed; therefore, your voice then becomes part of a movement for demanding better protection. – This can't happen if you remain silent.

For those victims who are continuing to adjust after such an unimaginable ordeal, then together we will find the way to get you back on your feet both emotionally and physically. This transformation will begin almost immediately once you discover the little things in life that you possess that have the greatest impact on human beings, that being our fortitude. This can easily be accomplished by becoming completely open-minded as you read through these pages. Whatever jumps out, first process then look for inspiration on any particular matter, and watch things fall into place, steadily becoming the person you want to be. If the truth is known you haven't been applying yourself as well as you know you would have liked. As a result, you have likely been denying yourself the discovery of the real benefits of reinventing yourself, all of which we will discuss throughout the following chapters.

Vulnerability

The sooner women embrace the meaning of the word vulnerability, the sooner they will understand that it exists around the clock, around every corner and during almost every situation in life—particularly where men are concerned. – This is not men bashing, we are discussing Rape.

In relationships, vulnerability can help a woman form meaningful connections with the right kind of man. However, it can also make her susceptible to opportunistic individuals who attempt to hijack the situation. In the worst cases this type of manipulative male will be looking to carry out non-consensual acts, such as rape.

Sexual Abuse

Whenever females venture out to socialise, males will naturally be out and about looking for sex. As well as the rapist who is also interacting but keeping a low profile. Therefore, before stepping out question yourself as to why you have made the decisions you have, regarding where you intend to go, will you be on your own, and what time do you expect to be home? Then put some control measures in place. A text or a call being a simple arrangement between you and a trusted friend or family member. Well-thought-out plans are crucial when looking at ways to reduce a woman's vulnerability and indeed the risk of meeting with foul play, particularly when commuting on her own. It's not just crucial, it's imperative.

— Men often sense when a woman is carrying an aura of being self-aware and self-assured or whether she is carefree—an inherent male behavioural instinct tied to the pursuit. —

When out socialising, if your instincts aren't prompting you to exercise caution when in the company of strangers, it suggests that your sense of being vulnerable has been overlooked—and as a result your vulnerability remains high.

The mature woman is more aware, or she should be, while for the younger female, it's often nativity, especially in cases where there's drugs and alcohol. However irrespective, there's one underlying and undeniable fact, and that is most women meeting a male for the first time do not know his motivations or intentions. We all want to believe in the common good because we don't want to think about the negatives associated with dishonesty and deception, particularly when out socialising.

Ques: "When I was young, I was always out with my girlfriends, and I remember on one occasion leaving my friends and going with a male back to his place who I had met in the nightclub. At first, I felt comfortable giving no thought to being vulnerable. Maybe I was just lucky, but had I not just gone along with his slightly forceful advances I'm not sure I would be here today. I played along, telling him I had to use the bathroom, and made my escape. I have never been so scared in my life, telling myself never to put myself in that position ever again. So why was I feeling ok with it before I went with him?

Ans: "As mentioned, maintaining your intuitive instincts is key, particularly in an ever-changing world where sexual predators can keep ahead of the game. In your scenario, the male may not have been an apex predator, but it suggests he was on his way. As pointed out, the lesson here is for all women to risk assess before doing anything that potentially puts them in harm's way. This should also apply to other situations women find themselves in, not just when socialising. Therefore, always carry an imaginary antenna with you, and align with your awareness, alerting you to any situation that exposes you to any type of vulnerability. You can reduce your risk significantly by getting to know him, other than going home alone with him. By using your mantra to pause, reflect before engaging, meaning to stop, and think about your circumstances in terms of your safety, before saying or doing anything, again significantly reducing your risk."

This conscious awareness will stay with you forever if you allow it, continuingly discovering the challenging and changing temperament within human nature, and the potential dangers it represents. Whereby throwing caution to wind during flirtatious encounters can lead to serious and regretful consequences.

-Always carry your mantra wherever you go-

Remember this adage – 'Stay alert, stay alive'.

Prevention is better than cure!

While we experience situations we can't control at times, there are many we can. Not everything is how we see or perceive it to be, therefore understanding then adopting the well-known adage, prevention is better than cure' has strong merit.

— If you are young, then there's no better time than now to digest what you believe aligns with your principles and values and stick to it. —

There are the single males who when out socializing- under normal circumstances behave civilised. However, when you put that same male side by side with a group of other males, mindsets change. Becoming influenced by peer pressure along with bravado, drugs and alcohol, and the lust for a female, the male can seldom control his libido. Escalated further by egocentric competition and his own level of testosterone. – A formula for trouble when like-minded males form a wild pack alliance.

— Human nature, from saint to sinner —

Primate behaviour

These males now hang their heads in shame. Each one of them wondering what caused them to act the way they did, realising the severity of the charges against them for gang rape. Despite our natural instinct to defend ourselves or justify our actions, many men face an additional internal battle — the primal side of human nature. It's for that very reason, that every woman should realise there's an extremely fine line between what represents as acceptable behaviour and again, that of the wild beast that lurks within. Males have been acting out this type of behaviour since the beginning of human evolution, therefore the change needed to keep abreast of civilised cultural change almost remains suspended in time.

One shocking example involves a beautiful woman who dedicated her young life to helping others. On this occasion she made the fateful decision to walk home late one night alone in the dark. When a pack of wild beasts disguised as human beings descended upon her. Raping her and carrying out indescribable and despicable acts, before they took her life. These sub-humans were rounded up and locked away for life.

Although this young woman may have had a sense of her vulnerability, she may well have been thinking more about her hospital patients than her own safety, we will never know. This tragic event should for evermore remain etched in the minds of every woman as part of their own enduring legacy, to exercise her mantra before venturing out alone in the dark.

Risk assessment

A quick personal risk assessment helps you analyse any task or situation you're considering. It's simple to do — just a simply mental rating between one and ten, with ten representing the highest level of risk.

For example, you receive an invitation to a secluded nighttime beach party with men, knowing alcohol will be involved. On the surface, it seems like an innocent social event. But once you assess it, the potential hazards become clear:

- a) Travelling to the beach party
- b) The seclusion, beach, and ocean environment
- c) Alcohol consumption
- d) Male bravado and group dynamics
- e) Getting home safely

Given these factors, the overall risk rating is high — a ten — because without controls, these hazards could lead to serious harm. That may sound pedantic, but it's not. It's about your safety.

Your next step is simple: put a few basic control measures in place to bring the risk down to an acceptable level. Think of this as your personal safety insurance policy.

Start with the first control: how you're getting to the beach party, and more importantly, how, where, and at what time you're being picked up. Then add a welfare check — a scheduled call to a family member or close friend at a precise, agreed-upon time during the night.

Take your first consideration in getting to the party- you initially considered hitchhiking, which carries a high level of risk. But now you have controlled that risk having eliminated it altogether and substituting it with a safer plan having arranged a lift with a friend instead. By doing so you significantly reduced both the likelihood of something going wrong and the potential severity of the consequences had a stranger given you a lift and meaning you harm. It's all about developing the habit of being a forward thinker, again by identifying and mitigating hazards.

It's not rocket science and there's no formula, its subjective, meaning it doesn't matter that someone else might think differently to you regarding how they identified hazards and the controls they chose.

Again, it's all about reducing the severity of any potential harm by using simple, commonsense risk assessments. By identifying potential hazards and putting together a set of safety measures you feel comfortable with, you immediately lower the risk. Now that you understand the logic behind arranging a lift to the beach party, try identifying controls for the remaining hazards (b–e) and you'll see how straightforward it is.

Nobody is suggesting you analyse every moment of your life this way, but it's worth considering when your instincts tell you the risk is higher than normal. When that feeling arises, it deserves to be taken seriously.

However, you also have the opportunity to take extreme measures by simply eliminating all risks by not going to the beach party, however, no one wants to be a party pooper do they.

Anyone who believes the above safety measures are a waste of time, should tell that to the many women who have adopted that same measure, through self-disciplined education, having remained safe. During the day, as you get ready to go out—maybe for shopping—your risk level is low, so your conscience remains at ease. However, when you contemplate other activities that have a greater risk, your senses will now instinctively alert you. This is something you may have never given any previous thoughts too, being a real game changer that can save your life. That's when you take a minute to call on your mantra and your fortitude and put controls in place.

-A suit of armour like no other-

Without these safeguards in place, we will continue to hear that all too familiar story line, 'yet another female has gone missing, with authorities announcing her whereabouts is unknown'. If only they knew where she had gone, and at what time, and who she was with, it may well have resulted in a better outcome. Instead, they found her deceased body behind a sand dune days later, having been raped and strangled. – The beach party is now all but a memory.

When a male is out and about on the town a woman can unintentionally give the wrong impression, whereby the male presumes he has been given the green light. This is usually the case when a female accepts a drink from that male who – in many cases - now believes his chances of having sex have increased. As the night wears on, the male's thoughts on achieving his goal of having sex intensifies, since his mentality reminds him - there has to be pay back.

Ques: "What's wrong with that, all us girls meet boys when we go out for drinks and have a good time?"

Ans: "No suggestion that there's anything wrong with socialising, drinking alcohol and having fun. It's in keeping with the commitment you hopefully made to yourself and a contact who knows where you are and what time you will expect to be home. That's along with one other very crucial pact to make with yourself - that is - to never go home with a stranger. Instead, use your discipline and willpower to remain patient, using the time you have to get to know him first. By doing so, you may well experience a feeling of relief, the following morning with no regrets, perhaps having kept your innocence and avoiding potential harm. Having controlled your urges and indeed your emotions you can meet your new friend at another time in the light of day. Thereby allowing your senses to be used without obstruction, all the while having maintained your dignity. That's if indeed he shows up, and failing to do so then you have your answer had you been looking for a relationship, other than a one-night stand. As for the girls looking after one another, there is no better way to ensure everyone remains safe."

It doesn't matter how charming a male appears to be, how neat his attire, how influential, wealthy, or easy on the eye, he can still be a wolf in sheep's clothing. Temptation as mentioned can at times be overpowering as it is for some men to believe there's more to gain in life by crossing over to the dark side. Once he changes into his alter ego, he becomes the sexual deviate rapist, that somehow excites him into planning his next move. Whether that's to force his wife/partner into non-consensual sex, at a bar or lying in wait in a carpark, he carries out his fantasies usually on unsuspecting females.

– *"Always remain suspicious and only reduce that suspicion having carried out your risk assessment with your controls in place i.e. controlled emotions, observations, instincts."* -

As mentioned at the bar he may try to work his charm, by showing his generosity—supplying alcohol even drugs, sometimes without your knowledge. Meanwhile calculating his next move, as to how best to get his prey back to his place of residence.

– *This all too familiar scenario is extremely high-risk, even life threatening.* –

There is no clearer example of the unpredictability of human nature than when a male is driven by sexual desire. However, on this occasion you have acknowledged and adopted the belief that your vulnerability must align with having control measures in place. – Smart girl.

Therefore, any male heading in your direction to be sociable knows nothing about your mindset, as you of his. He's completely unaware that your self-awareness has already been triggered and is now active. Unlike women who inadvertently remain vulnerable, and by doing so abandon any safety strategy.

Who then become social victims becoming caught up in emotionally driven conversation, flirting and intoxication, with vulnerability having reached flash point. Overtime becoming susceptible to further non-consensual manipulation, eventually coming to terms of being molested. It's generally at this stage she has become more alert to being in unfamiliar surroundings, further realizing she is being raped.

Unlike you, remaining vigilant and now better poised to either make conversation or simply walk away. However, we need to remind ourselves that not all men are sexual predators. Therefore, although it may seem unlikely that you will ever become a victim, someone somewhere is not so lucky and being raped, this very second.

Processing anything different in life offers challenges, granted. But now having gained the knowledge of how to assess risk by identifying potential hazards, and putting control measures in place, isn't that far better than becoming a headline story. We also need to remind ourselves we are discussing sexual abuse in the context of rape—part of the fight against preventing and ending domestic abuse.

Again, if you're uncomfortable or unsure of a male's intentions, walk away allowing your instincts to do the talking, with a reminder of the adage – 'curiosity killed the cat', so best not to tempt fate.

Ques: "I have been single for most of my life and there's not much I haven't seen when it comes to men wanting sex. When I look back, I could have done with some help, having had my share of troubles. This includes having been forced upon, therefore technically raped. I have found solace having taken some responsibility for allowing myself to get into that situation, not that I condone his behaviour but to help me cope through life when making decisions. The biggest problem today is how to get the younger ones to comprehend the dangers that exist out there, before finding out the hard way, as I did?"

Ans: "Hopefully by listening to people like you, who I suspect were also raised in an era without having been provided with any education on sexual abuse or social awareness. Statistics tell us sexual assault cases have increased over the years, all the better for starting a movement for early training and education. As for accepting some minor responsibility—acknowledging you're not condoning his behaviour—is a personal triumph, and if doing so provides you with some contentment that's so important for your well-being- which I suspect your already aware of."

This is not a book on averages or suggesting you do something you're not comfortable doing. Rather it's about understanding what you have, a woman's intuition, her new mantra, her fortitude and now her personal risk assessment. So, consider taking a fresh approach and using these skills that are interchangeable, providing you with exceptional empowerment whenever you need guidance to make decisions. In doing so, you continue to lower your risk across the board, whilst maintaining your personal safety.

When the risk rises!

Getting back to the female who remains completely vulnerable, never questioning her own behaviour or safety, continuing to drink alcohol at the bar remaining putty in the hands of her new acquaintance. Why would she? she has never experienced the type of thought process of being vulnerable before as nobody has ever mentioned it or discussed it with her.

We don't know what we don't know, correct? and for those who would say, "Anyone with any common sense...", probably has had the benefit of time to better understand their own vulnerability to make such a comment. However, there are many younger females that haven't been given any education on life skills and sadly may never get that opportunity. As a consequence- in this scenario- she agrees to go back to his place, where she has no idea of the life and death struggle that awaits her.

Consider a hypothetical situation. If you were that female, would you have taken a greater interest in understanding your vulnerability? Along with calculating the potential high-risk situation you are placing yourself in, before you decided to go to a stranger's home late at night?

Well now you can, because after all you have the benefit of hindsight having now realised the importance of carrying out a risk assessment, especially when you soon discover what this woman is about to go through.

– A moment of insight can be worth a lifetime of experience! –

This woman did in fact go back to this stranger's place of residence, who simply gave in to his initial advances with an innocent enough kiss? Only then did she suddenly experience a sudden and terrifying reckoning that something was not quite right and began resisting. When in a split second he felt that resistance, instantly exchanging his firm embrace by becoming more like a wild animal as he commenced raping her.

That reckoning she had come all too late, and sadly she was never heard of or seen again. With the authorities being only too aware that unless there's a body, there is little chance of finding any pattern of events, and it is less unlikely the true nature of this horrific ordeal will never be known.

When females, particularly young females come to understand the true nature of some human beings, they will recognise some disturbing truths. That is how incredibly fast a seemingly joyous occasion can turn into a horror story. That's human behaviour, why? Because it's human nature.

Into the lion's den

Nor do these women understand the implications of their legal rights, or indeed his, having crossed the threshold into his domain. This is when his mentality tells him he can have his way, knowing you accompanied him voluntarily into his residence.

— Unlike had you been attacked in the street with the culprit being caught, we can assume it would be a less complicated case - for you. — However, of little personal comfort.

Ques: "How can I accurately assess the risks if social pressure, alcohol, or the excitement of the night when it impairs my judgment?"

Ans: "In moments where excitement and spontaneity blur the lines of caution, it's essential to use your mantra, - to pause, reflect and then engage by risk assessing first, putting control measures in place before becoming intoxicated, or becoming emotionally involved. Understanding your vulnerability isn't about fear, it's about empowerment. Therefore, you must navigate every situation – particularly in these high-risk situations when there's a mix of men and alcohol. Remember our earlier discussion, to ensure you have contacted someone responsible explaining where you're going and your expected time to arrive home, having made arrangements to be picked up. Taking these few steps to make a call, to communicate with updates or changes can make all the difference to your well-being. Likewise, if you notice a friend having left with a stranger, you should have taken a mental note of the situation."

In this final scenario you went to his home, changing the dynamics of your situation altogether without notifying anyone, then finding yourself within the confines of his four walls. Your senses now alert you to the danger you find yourself in, as he's all over you and threatening you with violence if you scream.

You're now extremely frightened and scared for your life, and all you want now is for it to end. So, at this point, you must use the only survival skill left to you, your cunning and your wits, so allow him to have his way. Yes, become submissive, he wants sex. Hopefully he wants nothing else, least of all any interruptions, so by antagonising him in any way will only intensify the already volatile situation.

If he is being violent with you, say to him "You don't have to be this way, treat me properly and you can make love to me". Don't stop there, say and do whatever it takes – within reason -to try and control the situation. His mentality is telling him he must be aggressive because he knowingly didn't get your consent to have sex.

Your life potentially hangs in the balance as you are now in too deep, so reverse psychology is now your best option, as being raped is generally temporary – however shocking - whereas being murdered is permanent. In a scenario as terrifying as this, staying composed - as difficult as that will be - is crucial. Appeal to his emotional side, if he has one, expressing yourself....

> – *"When I saw you tonight, I felt a connection, but because I'm pregnant, I was too scared to tell you, so you don't have to hurt me, because I wanted you as well."* –

Again, although extremely difficult, seeking sympathy or showing him warmth by making conversation may cause his sense of volatility to relax. Establish some level of connection, however small, that can increase your chances of shifting any thoughts he may have to become further violent. – Your focus is on one goal: survival.

When nature takes its course, and he has had his way with you, continue to gauge his temperament and make a risk assessment. If necessary, repeat to him he doesn't need to be aggressive with you, and maintain this charade for as long as you can. Slowly angle toward freeing yourself from this monster, but only when the time is right.

Up to this point this woman was successful being both mentally and physically restraining her rapist from further violence due to her survival skills. She does, however, remain as vulnerable as ever so now is not the time to become complacent. You need to fully understand where you are, are there neighbours, is there a street with passing vehicles? Do you have a phone, think about a course of action to escape - safely.

Planning to escape needs more than thinking of just making a run for it. So, unless you can find your way to approach other people without coming to further harm, and/or contacting the authorities without being discovered, continue playing the empathy card toward him.

Only the rapist himself knows what's going through his head. He may be completely over being the violent rapist he was earlier now he has had his way with you. Maybe he tells you to leave, accepting whatever comes his way, in which case you must exit the door as fast as possible, and call the police.

Should that not be the case, when you're uncertain of his intentions, again you must continue with the charade. Explain to him, the two of you can sort things out together, working on his conscience to the point where his mentality believes he could have you as his girlfriend. So, remain compassionate and keep the conversation going as the last thing any woman needs right now is to lose the connection whereby, he returns to his violent behaviour.

Carefully analyse his demeanor. If it tells you he remains volatile do not attempt to make your escape or get caught on your phone, unless you have made a deliberate and concerted decision to do so.

If on the other hand he has calmed down, use your wits and go to the bathroom locking yourself in to make a call without being detected. Even if you only get to ring the emergency services, it will alert the authorities to where you are- in most cases. Another ploy is to convince him to take you out to get some fast food, so continue with the physical intimacy that males can't resist, where your chances of making your escape have greatly increased. Understandably, it's case-by-case circumstances, however humans will be astonished as to how they can handle difficult situations when under immense pressure- as long as they keep their composure by once again risk assessing their mantra and their fortitude.

As mentioned, the very last thing a woman should do is offer resistance or fight back, unless she believes she can achieve the upper hand, or she has resigned herself to the fact he is going to kill her. In which case leaving a woman with no choice but to fight for her life, which is horrifying enough, therefore she must fight back with everything she has? This includes screaming, yelling, scratching, biting, and anything else you can think of, being your best hope for rescue or for the capture of this rapist through DNA.

In this scenario the male having knowingly committed rape decides to let his victim go and take his chances with the authorities. That's because any brazen male that has committed rape in his own home will understand – as we mentioned earlier - that the victim may remain silent, or she must prove rape was committed. That, along with his defense arguing you reciprocated, further implying you went to his home voluntarily with having sex in mind.

This is the reality for many victims who apply to have charges laid against a rapist. The publicised and personal cost of humiliation every woman finds herself in, having to endure being personally scrutinised in a courtroom and beyond. The reality is not just the verdict or the question of guilt or innocence, it's what comes later, the gossip and in many cases, the lingering status of notoriety for all the wrong reasons. Everything the rapist is hedging his bets on, so that you won't follow through. A difficult decision - if ever there was one.

So, the message is now very clear, if you are to expose yourself to some type of vulnerability – as we all do in life - carry out a simple risk assessment in respect to your safety; it only takes a short time. Start by simply pausing, reflecting or thinking about the situation, having then determined your level of risk, mitigate that risk by putting controls measures in place before acting on. Therefore, in conclusion, having come to a well thought out plan by reducing the level of risk.

Remembering that adage – 'when fools rush in'.

SUMMARY

- There's no mistaking it, that whilst males know how to treat and impress a woman, in some cases it may only be skin deep.
- Every woman should remain instinctively aware of a stranger's demeanor and her intuitive instincts, alerting her to danger.
- When a male is confronted with the possibility of not getting sex when he so desires, he can instantly become a chameleon, easily transforming himself into an entirely unfamiliar and dangerous creature altogether.
- Remain responsible by letting someone trustworthy know where you're going, who you are with, and how you're getting home. When circumstances change, provide updates.
- Never allow yourself to become so vulnerable that your safety has been seriously compromised.
- Become a forward-thinking woman, identify the risks, put in place control measures, and always have a backup plan, and if it doesn't feel right, chances are it's not—so change it.
- If need be, simply plan to disappear from any company you feel uncomfortable with.

- Finding yourself in a difficult situation calls for something special altogether, particularly if you suddenly become scared for your own safety.
- Finding yourself having strayed too far, having compromised your safety, remember to go into survival mode and act accordingly.
- Take on board the different tactics that were recommended. As difficult as it may be to accept, don't fight back unless sadly it becomes perfectly clear to your instincts, you must.
- Is there someone you know you would like to introduce to the next section titled perpetrator?

PERPETRATOR

Although we describe humans as being civilised, there are those of you who have chosen a vastly different path in life to that of what society describes as acceptable behaviour. Child sexual abuse is one of pure evil, whether you are sexually abusing your own or other children. It's the type of behaviour that only has a place in the sub-human world, a description you have labelled yourself.

So why have you allowed yourself to stoop to the lowest depths of depravity, instead why not take a good hard look at what you are doing to either a defenseless child, a woman, and to yourself. When all you have to do is to man up and partake in discipline and willpower, and or seek professional help.

Unlike your victims who don't have such luxury having been both physically and mentally scared, you have choices you can make both legally and morally. Your victims are suddenly confronted with their own conscience in trying to come to terms with why this is happening to them. The more they question themselves, the less inclined they are to find the answers or to comprehend why they have been violated in such an intrusive and devastating way. As a result, they struggle to face the world, instead they fight against self-loathing with many tragically taking their own lives. All because of your soul-destroying debauchery against another human being, branding yourself a despicable creature.

Does that strike a chord with you? Can you acknowledge the pain and suffering you cause by sexually penetrating other defensive human beings? All because you fail to control your own sexual urges. Have you ever considered what it would be like to be a victim, constantly being reminded of the past and the pending abuse?

You may well believe there's something exciting in relation to your secretive abuse, however the reality is, you're slowly destroying your own life, by the following definitions….

The perpetrator's mentality is such, he is fully aware of the scale and severity of his actions, consequently believing there's no point in turning back instead of continuing carrying out his sexual desires. This belief is a fallacy. You have the power to stop, just as easily as you have the power to start.

Difficult to image, but by doing so you will receive a greater feeling of self-satisfaction when ending this behaviour than continuing with it. If only you could comprehend that by doing so, saves you from yourself, and free's your victims from any further abuse.

You are denying yourself any genuine quality of life, continuing to look over your shoulder, remaining paranoid. Becoming overcautious, while masquerading against the usual simplicities of going about your life in a normal, confident, and carefree fashion. What a high price to pay when all you need to do is to stop and think about what you are really accomplishing, by paying attention to your conscience. You will then realise there are other alternatives to your current sexual preferences, without having to destroy the lives of other human beings.

Remaining unchallenged only reinforces the false belief that your actions are justified, creating an illusion of invincibility- a thought far from reality. As a direct result, your mindset continues to spiral unchecked, unknowingly leading to a loss of control over your own life. Instead of being in control you have become trapped, a victim of your own downfall.

Sexual Abuse

We all harbour a vice of some description, a habit which is generally regarded as a weakness in someone's character. However, regardless of whatever weakness you have, -and as mentioned- every human being has the capacity and the inner strength to find and assert discipline along with willpower to defeat it. The human body provides it all, you only need to call on it to do so. Just start by understanding and agreeing you have a problem, then follow through with what your conscience instructs you to do, because your conscience instinctively knows right from wrong.

Since your vice is sexual abuse, simply pause, reflect – in your situation on the consequences- by consciously questioning yourself why you engage in this type of behaviour. You will discover conflicting messages and reasoning, meaning you don't sit as comfortably with the idea as you think you do.

If you first have trouble, don't think negatively by saying to yourself, "It's too difficult for me", instead think about finding the confidence to say to yourself, "This is something new and I will make it work", and remarkably by putting your mind to it, you have set yourself up for success. It's how human beings have evolved over thousands of years, by continuously thinking of positive ways to overcome issues that need resolving. That's because human beings inherently know the difference between good and bad, right and wrong. Therefore, there's every reason to believe you know you're doing wrong and you're suffering in silence for it, finding it difficult to discuss.

This is a golden opportunity for you to come clean and accept you are on the dark side of life and cross over to where you know you ought to be, making conscience decisions whilst basking in the sunshine. It's easy enough to do, just imagine how you would feel being a victim knowing that at any time the same person who has been sexually penetrating you will be back to doing it all over again. How does that make you feel? Now you can see through the eyes of the victim. A horrifying thought of it happening to you, don't you think? You also know you're not getting the type of satisfaction you hoped to enjoy.

Preventing and Ending Domestic Abuse

The pain you currently harbour inwardly reflects on your entire demeanor as you go through life, and it shows. Without you knowing or understanding how your life has become fragmented, eroding your character and personality. You're not the person you once were or were designed to be, causing you the inability to function normally. Those who know you, are all too aware of your changed persona that's because you inadvertently conduct yourself as someone who is false and conniving, always with something to hide – reason being, it's your conscience poking you, telling you the time has come to make that all-important change.

Is that what you really want, living a sub-standard life, unable to express yourself naturally, always hiding, all because you have a dirty little secret? Isn't it time to man up and take control. Start by learning how to appreciate yourself again, become responsible and become the real you. Once you're in control, you'll soon discover how you will naturally become defensive against losing control of your better judgement ever again.

If in fact you have suffered from sexual and other types of abuse perhaps during your childhood, then have you ever considered using those memories as psychological leverage for your future, using the adage, something good comes out of something bad'. Because anyone who has suffered as you have, would only have to put their mind to it, and with the right guidance from a professional, you can accomplish absolutely anything you want in life. - That is a fact.

So just have a think about that, whereby you will rise up, becoming determined to steer yourself towards greater goals. By doing so, regaining your self-respect and finding your self-esteem that has been lying dormant and just waiting on you to come to your senses - which can be right now. By making a simple decision to end this behaviour today is your pathway to redemption, whilst giving yourself and your victims their freedom back. Along with the hope, those women and children you have sexually abused can continue with their lives receiving the healing, love and attention.

-This is one enormous opportunity in your life, particularly since you have probably never faced a challenge from anyone before- or indeed from yourself-.

As mentioned throughout this book, we all need a wake-up call in life from time to time, even though we can be stubborn by our very nature. Often, we lack the foresight and courage to listen and accept other points of view, even when we know the advice is constructive criticism. In your case accepting this advice and acting upon- particularly on such a harmful matter as ending sexual abuse- is a giant step in the right direction. So again, why not look at life from a different angle and compare it to the life you have now, then come to terms with the fact you simply headed in the wrong direction?

So now all you have to do is to adopt a new mindset, a pathway that offers you genuine prosperity and a new direction. You can come out from behind that secretive yet destructive world you live in and let those lives you currently destroy, to live in peace.

– Including your own –

DYSFUNCTIONAL FAMILIES

So why are so many families dysfunctional? Is it inherent from generation to generation, or does it just mysteriously happen whereby human beings suddenly find themselves becoming a part of.

In most instances we needn't look any further than our childhood, being the very essence of our upbringing. Thankfully, for many children it was a happy, joyful and loving experience, remaining free spirited and becoming educated. Having learnt how to be respectful along with understanding the benefits of showing care and compassion, becoming ambitious with the confidence to reach our goals.

Then looking forward to emulating that childhood experience one day as a parent and raising a family in the same way, all because of that well-balanced upbringing. Sadly, far too many children miss out on the type of love nurturing and the attention they deserve, becoming deprived of the emotional support essential for healthy development and denied proper guidance and good education that every child should receive.

Dysfunctional Families

With a broken spirit, rebellion rears its head as a natural catalyst for those young adolescents and adults, having been subjected to a sub-standard environment. Consequently, remaining unhappy within, and becoming angry for no reason. As a result, unashamedly, remaining unaware they have adopted a mentality in believing that everyone and everything is against them.

This anarchy mindset is more associated with the male, who then chooses to get married only to orchestrate a dysfunctional family lifestyle. All in the name of raising a family, in many respects to convince themselves they are self- entitled authoritarians for the greater good. Which amounts to very little other than continued hardship, particularly for those innocent unfortunates, trapped whilst living together as a family under the same roof. Again, as a result many adolescents become destined to carry on with this very existence, sadly under the illusion of living a normal family life.

Is there a more damaging mindset than that of a person who unknowingly embodies narcissism? Who firmly believes they are raising their family just like any other family, while remaining oblivious to the harm and suffering they inflict.

This human behaviour has continued throughout the ages, with many an innocent young life not given a fair go. Instead, they are inadvertently caught up in a hostile environment, never to be shown or to understand anything different. Other than acting out what they themselves have been taught and are now subjected to, by maintaining a misperception of what is and what isn't acceptable behaviour.

It's extremely difficult for those that have been fortunate enough to have had a happy childhood and upbringing to comprehend that it could ever be possible for a young person to be brought up as just described. Yet it's a fact of life that for many children who display anti-social behaviour under these circumstances, do so as a direct result from being raised in a dysfunctional family.

Parents living under this type of regime have little concept that their own children are becoming desensitised by how they interrupt acceptable behaviour. These children become increasingly brazen living what they learn, with their natural instincts having been compromised, therefore unable to show any compassion. Incredibly, parents fail to comprehend that their own behaviour is the root cause of their children becoming dysfunctional in the first place. Sad but true, many parents remain unaware of the circumstances under which they live and instead continue to believe it's just normal behaviour— 'nothing to see here'.

Therefore, this type of dysfunctional lifestyle continues to thrive almost unnoticed to the outside world, almost comparable to a cult-like existence.

Am I living in a dysfunctional world?

Does mankind mislead itself in believing all humans are civilized? Since the facts clearly show many are not. The one major underlying fact that contradicts this notion is the common occurrence of children throughout all walks of life, being raised in a dysfunctional manner, – are you a part of that equation?

Then, there are those people who are caught in-between, having experienced a balance of both good and bad during their childhood upbringing. Fortunately, through time many come to understand and accept the outcome, believing parenting was merely a stepping-stone through life. Therefore, throughout this period, going from adolescents through to young adulthood by their instinctive nature, becoming comfortable acknowledging the good far outweighs the bad.

– However, that ratio favouring the good over bad is constantly challenged. –

Therefore, having realised the complex characteristics and balances with being raised from a child, they then move on to discover all that life offers with a positive mindset. As a result, seldom dwell on the former less unsavoury times. Sadly, for others, the past and the memories have gained a foothold in their psyche, causing mental anguish we know as psychological trauma. As a result, it becomes the catalyst for many individuals to continue with their dysfunctional and uncivilised behaviour, sadly throughout their entire lives.

Dysfunctional Families

It's clear that whilst many people pull through from the adversity of a downtrodden upbringing, there are many who simply don't make it, hence the never-ending trend of the dysfunctional family. While many achieve stability, others remain impoverished and lack the desire to improve their lives. Arguably mankind's greatest failure which continues today, with authorities offering little beyond mere recognition for the stigma it carries.

For many their upbringing is now set in stone, since their mindset is unable to steer clear from their tragic introduction into adult life. Therefore, depriving themselves little chance of harmonising in the future with a self-respecting family environment, only to continue living - the only way they know how.

Irrespective of upbringing, human beings who initially adopt this type of intellect also have the capabilities to rise above its adversity and better themselves, but only if they really want it badly enough. Fortunately, being human we were all given something at birth more powerful than imagination itself, being our forever protector, our fortitude.

It shouldn't be too difficult for anyone to decide on their preferred living standard when we realise the many children who are trapped in a less-than-ideal family environment. Forced to listen to adults talking down to each other, shouting, and arguing. Fortunately, very young children often can't fully understand these outbursts, instead they simply believe it's a normal part of life and retreat into their own little world.

-It's in their later years in life the consequences begin-

The consequences of embracing such a self-styled dysfunctional mindset marked by abuse and disrespect are far-reaching, affecting nearly every aspect of life. It manifests not only within the family, but spreads across communities leaving a lasting imprint. In time, it becomes an ever-present force, trailing individuals wherever they go, ultimately eroding the fabric of civilized society.

— And so it goes, resulting in a tirade of verbal aggressive abuse on decent unsuspecting people, perpetrated by those who have little in common who have become entrenched in anger and hatred. —

Profoundly tragic, as those who behave in this manner often fail to recognize the lasting consequences of their actions. Over time, their behaviour shapes their character, their personality, beliefs and values in ways they remain unaware of. Their perception of reality becomes deeply compromised, influenced and moulded by unknowingly accepting what they see and hear. This belief not only occurs within the confines of the dysfunctional home, but also tragically demonstrated out in public.

This mindset spreads easily, especially among the young, who lack the foresight and awareness to recognize or distinguish its effects. Unfortunately, those deeply affected by it often struggle longer than others to reclaim their own identity and pathway forward in life- if at all. However, they can find their way more quickly by embracing love instead of hate, kindness over harshness, encouragement in place of criticism, respect rather than arrogance, and empathy instead of indifference. – If only shown how.

As mentioned, dysfunctional behaviour spreads across generations, seamlessly passed down infiltrating family life. It persists without individuals truly grasping its origins, as they unknowingly continue the cycle. Left unchecked it fuels itself, continuously growing and evolving. Sadly, lack of awareness and understanding leaves little chance for many to transform countless lives instead destined to remain who they are.

Social skills versus dysfunctional behaviour

This mode of existence will remain in the 'too hard basket 'ignored and unaddressed—unless authorities choose to act. By illuminating positive changes and offering clear perspectives on the immense contrast between dysfunctional and functional living standards, we can then inspire hope in future generations, starting as early as possible in young lives.

Whereby gradually through time itself this initiative would spread throughout society providing all young adults with the skills and knowledge they so desperately need. In doing so, to make their own conscious decisions with additional clarity, having discovered the truth in the benefits of living in a civilized manner.

Early education of this nature enhances the way people think about finding a compatible partner, raising their children and becoming respectful law-abiding citizens. This would produce a knock-on effect that profoundly changes the entire dynamics for a greater success rate in relationships. This initiative also aims at alleviating the current almost incalculable measures of cost and resources associated with anti-social behaviour throughout the whole of society.

In broader terms, the training program will be tailored to include…

Social and Emotional Learning – Helping children develop self-awareness, emotional regulation and interpersonal skills, preparing them for positive relationships.

Relationship Education – Teaches effective communication, conflict resolution, and mutual respect within friendships, partnerships, and family settings.

Family and Life Skills Education – Covers topics like parenting, empathy, cooperation, and financial responsibility to prepare individuals for real-life challenges.

Psychology and Behavioural Studies – Offers insights into human behaviour, decision-making, and emotional well-being.

Ethics and Value-Based Education – Instils moral reasoning, respect, and social responsibility.

– We all want our children to grow up being respectful, happy and successful. Yet, without equipping them with an acceptable level of social skills, we knowingly send them into the world at a great disadvantage. –

This framework can be shaped with clarity and purpose—complete with defined objectives, learning modules, and development milestones—within a "Foundation for Life" pathway connected to Social Skills.

Results of which would change the face of societal growth by fostering firm yet emotionally intelligent individuals, strengthening relationships, and reducing generational cycles of dysfunction. Again, and over time, this education initiative would empower young minds with the knowledge and skills needed to build fulfilling personal lives, respectful communities, and a more compassionate world.

While some schools offer early programs in respectful relationship education it only touches on a broader scale and not the intricacies covering early warning signs throughout the initial stages of young adult relationships. i.e dating, courtship, and engagement; subtle behavioural shifts that signal risk; the mindset and patterns of abusive men; how coercive control develops; the influence of dysfunctional families. How to safely end abuse in committed relationships; the impact of drugs, alcohol, and trauma; online dating risks; or the realities of sexual abuse, rape, and post-abuse recovery."

To truly support young minds, a modern updated, broader and standardised version must be rolled out across all educational institutions, again anchored in a unified and integrated learning framework. For this to gain traction and deliver meaningful results, the education department must formally endorse it as a compulsory national curriculum under the guiding banner- e.g.-'Foundation for Life'.

Unlike many academic subjects that currently prove impractical throughout a person's life, a subject dedicated to the 'Foundation of Life', would serve as the missing link so vital in addressing social skill behaviour. This should first be accomplished by explaining the meaning of social science, i.e as in the broader field of study that examines human behaviour, relationships, and societies. It explores on how people think, interact, organise themselves, and shape cultures, institutions, and communities. Can there ever be, a more purposeful and profound learning curve in the life for a young adult preparing to step out into an uncertain world.

Ques: "For over thirty years, I have dedicated myself to teaching English, having witnessed countless classroom and schoolyard disruptions. While most of these disturbances were frustrating, they were, however, manageable. That said, a troubling new trend has emerged, one marked by aggression, abuse, and outright violence. What is disturbing is the law makers' unwillingness to take control of the situation. Their lack of action left me with no choice but to resign from a job I loved dearly. How have we reached a point where such intolerable behaviour appears to be openly tolerated? There was a time when respect was a fundamental part of life and education—where has it gone?"

Ans: "The authorities have failed us—there's no denying it. They do not hold the parents of these offenders more accountable, and the justice system hesitates to sentence adolescents. Dedicated individuals like you, who have spent years shaping young lives for the better, now find themselves feeling victimized and abandoned by the very system meant to uphold justice. Had this occurred in any other workplace, where aggressive, abusive, and violent behaviour existed, it would have led to swift and decisive consequences. Yet, in this case, accountability is absent, both from the authorities and the parents and the perpetrators themselves, who all share responsibility for this ongoing crisis. Failing to address such behaviour has allowed adolescent crime to escalate unchecked, stretching far beyond the classroom into home invasion, armed robbery, violence, and murder. It's time for strong leadership, someone that will challenge the status quo that currently continues to allow these young offenders to act almost with impunity".

Digression

The reason adolescents commit these atrocities - in many instances - is because this type of behaviour is advertised daily by the media on our televisions. This creates a sense of glorification in the undisciplined immature mindset of adolescents with their - live and learn mentality. It's telling them, 'It's all the rage' to go out onto the streets and cause anarchy. Our authorities are therefore arguably complicit since they don't understand human behavior, instead allow the term 'democracy at work' make excuses on their behalf, therefore continuing to exercise poor judgement when making decisions.

Instead, what's needed is to legislate a twelve-month blanket ban on the media that report these criminal behaviours, again seen as an advertisement for undisciplined adolescents, to continue carrying out criminal activity. The use of guns and knives, home invasions, vandalizing businesses and burning cars, all of which carry little consequence, being all too common. The next stage is to introduce a two-year minimum non-parole period for any offender who is found guilty regardless of age.

– Then watch over time as parents -and adolescents- start to take notice of the severe penalties-

We then change our own mentality by introducing rehabilitation centers, teaching our youth discipline and respect, along with providing them with the inspiration to discover themselves and find their way in life. By doing so they can be trained through something as simple as being shown encouragement, remembering that so many of these people live and breathe in the capacity of a dysfunctional environment.

Teaching them self-respect builds on their self-esteem, whereby they can re-enter society with a new outlook on life. Unlike the current trend whereby allowing juveniles to immediately return free into society with the mindset that they never had to be accountable or experience any consequences for their bad behaviour. Therefore, we could all be forgiven believing the authorities are not only again- complicit by allowing these offenders to do as they please but are also incompetent as leaders.

As of the year 2025, politicians have allowed sentencing laws to be turned on its head, allowing criminals that have been incarcerated to be given the type of leniency that goes against the wishes of the very people who gave them their power. A blight on the processes of democracy and a slap in the face for every voter. Because of this leniency criminals have more say, more entitlements with better treatment and modern facilities, than many on the outside. As a result, whilst criminals feel empowered, the police force is ham strung, being all too aware that the lawmakers are failing to provide the support they need.

As an example, the police continuously arrest the same criminals over and over again, as a consequent many innocent people continue to lose their lives due to inept law makers again allowing early parole for these criminals- in the name of democracy.

Back to our teacher friend...

– The deepest injustice lies in the emotional burden this former teacher carries, having been forced to make the decision to walk away from a career much loved and cherished, solely because safety was no longer a guarantee or seemingly of little importance. –

While the authorities remain inactive on this issue, it's left to those professional people who have also dedicated their lives to educating children. Those caring people who have recognized dysfunctional behaviour, having been brave enough to step up. Although often fraught with danger and difficulty, at times at great personal cost, with many teachers being chastised even losing their jobs. The authorities should hold their heads in shame.

Addressing the dynamics of dysfunctional families

Scenario One – It's a situation whereby a woman lives a dysfunctional lifestyle, whereby a confident and courageous female friend wants to talk to her about it, since she believes her friend hasn't been herself lately.

Whenever personal situations are raised in conversation, there's the possibility for people to get their feelings hurt, whereby defenses are raised, exclaiming, "what business is it of yours." So, there needs to be a plan before any attempt for this type of interaction, including a time and place, together with awareness and showing sensitivity.

Offering support could be seen as interfering that leads to lasting tensions between people, however isn't it worth trying rather than avoiding something you may be passionate about? Especially if you have experienced this type of unorthodox lifestyle yourself, having come through the other side safely. As a result, understand the profound impact those sorts of changes can have on improving and empowering lives.

Best-case scenario during this initial conversation would be for the person living in a dysfunctional manner to acknowledge that their family life is far from being what is regarded as acceptable behaviour. By becoming transparent and understanding the time has come to open up and talk about it, which is then a golden opportunity for the two women to discuss the matter.

Should you ever contemplate this type of confrontation, you should avoid being overly judgmental or letting personal biases cloud your perspective, as that could distract you from your true intentions. Instead, give the person space to express themselves freely, allowing them to talk for as long as they need to.

—- *Regardless of the outcome of this first initial confrontation, you have planted the seed.*—

Intervention takes real courage

The ideal moment would be after you have lured your friend into having a sit-down moment with you, perhaps at a coffee shop to have a casual conversation.

For this conversation, we will mark the friend F, and the woman living in a dysfunctional environment D.

With the friend asking…

F -- "Is everything ok at home?"

D -- "Yes, it's fine, why do you ask".

Perfectly normal answer and a convenient way to defuse any further conversation on such a sensitive topic. However, your instincts tell you differently. Assume you're on the right track, and if not, don't worry, as it's also as good a time than any to let your suspicions be known by asking…

F -- "Are you sure, because I've been wanting to talk to you, but it's a little personal, and I don't want you to get upset,"

D — "About what?"

So now you have created some curiosity, so no backing down now,

F – "Well, we have known each other now for many years and I care about you, I really do, and I would like to know if you are happy at home, because I get the feeling, you're not, so I thought we could talk about it."

Dysfunctional Families

At this point, you have made it quite clear where you're going with this, and if there's a frown or a delay in getting a response, just continue.

F -- "Is living the way you do with Bob and the kids getting you down? If so, I just want to help you; all you have to do is just talk to me about it, and together we can try to sort it out."

Getting someone to open up and talk on such personal issues can be difficult at the best of times. But once the conversation starts to flow, and the person you are with remains comfortable and rational, then that person may just have been itching to talk about it.

D -- "I'm just not happy at home, there's always a shouting match then slamming doors, and that's just the start. I'm just not coping. It's day in and day out. The kids are arguing with one another non-stop. They never do as they are told, and when Bob comes home from work, he usually just shouts at them, or me. Then we end up shouting at each other, which is happening all the time. I'm truly exhausted."

What a nightmare, and it's not fiction either, as this type of behaviour is more common than what many people could ever imagine, an out-of-control roller coaster that seems to have no stop sign in sight, taking a huge toll on the entire family.

The instigator in this scenario has inadvertently opened a pandora's box, that being the man of the house showing a lack of responsibility for this ongoing behaviour. His failure to handle situations allows his type of abuse to spread, consuming everyone within its path. Comparable to contracting an unknown and incurable disease that infiltrates the mind, body, and soul. Those who become unwitting participants become infected, passively accepting this toxicity as just another part of everyday life.

Anyone not associated with this type of lifestyle would clearly have a breakdown, if knowingly, it was soon to be their new way of life. It's just too unimaginably horrifying, therefore difficult to comprehend. Yet many such families live in this chronically confusing world, on a daily basis, without understanding why. Therefore, more reason for someone to intervene, helping to resolve the situation.

So, your friend has opened up, therefore it's all the encouragement you need to keep the conversation flowing.

F – "Have you ever mentioned to your husband Bob how you feel?"

D – "No, Bob can be very overpowering and quite aggressive. I wouldn't dare question him on anything like this."

All too familiar, where the woman feels she is at a roadblock not knowing where to turn. Instead, it's now time to look at that roadblock as nothing more than a crossroads, whereby you will soon decide which direction you need to go in.

First, acknowledge you're living within a dysfunctional household, but don't allow the bigger picture to overwhelm you, one step at a time. It is important to ask yourself what role you play - if any, in this dysfunctional environment, by further acknowledging whether you're a participant. Being honest with yourself from the very start allows you to move forward with a clear conscience. Doing so provides comfort in knowing there's no need to play the blame game. A process that will then further provide you with a feeling of intense relief that will reduce stress and anxiety.

There is no better time - when finding yourself in this type of lifestyle- to call on your fortitude than now, that allows us to bounce back from adversity by providing the tools to accomplish our goals. Seeking support, whether through friends, advocacy groups or professional counselling, that provides much-needed guidance and validation.

Possessing self-respect and self-esteem are critical, as they help us maintain our dignity and confidence. As is our self-worth by demonstrating discipline being essential in implementing consistent and constructive actions towards change. Having determination and courage empowers us to take active steps toward creating a healthier environment and ultimately achieving a life with dignity. Embracing these tools can transform our approach to living decently despite the challenges we face, particularly those associated with dysfunctionality.

Are there any other species that come close to having access to such an extensive range of resources to support and balance life? It is therefore reasonable to assume that those who feel they've reached a dead end haven't fully tapped into, considered, or perhaps even recognized the immense strength that comes within. The power of human resilience has the potential to elevate individuals from a state of despair to extraordinary, almost superhuman heights. - It's there for the taking.

Continuing with this substandard behaviour is to give in, allowing yourself not only to remain consumed, but it has also has absolutely nothing at all to offer, either in the short or long term.

Remain mindful -having recognised a serious issue in your life-, you already possess the inner strength to make meaningful and positive changes. With careful planning and determination, transforming your circumstances is entirely possible not just for yourself, but also for those around you. In time you will come to be admired, carrying that respect for a lifetime having finally broken free from living a dysfunctional existence. But this transformation will only happen if you commit to it, and when you do, that feeling of accomplishment breaks the cycle of every going back.

Adopting a new demeanour and talking to your partner, husband, and children calmly is an excellent first step—one that will prove to be highly effective over time, although it takes real discipline. While desired results may not seem to be immediate, finding patience ensures the experience will become more fulfilling as time goes by. Not just for your cause, but for yourself.

So, what is the crux of the problem facing dysfunctional families, and the immediate first step remedy, other than portraying your new demeanor. Most people would agree, it stems from the way humans talk to one another, therefore invariably coaching and mentoring those family members into talking to one another as they would expect to be spoken to themselves.

Taking this approach pays big dividends as it sets you in good stead for maintaining your own self-preservation and installing a positive and calming effect on yourself and others. In total contrast to raising your voice, which only encourages further verbal aggression that can lead to an escalation of abuse. This subtle action will naturally unfold in the minds of your family, gradually shifting their mindset without them even realizing the change.

Human beings inherently scream and shout, we all have our moments. So be sure to recognise that type of behaviour is the exception rather than the rule. Let there be consequences of a different kind, explaining to your family that unless they speak to you with a calm and rational voice, you will not answer them.

Cruel to be kind

This procedure is good therapy, and although it may be frustrating to begin with, you will eventually receive the tone you were looking for. Particularly when that person wants something bad enough.

How desperately sad it is for a mother having to go to these lengths in order to get her family talking to each other with respect.

– It only takes one other brave family member to support their mother on such a courageous journey. Could that person be you? –

If you have the strength and courage to chastise someone who shows aggressive and/or violent behaviour, it's essential to have some understanding of the level of potential danger you face. However, it wouldn't be the first time someone with this type of courage has put an obnoxious male in his place. – If only half his size.

Ques: "My dad shouts at me and my brother usually over nothing. I can handle it although I get upset, but my brother cries and hides in his room. Why doesn't my mum tell my dad not to get so angry?"

Ans: "When husbands/fathers shout, people are usually too frightened to answer back, possibly including your mother. Ask your mother if she will talk to your dad and explain to him the effect his shouting has on you and your brother. Try to understand that your mum may not be strong enough to confront your dad on this issue, as there are many mothers just too afraid to get involved. Should that be the case then the next time your dad shouts at you, say to him calmly "you don't need to shout" then don't make any further comment. Don't become disrespectful, instead go about your business knowing your father heard you. That's all you need to do each time he shouts and hopefully he finally gets the message. If your father gets physical with you, and you believe he has crossed the line then explain to him without raising your voice, that he's not to get physical with you. If your father's physical abuse escalates then talk to your teacher, or if no longer at school, either call the police or walk into a police station and make a complaint. Remember, feeling sorry for your father and not reporting his behaviour will not end the abuse. That is why you must report it, otherwise your father will never understand or receive any consequences. On the other hand, try to understand the difference between Fathers who at times seem to be heavy handed, and those who again have overstepped their mark- so trend carefully"?

It's normally the man of the house that's looked upon as the leader, the "protector". However, since he is probably also the instigator, it's a good start to try to understand the reasons behind his behaviour. Whilst he may well be mild-mannered while at work or around other people, he believes he must become some authoritarian type of tyrant when at home. Unfortunately, it's a common trend amongst a lot of men although admittedly it takes some work to resolve, however it's a worthwhile pursuit, but only if you truly see a future with this man.

The loudest voice is often the weakest

His mentality is one of wanting respect as he shouts out his demands in his intimidating tone, while relying on receiving a response. While some respond immediately fulfilling his demands, the ones that stand their ground are not so forthcoming.

Often, outbursts are a spontaneous reaction because of failing to control their emotions. This behaviour is ingrained in them, it's what they've learned and will continue doing so, unless challenged by someone that can offer them more than verbal retaliatory aggression.

As mentioned, an excellent strategy for any woman that can confidentially hold her own ground when in earshot of the loud obnoxious abusive male is to remain defiant and ignore him. Don't take the bait and fall into the trap, instead show complete defiance of being someone completely at odds.

> **AWARENESS –** Showing the aggressor your matter-of-fact reaction, after listening to his outbursts diminishes the type of response he was looking for, showing him that his antics are wearing thin, and of little consequence. - It's important you maintain that stance, while he maintains that belief.

Remind yourself of the adage; 'Slow and steady wins the race'.

– It's ironic, that when a male engages in verbal abuse and making people feel frightened and expelling all that energy, he could have otherwise used to generate love and showing encouragement. –

Again, it's the knee jerk reaction of falling into the trap of verbal exchange that always comes back to bite, instead complete silence can be the best course of action. You can accomplish this by simply exercising your mantra, to first pause, reflect on the matter at hand, then act by simply walking away without comment which again - speaks volumes.

That said, it's a double-edged sword, so be extra careful- because whilst one abusive male gets the message – when being ignored-, another may well become infuriated. The latter reaction can cause escalation in his unpredictability, so as previously mentioned, far too many women have lost their lives due to underestimating the beast within.

It's a big wake-up call when you suddenly realise that the person or person's you have been living with are abusers. In all likelihood, having been that way for some time, yet unfortunately you have remained oblivious – or in denial - to what has been happening around you and accepting it. Under the circumstances it's a sad reality in life, and one that's further exacerbated by the many women who believe it's simply their place to accept their situation.

When all it really takes is for those women who are affected to come to terms with the fact their lives are well below what they had expected or had always dreamt about. Then come to terms with, it's time to do something about it. - Isn't it time you did?

An abuser who remains unchecked will only grow bold over time, pushing boundaries without consequence until the inevitable moment arrives when everything unravels, often with severe consequences. It's usually at this point that victims question why they didn't take action that much sooner.

-As emphasised throughout this book, why do we wait for a serious adverse incident before finally taking decisive action? It's our ongoing emotional attachment — interrupted only by brief moments of detachment — within the family unit that prevents us from making clearer judgement-.

Humans can truly be their own worst enemy at times, particularly when they know something is wrong and fail to act, instead take the watch and listen approach. The worse action to take when abusive behaviour continues.

Make no mistake, the grind of remaining in a dysfunctional family is unimaginable and no different to being slowly tortured, not once or twice, but on a continuous basis. There are many people under these circumstances that become deeply affected, having endured so much, sadly ending their life.

Many of these troubled young adult victims have few friends, going from job to job, with failed relationships and turning to alcohol and drugs. Becoming desperate and engaging in criminal activity, with the additional bitterness of feeling guilt and self-loathing. That's just the beginning of this hellhole, because in many instances, this downward spiral continues throughout their adult lives. A continuation to live and breathe their hatred, spewing the same meaningless rhetoric they were taught during their childhood. For many the result of not having been shown ongoing love or given any encouragement that generally results in a complete breakdown of the vital skills necessary to maintain civilised behaviour.

You only need to listen to the daily news to understand the extent of criminal behaviour perpetrated by human beings that have steered off course, having lost their way. Someone raised and taught many of these people to become -in part- who they are today, failing to provide them with the alternatives and options that could have led them down a different path.

Is living lower class to remain lower class?

Topics on class distinctions are seldom openly addressed, particularly in contexts that involves domestic abuse. Yet they profoundly influence how we navigate life and the degree to which we let our circumstances shape our destiny. Being in a less privileged financial position doesn't mean adopting a less self-styled image or behaviour compared to those who are more affluent. Defining yourself with a preconceived lower status, believing it's inevitable in becoming your destiny, only reinforces a damaging mindset that keeps you trapped in a cycle of limitations, imposing unnecessary restrictions.

Class distinction has long fueled division and segregation in society, yet a fulfilling and better life is within reach through a simple shift in mindset. Material possessions may appear to measure true wealth, but the real richness lies in the integrity and depth of one's character. These qualities hold far greater value than money or social rank ever could, with those who possess financial wealth and riches willing to trade their eye teeth for.

Ques: "My upbringing was one of chaos from start to finish and I often reflect on the misery my father brought about on us kids regularly. We lived in a rundown home in a poor area for many years, having had a terrible effect on my brother being in and out of jail. Fortunately, I married a good man, and we raised our family totally differently, unlike my brother who remains badly influenced and traumatised. What I don't understand is the serenity and peace my elderly parents now live by, as if their entire lives had been one of rationale, love and compassion, which could not have been further from the truth"?

Ans: "A heartbreaking reality and a familiar fate for those males through the passages of time, now retired, having finally beaten themselves into submission. Now surrendered to a life of quiet acceptance- as you so aptly described- in serenity, but never understanding the trail of their destruction or able to grasp the reasons behind their own son's fate. Yet, the hope in this story lies in the fact that you overcame this deeply demoralising existence and found true happiness".

For many, living in a substandard environment falls into the realms of having reached a rock-bottom existence. Men who live in this world are possibly of the belief they may just as well find a wife and start a family. That's because in his mind, it's what everyone else does. Tragically these males seem to find some hapless female willing to get married, believing it was the thing to do. Consequently, the male gradually infiltrates the minds and souls of their own family for one reason only- their own selfish needs. By doing so, missing out on the love and warmth the family was so desperate to both give and to receive, instead these families become destined to live their life feeling rejected.

Mothers in this situation pay the heaviest toll, as not only does her man show her little attention along with little respect, but she also must also put up with the demands of her children misbehaving. What a devastating set of circumstances for these women who keep the very fabric of the household together with many also being employed. When all she ever wanted was to be loved and respected by her man and her children.

Poignant mix of guilt, relief, & resolve

Are you a woman who has inadvertently aligned herself with your husband or partner's indiscretions? Having fallen into the trap of partaking in verbal and emotional abuse in a family environment? If so, now is the perfect time to stop and ask yourself, 'what is your real purpose in life', and 'why are you allowing your world to be controlled and turned upside down?' Therefore, instead of waiting for someone else to offer you an explanation, you can easily find it yourself, and throughout the pages of this book.

Let's remind ourselves of the male who may have been a victim of childhood abuse, now suffering with long-term mental health issues. One who has completely adopted the mindset of being abusive, he now directs at the very people who love him—his wife and children. Irrespective, this man is the husband, the father, the leader, a person of status, the very person the family looks up to for encouragement and support. What an absolute travesty it must be for these men genuinely believing they are on the right path when their ideology could not be further from the truth.

Bob's wife has not only recognised the dysfunction in their family home, but she has also clearly opened up and expressed a desire for change. That is a powerful beginning and a major step forward, and something to feel genuinely encouraged by. It's also the type of response that every woman living in similar circumstances should adopt.

This journey, whilst being a long-term commitment, is a deeply transformative and life-changing experience. One that hopefully continues to fuel your imagination and motivation to remain inspired and see the process through to a positive resolution.

—Equally important is to acknowledge your genuine feelings toward him, rather than convincing yourself you are in love simply because you feel obligated to do so —

Any form of confrontation can be unsettling, but in this situation unwavering resolve is key—you must be certain that you will not give in, not even the slightest. These men are experts at manipulation, effortlessly shifting between intimidation and charm to get their way. Standing firm against their tactics is the only way to break the cycle of his control.

Let's return to our caring and thoughtful lady wanting to help her close friend, who she believes has fallen into the abyss of living a dysfunctional lifestyle. Fortunately, she has openly admitted there are in fact serious problems in the household, but currently she is too scared to discuss with her husband Bob.

Returning to our two ladies…

F – "So if you believe you can't talk to Bob regarding your concerns at home, have you tried doing anything else?"

D – "No, Bob's always at work, and when he's not, he's doing other things."

F – "Have you ever mentioned anything to Bob in the past about your feelings?"

D – "No, never, but I really want him to know how I feel. I just don't know how to do it, and that's why I haven't mentioned it to you, or anyone else for that matter."

F – "Well, I would like to tell you something I have never told anyone before. As a young girl I was brought up in a dysfunctional family environment, and I witnessed my mother's suffering. One day she made a pact only with herself with no one else knowing, determined to put an end to the way my dad treated her, and she did."

D – "What did she do?"

F – "Well, I didn't really understand at the time but many years later she told me the story of how she tried talking to my father, but he remained obstinate and just wasn't interested in listening to her, and that's how it all started, or rather ended. Anyway, from an early age I remember how my father always seemed to be in a bad mood, raising his voice and he would throw things around. Then he would start arguing with mum and shouting at us kids. Well, my mum told me she put up with his abuse for many years trying everything to get him to be a different person. She went on to tell me that sometimes he was ok, usually when other people were around, but when it was just us family he would then soon slip back into his old ways."

D – "Did your father drink alcohol?"

F – "Yes, but I can't remember whether he drank all the time, but when he brought the alcohol home, soon after the arguing would start, and we would go to our bedrooms having to listen. I also remember my brother causing trouble at school, they caught him smoking and drinking, and when my father found out he hit him. Then on other occasions the police came to the house, and not for the first time. My mother was a good person, and she told me how she had been thinking about leaving my father and taking us kids away for good. That's exactly what she did, and she has never looked back to this day. We never really knew what was happening, as we were only young and didn't really understand what my mother was going through."

D – "I sometimes wish I could do the same and just pack up take the kids and leave Bob, but I don't know if I could do it."

F – "Do you love Bob?"

D – "Yes, but I just hate the way he treats me and the kids."

F – "Do you remember when I told you my mother tried to talk to my father, and he just shrugged it off, well I'm sure he must have lived to regret it, because when we moved out my mother told me years later, he nearly went mad trying to convince her to let him come back, but she refused."

D – "How did your mother manage finding somewhere else to live? Did she have any money?"

F – "I remember my mother having a part- time job and that's all, but she was obviously determined to give us kids a better life, and she has done just that, and I am so proud of her. That's just the start of the story because my mother told me she had planned and confided in close family and friends. Biding her time, and saving what little money she had, the day came when we all moved into a small apartment where she managed to get a full-time position and brought us kids up on her own. I have a lot of respect for my mother for the life we all had together after that. That's why I wanted to talk to you, because I felt you were possibly experiencing what my mother was going through during that stage of her life, when she was about your age."

D – "So, what do you think I should do?"

F – "Well, if I were in your position, and believing you when you tell me you love Bob, I would be sure about one thing before I spoke to Bob. I would be as direct in my thinking as my mother was and make a solemn promise to myself. That regardless of whatever happens, I would put an end to this type of dysfunctional lifestyle once and for all, with or without Bob."

It will be a huge weight off the shoulders for this woman, having finally discussed her problems and receiving encouragement to put an end to her dysfunctional way of life. As it was for the woman confiding in her friend, reliving her experiences and that of her mothers.

Dysfunctional Families

Although this subject on the home front may appear to be heavy in the moment, it's the after effect on the human psyche that produces clarity, since the genie is out of the bottle. What gives this suggestion more merit is the fact you would hardly expect men to sit around debating such a topic, therefore keep the positive momentum going.

Humans are generally emotionally driven; therefore, there's nothing more difficult in life when the time has come to say goodbye to a loved one – still living. But although ending a relationship with a tyrant comes with its challenges, amongst other things it offers psychological escape. Gaining freedom and choosing to surround yourself with like-minded people who offer uplifting conversation, care, compassion and encouragement, being such a vital part of healing.

– Don't allow your emotions to cloud the greater cause –

Imagine life as it should be, being treated with respect and shown the love you deserve, whilst giving and receiving all those vibes that make us feel good. In complete contrast to the anxiety and stress, alongside that constant empty feeling inside, caused by knowing he will be home soon, along with his unpredictability.

– Is this how you should live, day after day, week after week, year after year? –

You don't need this type of man in your life. You need a man that shares your values and beliefs, because it's what you deserve, and not what the Bob's in this world want. Instead, the Bobs of this world will have to learn the hard way like so many men do, discovering the sheer despair when coming home to an empty house and realising, it's all just too late.

Returning to our two ladies…

D -- "I believe I can follow through I really do. I have been thinking about this for some time, believe it or not, and I feel so much better having talked with you. As I mentioned, I just need to know where to start."

F – "Well, just as my mother did with my father, I suggest you talk to Bob, even though I appreciate what you say about him not being the type to want to talk about it. The only reason he acts the way he does is because he can't see what could happen. The same mistake my father made. By refusing to sit down and talk with my mother, my father made my mother's situation easier, whereby she never had to make any idle threats to leave. She just did it."

D – "You make it sound so easy."

F – "No, not really, I just know my mother with three kids did it and has lived peacefully with no regrets ever since."

Women with real determination can accomplish anything they put their minds to, irrespective of what they may see as insurmountable pressure.

There are the men who dismiss women the minute they believe there could be a conversation that may expose their indiscretions. Humans by nature dislike to be challenged when conversation activates their guilty conscience, so this type of man believes deflection is the best course of action. However, in the event he remains defiant, don't see this as a setback, other than a delay. Move on with a determined attitude to mentor and coach your family, including your husband/partner, being the best cause of action.

Regardless of the method chosen, prioritizing your safety and recognizing your own limitations as being essential. As mentioned, there is a time and place for everything, and resisting the urge to engage in his style of dysfunctional rhetoric will be a powerful statement.

There's nothing more important, than for a woman to show herself with genuine conviction in front of her man, whilst in this situation. Why? Because no one has likely ever challenged this man in his entire adult life, and you are the last person on earth he would have ever expected to oppose him.

Returning to our two ladies …

D — "But as I have said, there are times I fear Bob."

F — "Then why would you continue to be intimate with someone you are scared of?"

F — "I often ask myself that."

D —"I understand you love Bob, which makes the situation a little more complex, however what made my mother's decision so much easier was the fact she had fallen out of love with my father. So, if I were you, I would take another look at Bob's true feelings towards you, remaining blindsided to the truth could be very disappointing.".

D -- "I feel he loves me, but I guess I could be wrong."

F – "How do you think Bob would react if he came home, only to find you and the kids weren't there, and he could see that you had packed and took your belongings?"

D – "He would hit the roof; I know he would."

F – "Well, there is only one way to find out, so I would start off by having a talk with Bob away from home, and lay it all out, do you feel you're up to it?"

D – "Yes, and I'm so grateful to you for talking with me, and I will let you know how I get on."

Although no one wants to face situations like this, human beings are remarkably capable, however the tradeoff is that stress, and or anxiety often comes with the territory. For that reason, she must again approach this with full conviction rather than making a half-hearted effort, otherwise he will sense any hesitation you make and use it to his advantage. Again, if the response is weak or inconsistent, most men seize the opportunity to push back even harder, which can quickly undermine any chance of achieving the desired outcome.

— You are calling the shots now, remember that —

As mentioned throughout this book, never get disheartened over what may appear to be overwhelming odds. Disappointment is only the result of a singular one-off attempt to solve a particular problem that provides a temporary setback. Finding the right solution that suits your specific circumstances is out there, you only need to find it, so never lose faith.

Regardless of what you may perceive to be working or not, take some comfort in knowing, there is a greater awareness playing out on his conscience once he discovers you're on to him. So never think it's all in vain, as it's unquestionably a great start, but again, the answer is to keep at it, slowly wearing him down, until he changes his ways- or you have finally had enough of the relationship.

Returning to our two ladies...

F -- "So how did it go?"

D -- "Well, not so good. He basically just sat there, not showing any genuine interest in anything that I had to say."

F – "Did you explain to him why you can't live this way anymore?"

D – "Yes, I told him we are living a dysfunctional lifestyle, whereby he basically looked at me strangely, probably wondering what I was even talking about."

Considering this was just the first discussion between husband and wife on such an important matter, the male will mull over the situation he now finds himself in. He will undoubtedly question himself as to whether he is indeed suitable as a husband and a father, if only briefly, however he understands the matter will surely ignite future discussions between himself and his wife.

There is no question you are potentially putting yourself in harm's way, as only you know the potential level of risk you are putting yourself in. Therefore, you must decide on the safest way of delivering and expressing your future concerns either again face to face, by letter, or through an intermediary. What you can be sure of, is this man now sees and hears you like never before. A challenge he never saw coming, therefore providing him with a letter in your absence is by far profoundly safer than any other type of intervention.

Returning to our two ladies...

F – "Well, at least you had his attention, even though he had little to say since he may well not have had any answers. Think of it this way, his silence speaks volumes, so why not assume that's the case this time around and make future plans?"

D – "I don't intend to give up. I've made my mind up, I love Bob, and I believe he loves me, so I will talk to him again soon and keep you informed."

F – "I hope you do because you are onto something now, and I guess you already know that Bob has had time to get both a little hot under the collar and to cool down. I'm guessing it should be okay for you to attempt talking to him soon, so be careful and I look forward to seeing you again."

This brave woman is having a go, reassured with the support from a good friend, giving her the inspiration and the confidence to open up, discussing her dissatisfaction with living in a dysfunctional family. Having now made it clear to her husband concerning her grievances, unlike the many women in this world currently sitting on their hands. For those women who do not know which direction to take, they only need to find the desire and a little courage then understand there is a whole host of different options to consider. By simply contacting family services and talking to a councilor—with or without him. Or as in this scenario confiding in a close friend or family member along with making entries in your diary, it's so important to first break away from the silence and start the ball rolling.

As mentioned, human beings are usually uncomfortable when approached to discuss such personal matters, particularly with family services. A hurdle that needs to be addressed if in fact chosen as your option to act as an intermediary. Particularly when you have made earlier attempts to talk to your husband that fell on deaf ears. It really is a matter for your man to understand the seriousness of the matter, and for that to happen he must first feel the effects of losing you. However, regardless of the method you choose moving forward, you can't be denied, instead you must turn up the heat.

Otherwise, it is just business as usual, and rest assured—that's just what the male is hedging his bets on, particularly when suggestions are made which he believes are a waste of time. It may also be the case where he suddenly receives a wakeup call and decides to take a closer look at his wife's concerns. It's a situation whereby, nothing ventured nothing gained.

-- Such is life, when we first discover our initial beliefs are one thing, only to discover the facts are completely different altogether. As it may well turn out to be in this case, particularly if the wife discovers her man voices real concern and shows remorse over his behaviour. --

Regardless of what challenges you're facing, continue to remind yourself that there are many families in your neighbourhood who live together in harmony. Respecting one another and exchanging pleasantries in a dignified and compassionate way. – Your mission has real merit.

Returning to our two ladies…

F – "So how did you get on."

D – "Well, better than I first thought. I just came out with it and further explained to him I can't live like this anymore and he knew I was serious. Anyway, he has agreed to come with me to talk to a family services councillor, and we have already made an appointment."

F – "That's great news, I do hope everything works out."

If you find yourself relating to this story and feel ready to take some sort of action in your own way, remember the importance of a holistic approach, otherwise your plans just won't work. Again, note the initial planning stages taken by Bob's wife, having been inspired by her friend, that provided her with the further encouragement she needed. You can do the same, by allowing this moment to inspire you. First acknowledge you're living a dysfunctional family life, and that will provide you with the inspiration to put your own plans in place.

– Train your emotions and discover real control –

However, let's not get too far ahead of ourselves, so again remember to make those all-important entries into your diary, especially now you have decided it's time to put a plan together, in your quest to finally end this dysfunctional way of living. As we have constantly stated throughout this book this step is vital, because on reflection when reading your diary, you will then find the answers you are looking for without too much trouble.

Consider your diary as the golden goose that keeps on giving, so whenever you're feeling a little low, all it takes is revisiting, writing and reading. These reflections can spark insight, stir inspiration, and change perspectives. And that's why keeping a diary is such an indispensable, and personalised companion.

In the first scenario, Bob finally agreed to address the dysfunction in his family's life, fully aware that he bore much of the responsibility. But this turning point only came after his wife stepped in—proving just how resourceful a woman can be when it truly counts, without her intervention it's likely they would have remained trapped in a toxic cycle, feeding off each other's struggles. Bob's brave wife, who despite acknowledging her role in their unhealthy dynamic and facing deep fear, chose to believe in herself. With quiet determination, she's now on the path to transforming not only her own life but also that of her husband and her family.

Empowerment is within your reach

In this second scenario, the initial planning stages - prior to any confrontation, remain the same as in the first scenario. But sadly, the meeting with Bob provided less than the desired outcome for Bob's wife. Bob is steadfast in believing their lives are normal and has no intention of seeing any type of councillor or making any change. A seemingly insurmountable task for any woman is to change the mind of the adamant male who's set in his ways. Or is he? The good news is it's only on the surface as he is about to experience that empowerment delivers an unparalleled awakening.

Returning to our two ladies…

F – "So how did you go talking with Bob?"

D – "Not good I'm afraid, Bob wasn't interested in anything I had to say".

F – "That's disappointing. Did he say anything about living in a dysfunctional family?"

D – "Bob acknowledged nothing I said to him. As hard as I tried to be convincing, he once again told me I was carrying on about nothing.

Bob lacks understanding of the kinds of conversations that should come with having a wife/partner and raising a family. As a result, he finds it difficult to engage in meaningful discussion or thoughtful dialogue, especially when it comes to complex issues that involve cold hard truths.. To him, such matters don't even register as real or relevant. – A man incomplete denial showing zero respect for his wife and himself.

Returning to our two ladies…

F – "Do you know what you are going to do, now that Bob has chosen not to support you?"

D – "Not yet, I'm still thinking about it, although I realise I can't and won't give up trying at this point. If I fail to turn Bob around, I will have to consider leaving him and live a different life."

Meaning there's no magic bullet, however there is and always should be belief in that adage; "different strokes for different folks". Meaning of course, what works for some may not work for others, so if at first you don't succeed, - it's time to up the ante.

Even though Bob has his views he now has yours. So, the next move is to continue—with or without Bob's consent—driven by your sheer tenacity and determination. Again, start by chastising anyone in the family home who behaves badly, by doing so without raising your voice. As we have stipulated throughout this book, staying calm and remaining composed puts you at a different level, one that universally commands attention and respect.

Until you accomplish your goals, you will have to adopt the cruel to be kind method. This can be accomplished by holding back from expressing love and affection, especially to those who aren't deserving. Other than when there has been some form of improvement on their part.

As difficult as that may be, it's imperative you work on your family's conscience, showing them, they need to show love and respect before they can receive the same. This will provide the crucial foundation you need when your family discovers you're not your usual self. It's a battle of the wills, and one you will win.

As mentioned, when people use verbal aggression, they usually seek a reaction or look for some type of support.

Therefore, when the family notices you are remaining quiet, it will play on their minds, so continue with this one very important proven control measure. Only this time, it will be on your grounds, as you are going to take control, subtly to begin with, and in total contrast to engaging in any sort of abusive behaviour. When the time presents itself, calmly announce, "Has everyone had enough of abusing one another? Has everyone had enough of being abused?" There's probably silence, since humans have a built-in trigger, caused by our conscience we are all too familiar with, called guilt. The normal reaction is to instantly remain quiet and hide in their shell when they know they are in the wrong, particularly having heard an unusual authoritarian yet softer tone.

Since the chances are you won't get a reply, continue with, "I won't have that sort of talk in my house, do you all understand?" whereby the silence will most likely continue to be deafening. This will only occur by remaining calm, maintaining your voice at a low-level pitch that comes across with authority. Doing so lowers the risk of anyone becoming enticed into continuing with any further verbal bad behaviour, instead they receive a feeling of being disarmed, if only temporarily.

Yes, that's right, your house. No more playing second fiddle to any man who doesn't know how to run a civilised household. This action will show the family how things are going to be from now on. You have made a good start and a big first impression.

As a result, you have given yourself a confidence boost and emotional uplift, where you will be wondering why you never took this course of action earlier. You won't know yourself, - in a manner of speaking- and hopefully neither will your family, at least in the short term. That's because something very soon will come over them, a type of curiosity that they can't quite put their finger on. There's a change coming, the type of thought process and psychology lesson they so desperately needed to have- sadly without understanding why- at this stage.

Admittedly, and from time to time, particularly during the initial stages of laying down the law, there will be some resistance, but you're up for it. That's because you are now seen by the family with an aura of authority about you, along with having already put some planning in place with the following new policies and procedures.

Forgive them as they know not what they do

Become confident about educating and motivating your family against living in a dysfunctional way. Continue with your new style of belief by teaching your loved ones to pause and reflect before reacting. Doing so will help them to understand how their words impact on themselves and those around them. Other than their continuing failure in given it some thought on what they are about to say.

—A household filled with encouragement instead of criticism nurtures emotional security-

Make a personal pact with yourself to maintain your composure during verbal outbursts by others, then choose the moment to make a profound and meaningful statement. "I want you all to know how much better we would all be as a family if we talk to each other decently, so from now on we will all be under some new house rules. The first rule is, if you have nothing nice to say about anyone or anything, then say nothing at all, does everyone understand." A silent stare by those in ear shot will be suffice - for now.

In all probability no one has ever given your family any such thought-provoking advice before, allowing them to hopefully begin questioning themselves and understand what's truly happening in their lives. This is only the start, because with your resilience and continued line of mentoring, your determination will ensure you remain on top. As a result, gradually seeing the changes in the family, all that hard work you were responsible for and at the same time becoming a refreshed person for it.

Being a caring woman is to be a mother, a wife/partner, and a teacher, which is something you can do and do well, because when a woman acts with dignity in the home while the husband and children misbehave, she will attract respect naturally. However, under the current circumstances she unfortunately needs to work harder at getting that respect, and when she does, she must never lose it again and use that respect to her advantage. There are a host of important changes that are necessary when transitioning from living a dysfunctional lifestyle to one of respectful behaviour. It doesn't start any better than with a mandatory (house rule number two), where everyone sits down together at the table for dinner. That's right, a proven yet old tradition that produces remarkable almost mystical undertones that reveal themselves both during and after a meal.

– Adjustment in the home, -no matter how insignificant it may first seem at first-, is crucial provided it leads to a meaningful outcome. If positive behavioural changes are not forthcoming, then remember there must be consequences- with control measures? –

By going about your own life, showing a little less interest in family life will also have a profound effect, increasing everyone's curiosity even further. Asking themselves what is going on, becoming inquisitive, and all because they aren't completely grasping what you're up to. This is an excellent position to be in, where the family feels a sense of uneasiness because of their inability to understand the change in you, and indeed what's installed for them.

Having initiated change, with your family witnessing your firm stance through statements like; "Don't speak to each other that way" and "It's time to learn some respect", to "I don't want to hear foul language in this house"—prompted your husband's surprise response, "What's got into you?" At this stage, you've gained significant authoritarian ground and the tiger by the tail. Take a firm grip and hold on tight.

Steadfast courage fuels your journey through adversity!

Let's pick up where Bob just left off, asking "What's got into you", being our second case scenario, proving not to be an easy adjustment for Bob.

"Well, Bob, I am glad you asked, because as you would recall when we spoke last week at the coffee shop, I told you I am no longer interested living this way."

With Bob replying, "You're not still going on about that again, are you?"

"Yes, Bob I am, and I don't intend to stop until you and the children behave like normal civilised human beings. Bob, we all need to talk and treat one another with the love and respect that is so important to me, as it will become to all of us. Don't you understand what is happening to us as a family, Bob? It's being destroyed, and once it's gone, we will never get it back. That's the direction we are all heading, so unless you stop and think about what I am saying to you, it will be too late."

"What is that supposed to mean?" Bob replies.

"Exactly how it sounded Bob, the children are off the rails, because you talk to them like dirt, as though they mean nothing to you, and they feel it, Bob. They aren't aware of it, but they are being emotionally abused by their very own father. Can't you see what you are doing, they are responding to you in the same way you talk to them, it's the only way they know how to react and defend themselves. I am no longer prepared to wait on you and the children hand and foot. From now on, there are going to be some big changes, so you'd best be prepared. Our children need your love, direction and encouragement so they can grow up and become responsible adults. Then to go out into the world feeling good about themselves, with love, compassion and respect in their hearts, which you are denying them. Can't you see what you are doing to the children and to yourself Bob? And as much as I love you all, unless there are immediate changes I am leaving you Bob, and that's the end, so I want to make myself perfectly clear on that point."

Having provided a well-structured non-negotiable and composed statement, simply walk away. Don't be drawn into further conversation unless he offers up a rational and calm response. Should he attempt to talk with garbled nonsense disguised as a pathetic attempt to defend himself then be aware it's what far too many women fall for. Instead, exclaim, "Stop, Bob, I am not interested in excuses, I want to see action. No more Bob, do you understand enough is enough".

That's using and bringing your fortitude to the forefront, demonstrating your strength, courage and determination to express yourself, without enticing a verbal slinging match. We can assume the Bobs of this world would find this surprisingly powerful approach bewildering, with the ball now firmly in Bob's court.

It's important to remember that Bob's wife described him as verbally abusive but not physically violent. This influenced her decision to confront him at home on this occasion—a crucial factor to consider in these circumstances. Therefore, always assess someone's behaviour at the highest risk level and work backwards until you find the balance of safety you feel comfortable with.

Also, it's crucial to remind ourselves of the importance of continuingly controlling both the situation and our emotions at such a time. Avoid falling foul to the antics most men see as their saving grace to relationship problems, which is by use of the charm offensive. Now that Bob is aware of just how serious you are it's imperative you implement and monitor your instructions and demands disguised as control measures. Any deviation or change of heart on your part will be seen as a failure in the eyes of the male. Therefore, don't become swayed, hoodwinked, or unwittingly coerced, instead remain vigilant and don't give an inch, and you will discover what the Bobs of this world are really made of.

It's now time you speak to the children, without Bob being present expressing all that needs to be said regarding their behaviour and your expectations. Approach the situation with both firmness and empathy, and do not simply chastise them without recognizing the deeper influences at play. Their father's conduct has shaped their attitudes, and while this is not an excuse, it is a factor that must be acknowledged. By doing so, they will help develop the clarity, accountability, and emotional grounding they have been missing.

Once again, find the right time and place, ensuring the children feel comfortable, because you want them to open up, feeling free to express themselves, while maintaining clear and honest communication. You must articulate their unacceptable behaviour, disrespect, defiance, and harmful actions—without allowing frustration to overpower the conversation. If your voice is too harsh, they may shut down, feeling attacked rather than guided. Instead, continue maintaining a calm but unwavering tone, ensuring they recognize the seriousness of the matter, whilst continuing to work on their conscience.

These children have had to absorb extreme patterns of behaviour again modelled by their father, and in doing so may not fully grasp the impact of their own actions. Make it clear that while they are responsible for their own choices, they have been influenced by an environment that hasn't always set the best example. Further explain to them, that while you understand why this has been happening, they need to consider their actions, and the effects which their verbal abuse has on others and themselves as individuals, now and into the future.

– By doing so, you are giving them the space to reflect without them feeling condemned –

Most importantly, offer them a path forward—one built on accountability, love, and change. Setting boundaries will be necessary, and as earlier mentioned there will be consequences for negative actions, just as there will be rewards for positive ones. However, encouragement is crucial, therefore other than simply punishing misbehaviour, instead emphasize the values you want them to embrace. Provide the reasons why they should adopt respect, kindness, and responsibility and why they are the pillars of life, then reinforce those beliefs through consistent guidance and encouragement. By balancing discipline with understanding, firmness with empathy, you can steer your children toward a healthier path—one that breaks the cycle of dysfunctional living rather than repeating it.

– At this point follow through by further explaining that if their behaviour doesn't stop, you have decided to leave home for good, to start a new life. –

"I need to say something that has been weighing heavy on my mind. I love you all deeply, but the way we are living- this constant tension, the lack of respect, it hurts me more than I can explain. I give and I give, but lately it feels like I'm running on empty. When you are disrespectful to me, when you fight and ignore what I say it tears apart something inside me. I'm not saying I want to leave, I don't. But if things don't change, I honestly don't know how much longer I can keep holding everything together. I need you to see me, to hear me, and to help me heal this family—because again I love you more than anything, but I can't do it all alone. As of right now I am asking you all to think about what it would be like if we lived differently by being respectful towards one another or think about what it would be like living here with your father without me, the choice is yours.".

Families don't want their mother to leave home, so having thrown down the gauntlet by keeping your charade like existence alive, will impress on your family they need to act. However, it's important to keep yourself mentally and emotionally stable throughout this ordeal. Do so by continuously reminding yourself of your personal goal to become that woman you now know you want to become, that women of substance, which is now within your reach.

Paying less attention to the family you love to prove a point is an emotional roller coaster, but one that's extremely necessary. Because when all your hard work has been completed, you can look back on what you have accomplished, being the greatest achievement, you are ever likely to undertake in your entire life.

Stay quietly confident as you are on the right track, and if you have any doubts, or feeling the changes aren't going as fast as you would like, get out of the house and visit the outside world. Never become consumed by family life as we have discussed earlier, instead help yourself by finding inspiration elsewhere. Through friendships, accepting invites, reconnecting with nature, becoming creative, learning something new, joining a women's support group, volunteering. Telling yourself nothing will come to you unless you go after it and by doing so, it will bolster your self-esteem and create a whole new mindset. This will inadvertently steer you further toward your goals while continuing to cause further curiosity amongst the family. At the same rewriting the way you want to live on your terms.

Staying true to yourself is key!

Having expressed your feelings to your husband and children, they now ponder what will happen next, and although at this stage the matter is still in its infancy, the family is filled with some type of trepidation and uncertainty. Think in terms of being the conductor whilst your family plays in the orchestra, placing you in a commanding position.

Continue making entries into your diary, expressing your feelings, recent events, your goals and future plans. It's extremely important to analyse what your earlier thoughts were and identify any gaps that need to be filled in, or any changes to what you previously had in mind. Doing so will provide you with direction and the desire to keep going. Don't forget to also make any diary entries about your own well-being, both in your mental and physical space. If you are using your fortitude as life intended, you will feel those inner strengths carrying you through just as long as you are using them when needed and to their full potential.

Think of the achievements you have made having used your inner strengths as a progress report in meeting schedules, reaching milestones and writing them down. Learn how to acknowledge and use those achievements as being personal accomplishments. Discover the self-satisfaction that comes with writing what went well and not so well, along with a- thing to do list. It's imperative you remain proactive, particularly during family sessions and your newly discovered lease on life, now as a more independent woman.

—Don't hold back, no one else will mark your work indulge in a little self-appreciation-

You have courageously opened up to a friend explaining why you can't live the way you do anymore. As a result, it has led you to make your husband and children know of your dissatisfaction with the lifestyle in which you all live. Again, pace yourself by engaging in the intervention process during times of real opportune moments, and don't allow yourself to be caught up in trivialities. Better to remain in the background for longer periods and keep the dream alive than to inadvertently get caught in the spotlight and become involved in inappropriate behaviour, retracting on all your gains.

Little by little, one travels far

Since the family hasn't joined you at the table for dinner as you requested, it's now time to up the ante, which is sure to attract some debate from our readers. So, let's be honest, serious situations demand serious action. That action is now based on the family having to help themselves if they want a cooked meal or to wear fresh clothes. They received fair warning, and now they must face the consequences.

Dysfunctional Families

— If those suggestions strike you as being too harsh, it's likely because you've never seriously considered taking such bold steps to bring about the required changes —

Most people would agree that in many households it's the woman who ends up handling the bulk of the housework, usually receiving little gratitude. That's not because others aren't capable, but because husbands and children often come to expect it— a tradition that must end. And if managing the cooking, cleaning, and laundry wasn't enough, now you're about to take on coaching and mentoring duties too. Why has this been happening? Because it's what's known as living in a dysfunctional family.

That stops now. You're about to master the art of delegation. It's a simple principle, if family members want to eat, and wear clean clothes, in clean surroundings, they best learn how to take instructions and carry them out. These aren't punishments, they're the consequences for every family wanting to live in harmony and playing fair. In well-balanced homes pitching in is expected, a necessary lesson in later life when children become young adults and having to make the same type of decisions themselves. In dysfunctional households, the load falls on the one who tolerates it, usually the woman. But not anymore.

These changes will hit home eventually, with Bob soon becoming all too aware that his wife is becoming less interested in running the household, even less interested in him. She's also making unannounced decisions to go out, leaving him and the children to their own devices, whereby they will soon realise the depth of those consequences. This will become apparent when unsurprisingly Bob makes comments, such as "How much longer do you think you can keep this up?"

This unrealistic attempt by Bob to offer some type of concern is what you need to expect. In Bobs case he is incapable of extending any meaningful conversation of any value or with any relevance to the real issues, other than hoping it just goes away.

However, it opens an opportunity for you to educate Bob further, by replying. "Let me explain something to you Bob, I can keep this up for as long as I like or as long as it takes, because I am now at peace with myself.

Unlike you, I have chosen a different path which doesn't include your pastime of being aggressive and verbally abusive."

With Bob replying, "Well, if you mean what you were talking about in the coffee shop, I thought you would be over that by now." No surprises there, it reeks of that all too familiar male mentality, dismissing something of high significance.

"Please listen to me Bob and understand what this means to all of us all, because the situation won't get any better unless you do. As I mentioned to you before, I will no longer be living in a dysfunctional household, having to continuously listen to obnoxious behaviour, or being verbally and emotionally abused. I am trying to make you understand Bob; it's time to stop it once and for all. So, unless you think long and hard about what I am saying and start questioning yourself and disciplining the children respectfully, I won't be doing anymore housework including cooking, washing and cleaning, other than what I choose to do for myself.

I have also made up my mind, Bob, that I won't be sleeping with you either, not until you have come to your senses and show me some meaningful improvements. You can carry on all you like about my decisions Bob, but that won't help matters, so if you want me to remain your wife you need to turn our lives around for the better. Will you do that for me Bob, will you really try hard so we can all live a happier life together, that's what you want isn't it, Bob?"

Bob – "I guess so"

"Just think about it, Bob, no more swearing, abusing one another, making threats and being aggressive toward each other. When we could just as easily talk to each other decently and with respect. None of us are happy Bob, just think about that the next time you hear the children arguing. Try to understand Bob, you are no longer in charge of your family, the children don't respect either of us, they speak to us as if were the enemy. All because you speak to them the same way, surely you get it by now Bob, our lives are all messed up. I'm asking you to look at me and tell me the truth. Do you want me to leave you?"

Bob – 'No, of course not."

Dysfunctional Families

"Do you love me, Bob?"

Bob – "Yes, you know I do."

"And I love you, so please help me turn our lives around, and together we can start fresh, raising the children properly before it's all too late. Spending more time together away from the home, enjoying each other's company as a family. We can teach our children to be respectful, to love and care for one another. We can all benefit from this Bob, so if you really do love me, then help me do this because I can't live like this anymore, so promise me you will?"

Bob – "If that's what you want, I'll give it a go."

Returning to our two ladies...

F -- "How's everything going at home."

D – "Well, it's been a little tough going, but I believe I have been making some headway now that Bob has agreed to change his ways."

F – "Oh, that is good news. What did it take for Bob to change his mind and what are you planning to do now?"

F – "In the last few weeks, I have been looking into my wellbeing, my self-preservation if you like, and I discovered exactly what I have been failing to do for so long. That is how to use my fortitude, and when I do it gives me the strength and the confidence to tackle anything that comes before me, the feeling is truly remarkable. But above all I have regained a sense of who I really am, my self-respect along with rediscovering my self-esteem, which I haven't had for as long as I can remember. On top of that, I remain calm before and during a conversation with Bob and the children. That's regardless of whether they are acting up, which has helped me in so many ways, particularly since the family has recently become more restrained and less argumentative.

F – "It sounds like you have been extremely busy, having had a productive heartfelt talk with yourself and Bob. What else has been happening?"

D – "Well, after the first conversation in the coffee shop with Bob when he was adamant we had no family issues, I knew I had to do some genuine soul searching. By further questioning myself about my feelings about Bob and realizing, as I mentioned, that I still love Bob. It was during that moment I knew I had to be the one to make the family understand what was happening. I explained to Bob the time has come for him to lead by example. I have put some control measures in place that have real consequences, because I can't take any further risks of the situation going backwards".

"So, I told Bob I wouldn't cook or wash clothes for him and the children until our lives changed for the better, and on top of that, I also told him I wouldn't be sleeping with him either. Despite that I really feel good about what is happening, although I fully understand that I must follow through. This is something I am so determined to do, until it becomes second nature for the family to maintain peace and order, and show respect to one another, and then the love will return. I just know it will".

"I have also planned to meet a girlfriend to start playing tennis again one night a week and spend a little more time socializing, and to try and feel less consumed by the family, - as much as I love them all. Although I know Bob and the children will miss me when I'm not at home, it will provide them with more time to think. I have made sure there's food they can easily put together.".

F – "Do you think Bob will do the right thing by you?"

D – "I am convinced I am going about this the right way and believe he will. I saw his face when I told him I would not live in a dysfunctional household anymore, and I would leave if he didn't change his ways. He knew what that meant, and I really believe he doesn't want me to leave him and the children."

F – That really sounds like a well thought out plan. I admire you for all your courage, and I wish you well. I hope we can talk again real soon."

Yes, not to unfamiliar tactics to earlier scenarios, but to anyone who may scoff at any similarities, it's because the time has come for all women to take a firm grip and not just some casual glancing interest at these suggestions and recommendations. - *Instead, remain constantly reminded.* - That's because, to counteract high level risk within domestic abuse there needs to be extreme safety control measures, and should that also mean some repetitiveness, then so be it.

It took a brave and courageous woman to take on such a challenge, to make life-changing decisions in order to put an end to the domestic abuse associated with living in a dysfunctional family.

The instigators of this behaviour, having been shown up for what they truly represent, chastised, then educated, have been steadily reprogrammed and are now on the path to reform, as if awakened from a bad dream. A father who now understands the benefits of following his wife's lead and talks to his children rationally, who reply in kind. Who are now going about their lives as civilised human beings, not wanting to be reminded of their past.

A woman's sheer determination brought about this extraordinary and successful intervention, which has now gained positive momentum. However, like anything we do in life to keep something running smoothly, there must be ongoing monitoring and maintenance. There must be ground rules in the family home for a family to live in harmony. Failure to do so becomes the crux behind why so many families spiral out of control. Caused by the lack of discipline, without consequence, which unquestionably breeds contempt that gives way to further anger and aggression. A breeding ground for human beings to become trapped and unable to escape- until now.

Remind your man of his responsibilities

It should only take the father with his new mindset and a common-sense approach to take some simple leadership steps to ensure his young family takes notice and stays on track. With ground rules that again are simply monitored on a daily basis, without being pedantic- it's as easy as that.

As mentioned, it could never be over emphasised the long-term benefits of sitting together at the table for dinner and bonding with one another in an orderly fashion. A great family tradition, a time when families got ready for dinner by first cleaning themselves up and wearing something appropriate, as a mark of respect for both the meal and for each other.

— Providing the parents with the perfect platform and the opportunity to engage with their loved ones. To make recommendations, to settle indifferences, discuss personal problems, express desires, provide support, share concerns, and to show encouragement. At its heart lay one quiet, unspoken truth, a current of love running beneath it all, not always declared, not always seen—but always there. —

Re-establishing this once great family tradition, and spending quality time together without digital temptation. The family will discover the priceless value along with the future rewards as the entire family becomes truly bonded. The effects of these ongoing family ritual shapes human beings into what they are and who they become- as life was intended.

SUMMARY

- Coming to terms with the way you live is the first sign of acknowledging that you may be living in a dysfunctional family.
- Where there's abuse, there's unpredictability, a type of danger that has no equal, a testament to many deceased women who remained unawares.
- The challenge is there, along with recommendations, suggestions and advice for you to consider.
- Remembering there's no immediate rush, instead exercise caution with your new mantra – To pause, reflect before engaging.
- Having done so, set out step-by-step plans, by first acknowledging his unpredictability and further understanding your safety.
- Discover your fortitude and practice using all those great tools, by finding your self-respect, the deep recognition of your self-worth.

- Be sure to confide in yourself by making entries into your diary, and most importantly, reflect on what you have written previously, and make new surprising discoveries.
- If you feel more comfortable talking to a family member or close friend, then just be careful who that person is. Humans love to gossip. If in doubt, consult with a professional.
- Taking ownership of past mistakes is a necessary step forward. Let the past remain where it is and focus your energy on embracing the future.
- This will be a life-changing moment if you allow it to be, even if you can't accomplish everything you want, as nothing can ever prevent you from becoming the type of person you really want to be.
- Remember, refrain from being an overzealous mother, partner and wife, instead become a more carefree woman who explores her other passions, and watch the curiosity grow.
- With your new persona, characterized by calm and rationale, you have created the perfect foundation to build on.
- Learn when to ignore obnoxious behaviour and knowing when to intervene or confront. Don't be drawn into any type of verbal exchange, other than when it's on point and equally amicable.
- Discover how your new stance on life affects your presence amongst the family. Watch for unexpected changes within the family, using those opportune moments to keep your style of chastising and mentoring alive.
- Remain patient, and you will gradually see the rewards.
- Remember, don't treat the suggestions and recommendations as something set in stone; instead,

> consider them a starting point and adjust them to fit your specific needs.
> - You can do this. Don't allow this opportunity to slip away, as it will have a significant effect on your life, as it will on your future family generations, all made possible by you.
> - Talking about you, if you have truly been touched by what you have read, perhaps you can be a powerful advocate in helping to introduce the much-needed social skill education into our schools to end domestic abuse. It only takes one confident person with self-esteem and dogged determination to start a movement and people will follow.

PERPETRATOR

I am a husband and father, having been told I am running a dysfunctional family, so where am I going wrong?

Any man who poses that question stands at a valuable point of self-reflection, able to examine the role he occupies within his family. Recognising a potential problem—or even just entertaining the question—is an important first step. From there, observe your behaviour at home, the routines you may take for granted, and place yourself under the microscope, being sure to clearly focus.

Start by looking at how you currently conduct yourself when in the company of your wife and family and do it with honesty. It may be that you don't know yourself that well, remaining oblivious to what is taking place around you. Since you're in a family environment ask yourself, do you ever offer your family any humility, empathy or compassion when you're engaged in family matters.

You can't recall, can you? Reason being it's unlikely you ever have. That's because you take less interest in your family and being only concerned about yourself. As a result, when you either see or hear something you immediately think you don't like, you instantly look around to find someone to take your frustration out on, isn't that right? The very people that love you most. To put this type of scenario into better perspective ask yourself this, when you eventually calm down do you ever question yourself about your behaviour afterwards? Probably not, so question yourself further by asking, was using all that energy during the last few minutes ranting and raving worth it? Again, probably not, because you have never previously given it any thought, have you?

If you're already thinking you fit into this category then chances are you do, but don't despair, because there's not a human being alive who hasn't seen something about themselves they don't like. Therefore, by answering some simple questions, you may once again discover you don't like what you see or hear. Only this time it may just prompt you into making some enquiries that may well lead to life-changing discoveries.

This challenge could be your greatest achievement, just as long as you follow through, and be honest. So, if in the meantime you need some inspiration and further encouragement, just think about why you are reading this section of the book to begin with. By doing so, you may well want to escape from the way you currently live, reshape your way of thinking and give yourself and your family the best opportunity in life. Even if you're not eventually convinced, remain open-minded enough to challenge yourself by further discovering more about how you currently live and making that all important comparison to how you could be living.

This is what you are now encouraged to do, so give it a go and start by adopting your new mantra to - pause, reflect then engage. Try this sequence of events before you attempt to speak or act. In other words, the second you feel your blood boiling urging you to respond verbally or physically, stop your immediate thought process and instead relax. Then take a few deep breaths, thinking more in terms of being positive and ignoring anything negative. You have now lowered the temperature, having given some thought on reflection, allowing you to think rationally. So, unless you have had a lobotomy, which I very much dealt with you have, your conscience will take over and instinctively guide you to what's right and what's wrong. So, listen and learn from what your conscience tells you, then having done so, only you can decide which way you want to go.

Let's get started with some questions you may think of as trivial, however, they are relevant and have a meaningful connection with what we are discussing. When returning home from work, or after some time away, do you call out to your wife or partner as acknowledgement that you have arrived home? Do you then approach her with pleasantries and or make a loving gesture? Do you then seek out your children to engage, and embrace?

Answering no to those scenarios reveals a severe lack of care, compassion and commitment to those who love you, because to them it's deeply personal and now disappointing. Your family is aware of your presence and thrives on you returning home, as you're the one person above all else, they look up to and want to draw inspiration from. They want you to be their hero, yet they are sadly let down, and the more times this happens the deeper the cut into their already open wound.

Can you understand the significance of your failure to bond in this way with your family, and the lasting effects it has on you all? How does it make you truly feel? Surely your conscience is prodding you at this very moment, and if so, then it's doing its job, and all you need to do is answer that call.

But don't despair, by simply adjusting your anxiety and relaxing your emotions, you will experience a sense of overwhelming relief. In truth, you don't know why your defensive mechanism leans more toward hostility or resistance. This is especially true in a home where there's a constant level of distrust when verbal conversation takes place, as it invariably becomes a misconception or perceived as a personal attack.

So, what is the benefit of this behaviour? What do you possibly get from making everyone around you, including yourself, miserable? You know the answer, yet you allow yourself to be controlled, when you could easily be the one in control. Simply confront this problem you have by putting in place a new strategy to take back your life.

Dysfunctional Families

— Having done so, chances are you will ask yourself why you remained on the dark side for so long, denying yourself and your family those lost magic moments. —

The good news is you can easily rectify your situation, but again, only if you open your mind and your heart, acknowledging there's strong merit in what you are reading. So, let's put some solutions in place that puts you in a much better state of mind. Let's remind ourselves again of your new mantra to pause - reflect then engage, being the best possible reset process there could ever be, by not allowing any type of conversation, action, or detail, become an instant problem for you. So again, by using your mantra regularly, you're creating a space to pause, to settle your emotions, to think constructively, swapping hostility with rationality, acting with real confidence, experiencing a deep feeling of satisfaction. Ultimately finding what's missing in your life- peace.

The time has now come—the moment you asked where you were going wrong-when it's crucial to stop and truly reflect on what's been happening in your life. You wanted a wife and family, and now that you have them, it's time to live up to the responsibility that comes with it. Being a husband and father isn't just about having a family, it's about being present, accountable, and emotionally attached to the needs of those who love you.

— Recognizing dysfunctional behaviour is a good start. —

The next time someone speaks to you, try to spend more time listening without feeling the urge to interject. Then take a moment to reflect on how that interaction affected you. Did it stir up any anger within you, if so, did the anger subside the spilt second you reminded yourself you have your mantra as further backup. All possible because you engaged in your fortitude that provided you with both willpower and discipline that aligns perfectly with your mantra. All of which empowers you by giving you the control to remain rational and responsible. It just keeps on giving, whereby you will discover the benefits of being caring and showing compassion, since it has its own way of rewarding those when they least expect it.

So, having addressed working on resolving your personal issues as they present themselves, you will settle down until the next time you feel you need to respond, however, by not responding also speaks volumes. Only the next time, you will instantly adjust by accepting and using your mantra and becoming rational. By doing so you will take control of your anxiety, by handling the conversation as the man of the house should. It's what's expected of you, and surely, it's what you would expect from yourself.

You may ask, "What's the big deal about how I greet my wife and kids when I get home from work?" and that's a reasonable question. Again, we all act, respond and see life differently, in ways that align with our own disposition, being our makeup, our characteristics and beliefs.

We all naturally develop our own individual personality without having to study or train, again shaped by our characteristics, our upbringing and life's influences. This provides us all with our own unique way in how we manage ourselves, it's what shapes our demeanor, allowing us all to choose our own path, as others have chosen theirs. The problem being, do we ever stop to consider the path we are on, and can our mantra and fortitude help us to go in the right direction- As sure as night follows day, it can.

— Isn't it time you thought more about the way you are programmed? --

It then comes as no surprise that men, perhaps like yourself, living in a dysfunctional lifestyle, have neither any concept nor thought process of how you could be otherwise living, because you have never given it any thought. It may be that you were deprived of the sort of upbringing every human being needs and deserves from early childhood.

It's what many of us take for granted, having received those precious family values during the many happy childhood years. It provides the means for long-lasting and fond memories that we never tire of, reminiscing and telling the same stories over again. So hopefully the penny has dropped, and you now realise that you have never been taught any skills or obtained any knowledge of how to raise a family and maintain a loving relationship. That's the missing link in your life and so many others like you, acting the way do you do, unfortunately you're in a confused state of mind.

When you're alone, it's natural to slip into a quiet, passive mental state. But the moment a stranger addresses you, your mind shifts into composure and rationality. This is part of our social programming — we instinctively present ourselves with calmness and respect around unfamiliar people. As soon as a voice is directed at us, we become alert to its tone, triggering an automatic internal assessment: do we respond defensively, or with measured curiosity.

Unlike the shattering nervous reaction, most humans experience when subjected to aggressive, loud, obnoxious ranting and raving, a behaviour that needs no introduction or further evaluation. It's that gut wrenching feeling we all prefer to avoid like the plague, pushing our anxiety, stress, and emotional levels to their limit. Worse still, when it becomes all too clear that the behaviour is coming from a family member, namely you.

So, before you get home from work, just imagine how your wife and kids are feeling, being consciously but cautiously aware of your pending arrival and looking forward to seeing you. Yet you fail to acknowledge your family in the way they expect you to, causing them to become disillusioned. Through time, your behaviour only draws on negative outcomes, rejection and resentment, causing arguments, being disrespectful, and escalating from verbal to physical aggression. The evolution of dysfunctional living.

Can you really imagine what this is like for your family, caught up in this reign of terror, inadvertently becoming co-conspirators? This is a tragedy brought on by human instinct for survival, only to perpetuate the scourge of your escalating aggression. You planted this seed long ago and now it flourishes because of your inability to control its growth.

This shared mindset has made it far easier for abusive behaviour to take systemic root—what starts out being subtle and sometimes innocent innuendos, which quickly escalates into insults, and verbal aggression. It's now spiralled out of control, reinforcing the very culture that you have allowed to overwhelm your family.

— It's what you are solely responsible for --

This family feud is soon over, temporarily, with everyone going to bed licking their wounds having no real concept of what the earlier confrontation was all about. Even in the quietest moments they now find relief alone in their bed, consumed by despair, wrapped in sadness and regret whilst beneath the covers—here lies the lasting impact of growing up in a dysfunctional family.

Preventing and Ending Domestic Abuse

Try to fathom the incredible benefits of giving just half of the time you waste on orchestrating in-house fighting at home, intentionally or not, and putting all that wasted energy into something so much more rewarding. Becoming respected by your friends and peers, reaching your goals, fulfilling your dreams, and recognising your accomplishments. By doing so, it comes with a greater reward, because all the while your devoted wife and children become proud, remaining loyal because they only ever wanted to love you.

Understand the logic in what you are reading. Would your employer tolerate that same conduct at work that you display at home, or would you be reprimanded and possibly issued with a warning? You know all too well it's the latter, because your employer would never put up with that type of behaviour, so why are you doing it in your own home?

It's because unlike being at work, you get away with it while at home and you know it, and therefore you also know it's a cowardly act, since no one has the capabilities of stopping you with your thuggish behaviour. A common trait by many men in your position, believing you need to maintain an authoritarian presence. - How wrong you are.

If, during this very moment in time while reading, you feel a sense of remorse, then this is the perfect time to sit with your wife and family and ask them what they like about living at home. Do this without being coercive or domineering, because that will only prompt them to provide you with the answers you want to hear. Doing so is only wasting your time and frustratingly theirs. Instead, try a genuine approach with a tone to match, so your family can feel relaxed and comfortable around you. Allowing your family to speak freely will provide them with the release they need, while you hear the truth. So, listen intently, and take in everything that is said, and hopefully experience the emotion that your family feels. By doing so, you have just crossed over into the zone of showing compassion and being caring. Why not give it a go?

— *It's time to stop fighting, and time to man up.* --

You may also hear grievances you were completely unaware of, while at the same time allowing yourself to demonstrate that you can listen without interjecting. Never a better time than now, for you to relinquish your normal way of life and allow this moment to take its course. When having a conversation with your family, during this time do what you know you must do, pause, reflect before engaging. Having done so, the chances are you won't mention what you initially thought about saying all because you gave yourself time to think it over, other than just reacting and blurting it out. By demonstrating your willingness to sit with your wife and family, it shows your strength and courage as a genuine leader and relaxes your insecurities. By doing so, you build on establishing respect for yourself and the trust you need from your family.

Continue to work on your temperament, as we just discussed, being so important for you to maintain your self-control. As a result, your family will sense there's a change in the air, which will make them both excited and relieved. However, your work has just begun and in doing so you will receive as much personal pleasure and enjoyment as your family will, by believing in starting a complete overhaul of the family's living standards.

Start by coming home and willingly greet the family with a simple "how was your day" with an embrace, placing everyone in an instant feel-good mood. Just think about how that would also make you feel. Once you start this process, the experience will be so uplifting the whole family feels the connection, the warmth, and the trust. It becomes less about fixing everything at once, and more about creating space for healing through small, consistent acts of compassion. These simple gestures could be the first ripple in turning former chaos into a happy home, sharing peace, love, and harmony—Something you will be proud of.

Other than having to remind yourself of the all-too-common scenarios many males in similar scenarios find themselves in when coming home from work only to find their wife and children have packed their bags and moved on? The irony here is, many men like yourself believe you have the family situation in hand only to find out the hard way, by discovering your family has had enough of you and left seeking a better life.

The reality of the family having left home can easily bring the hardest man to his knees. Sadly, in this case, that equates to the weakest man, because of his inability to have been strong, and failing to provide real leadership when it was most needed.

If you fit into this category, then it's time for you to act by continuing to read and make positive changes. It's so achievable, just think in terms of gradual progression, day by day, step by step. If you don't believe that your family is more important, then why are you prolonging the inevitable. Why continue to cause heartache when you know you should end the cruelty and move on with your life.

Or perhaps you can't be found because you're lost, making it extremely difficult for anyone else to reach you, other than giving you advice to seek help from a professional. However, the remedy is right under your nose, by leaning on your family differently, and exposing your vulnerabilities. This is nothing to be ashamed of, rather a way of showing a side of you not seen before, and your family will respect you for it.

— Are you ready to accept their help? —

This is an enormous problem for many men, having followed suit in the tradition of marriage, without fully appreciating or comprehending what they are getting themselves into. By first understanding what the expectations and the workings surrounding the responsibilities and the commitments that are needed. Then to experience the rewards being a wonderful trade-off when giving and receiving love.

'You don't know what you've got until it's gone'- such a profound adage, and so true, with far too many males destined to experience it firsthand. That emptiness, a feeling like no other, that could never be truly understood or described unless you find yourself in that position.

Such is this roller coaster ride you're on right now, feeling uplifted one minute having been brought back down to earth the next. This kind of emotional desperation tends to surface only after the damage is done. The realisation dawns—often too late—that many men having become their own worst enemy all along. Their mindset and short-sightedness led to an inevitable downfall, and once it all unravels, they're left grappling with the question - why me.

Hopefully, you haven't reached the point where your family has already left, although you just felt that pain, - isn't that true? If you indeed felt a dagger through the heart, having imagined the above scenario of losing your family, then rest assured you want your family more than you are aware. That shock horror you just experienced is all you need to make the changes you know must happen, and that time is now.

Assuming you still have your entire life in front of you, without restriction, that's something to be truly grateful for. If you're feeling somewhat a little overwhelmed then it could well be you are experiencing a quiet reckoning—not with regret, but with the emerging sense that something better is now possible. This is by far the greatest acknowledgment that your conscience is calling you out on. A powerful concept rooted in how we maintain our sense of self-worth, a reaffirmation. Especially when self-worth and integrity are under threat, as is yours.

So, what lends itself -in order- for so many males to live a counterproductive life, having almost kidnapped the rights of their own family. Life inevitably presents ongoing challenges, including maintaining steady employment, handling finances, and others, yet it's our innate resilience and adaptability that enables us to navigate our way through. However, due to your inability to act responsibly - as the head of the family should-, you allow yourself to become corrupted by stooping as low as possible and allowing dysfunctional behaviour to act as your keeper.

In many circumstances many dysfunctional households overextend their financial limitations, whilst managing their financial obligations and constantly struggle. Again, no excuse for your behavior.

Finding a solution makes much more sense by simply following your new mantra. Having become rational, contact the people you are indebted to -if it's financial- and simply explain your situation. They will understand your predicament and provide you with the help you need. Then seek help from a financial advisor to look into restructuring your finances. Living beyond your means is the biggest battle far too many couples face, a precursor for dysfunctional standards. By living within your means you will revitalise your entire life, releasing an enormous weight from your shoulders. As a result, you won't feel so inclined to become angry and looking to release frustration on others. - Swap credit cards for debit cards, and you will never look back.

Organise some time with the family away from home, the simple things in life like camping, and watching your family bond. Having fun and watching them grow, going back to basics, where you're not allowing home life to be the centre of your universe. Use this time to reflect on your conduct while watching your family enjoy themselves, releasing family tension allows you to relax, mind, body and soul. Use your senses and discover how your kids instinctively gravitate toward you, where aggressive behaviour is all but a distant memory. Imagine that for a while.

Discover how that type of bonding plays such a big part in the family home, while you begin paying interest into the children's schooling. Then to see their faces when their dad helps them along, giving them a quiet word of encouragement. Children are inquisitive and eager to learn; they want to hear their dads' stories and get excited by them. They want to ask their father questions and to hear honest answers. As they become more spirited, they gain confidence as they grow older. All the while they continue to admire and respect you for being there for them.

There is no better way for a father to audit his own progression than by sitting around the dinner table with his family acting as any father should. With the family now wearing what appears to be a new disguise, having become instinctively happier because of newfound happiness that continues to permeate throughout the home. The absence of frowned faces and digital temptations while at the table is clearly a great improvement you can be proud of. You will learn more about your family in one sitting at the dinner table than during the entire day.

Take advantage of the situation, allowing the family to talk while you continue with your quiet observation. Interjecting, only having exercised your mantra then to discover the conversation continuing in the same civilized tone around the table, as your family remains encouraged by your words. You will continue to guide your family and indeed yourself in natural harmony, with a renewed passion for family gatherings, and look forward

Dysfunctional Families

to sitting together as a family each and every day for dinner. Experiencing unforgettable moments while the reality of life slowly but inevitably shows it hand by revealing one less plate on the table until it's just you and your wife.

Should you have any doubts about restructuring your life and that of your family, then read over that last paragraph along with the earlier chapter on dysfunctional families and discover the woman who also sought change in her life. Having become inspired by her friend's intervention, she became empowered and learnt how to reinvent herself, using her fortitude to manage whatever obstacles crossed her path. Discover how this woman's friend told her the story about her upbringing in a dysfunctional family and her father coming home to an empty house, only to realise his wife and children had gone, never to return.

– Use the recommendations and advice given, again starting with rediscovering your own fortitude, which is coming up in a new chapter. - It's there waiting for you-.

So, why not go somewhere quiet to gather your thoughts and become inspired to read this section again and then talk to the one person you fell in love with, your wife. The one person in your entire universe who will support, love and encourage you, and together you can both change the way you currently live. Again, this can be accomplished with simple step-by-step procedures and start living as all united and loving families should.

Imagine growing old and knowing you raised your children to be respectful of themselves and others, a direct result of your influence on their lives. A father's most endearing legacy lives in the hearts of his family, not in monuments or history books. Through his honesty, he imparts a moral compass that shapes their choices throughout their lives.

Is the letter below the type of recognition you would like to receive one day from your children?

Dad, remember the hard times, the confusion, the tension, the moments when everything felt uncertain and heavy. There were days when it was easier to run away, because as kids we carried the weight of things we didn't fully understand. The anger, the silence, the mistakes—they shaped our world for a while. But what shaped us even more was what came after; your decision to change.

I want to thank you dad—not just for becoming the father we needed, but for showing us that people can choose a better path. Your determination for change provided the best path forward. You rebuild trust, you brought back laughter, and most of all, you gave us hope. Now, when we look at our family, we don't just see what we came through, we see what we became because of you. And that's a legacy stronger than any pain we left behind. We love you, Dad.

And from your wife, the hero in this story, who reshaped your entire world.

To my husband, your accomplishments can't be measured by trophies or accolades, but by the quiet strength you've shown in turning your life around. You chose growth over comfort, responsibility over excuses, and love over pride. You've created a home filled with honesty, safety, and care—and in doing so, you've given us far more than we could have ever asked for. I see the man you are today, and I'm proud—not just of who you've become, but of the journey we took together in getting there. Your loving wife-

— Is that worth fighting for? —

THE ELDERLY

When we talk about the elderly, we generally think in terms of love and respect for the huge contribution they made throughout their lives. Whilst many family members and friends acknowledge this by caring and making regular visits, there are those who don't, preferring to prey on their vulnerability like circling vultures.

Many elderly people are left feeling used up as though their purpose in life is no longer required. Therefore, a stark reminder for those who are entering their golden years, that whilst it's perfectly normal to expect and receive ongoing love and help, the reality as time goes on, can be quite different.

In many cases one of neglect and abandonment that can become an all too familiar way of life, and one you need to prepare for. Because unless our lives are cut short, we all must face reaching an age where increased support, dignity, and connection become more important than ever. Therefore, never take it for granted the older you get the more attention you receive, because if you do, you're either one of the lucky ones, or it's the sort of attention you never gave much thought about. Making inroads sooner rather than later into what your expectations and wishes are for your later years in terms of your health and your assets, keeps your life in order. By doing so, you stand a much better chance of achieving the outcome that aligns with your wishes, and indeed your mental wellbeing.

> **CAUTION** – Lets remain mindful, the perpetrators who haven't reached that age yet would do well to remember, 'What goes around comes around', another adage of significance. Because the day may come when they themselves become vulnerable due to old age, where they too could experience firsthand the feeling of being neglected and abused.

Time you looked at the bigger picture

Being an elderly woman, whether in a relationship or living alone offers no immunity from the many types of abuse. So, ask yourself, is it time I looked at the bigger picture? Many women have already endured ongoing domestic abuse throughout their lives, making this a heartbreaking reflection on the challenges they now potentially face.

Human beings can be unscrupulous, as seen by the actions of supposedly loving family members who go to extraordinary lengths to fight over assets and money—often at the expense of some unsuspecting elderly person.

– Is it time to become that wise old owl?

"The wise old owl lived in an oak; the more she saw, the less she spoke; the less she spoke, the more she heard; why can't we all be like that wise old bird?" –

The Elderly

Having your last Will and testament organized is essential and puts any unscrupulous family members, friends, and in some cases professionals on notice. Therefore, ensure you consult with a professional lawyer that comes highly recommended, and qualified in your circumstances. Someone who remains unbiased not associated with any of your family members, friends or acquaintances.

Consider the following…

The key difference between a will and a power of attorney lies in their purpose and timing:

Will: A will is a legal document that outlines your wishes for the distribution of your assets and belongings after your death. It may also:

- specify guardianship for children or pets.
- only take effect after you pass away.
- appoint an executor who is responsible for carrying out your instructions.

Power of Attorney: A power of attorney allows you to appoint someone to make decisions on your behalf while you are still alive. These decisions may be financial, personal, or medical. It takes effect during your lifetime, particularly if you are unable to manage your affairs due to illness, injury, or absence.

There are different types, such as…

General – for specific or short-term purposes.

Enduring – continues even if you lose decision-making capacity.

Understanding the role of the executor of your will…

Applying for probate: Confirms the validity of the will and grants the executor legal authority to act.

Preserving assets: Ensures the deceased's assets are secured and maintained until distribution.

Paying debts and taxes: Settles outstanding debts and lodges required tax returns on behalf of the estate.

Distributing assets: Allocates the estate according to the instructions in the will.

Handling disputes: Manages or defends the estate if the will is contested.

Organising funeral arrangements: In some cases, the executor may also oversee funeral planning and related services.

Being an executor is both an honour and a significant responsibility, requiring careful attention to legal and financial matters.

Appointing a power of attorney can be highly beneficial, providing essential support in managing your affairs when you're unable to. However, it also carries potential risks, as the decisions made may not always align with your wishes. This is why it's crucial to understand fully what it means to grant someone power of attorney before appointing anyone. Ensure you are confident in their judgment and aware of the extent of the authority you are giving them. It's that important.

A will ensures your wishes are respected after your death, while a power of attorney safeguards your interests during your lifetime. The executor manages and settles your estate once you have passed.

Ques: "I'm getting on in life and didn't realise how my situation could have such a big impact on me and so many other people, where do I start?"

Ans: "By simply doing what you are doing, thinking more about the impact and the potential hurdles you face from both a personal and legal perspective. There's no need to rush into anything, other than to get some advice from a third-party professional. Without the necessity for anyone else to know, unless you believe you are in a secure genuine and compassionate relationship. If you are a pensioner with limited funds, you can receive free consultation from your community legal centre who will assist you on a whole range of matters, so why not make a call right now."

Again, before signing any documentation, discuss with a lawyer and understand precisely the processes and changes a power of attorney can make while you are alive.

An all-too-familiar tragedy for the elderly is falling foul of the very people they would never have suspected of treating them in any other way than with total respect and integrity. Shamefully in many respects, that's human nature and a hard lesson to avoid at all costs.

— Greed never satisfies; it only craves more —

You have the lawful right to change your will and the power of attorney you have appointed, provided you are deemed competent to make such decisions. However, this introduces a contentious and often debated issue—mental health. Even if you believe yourself to be cognitively sound and in full control, there is a genuine concern that external forces may be at play. This equates to others holding differing opinions about your capacity, intentions, and vulnerability. These differing opinions can lead to disputes, delays, or even legal challenges, especially if family members, carers, or professionals suspect undue influence, confusion, or cognitive decline.

In such cases, your autonomy may be questioned, not because of your actual mental state, but because of perceptions shaped by age, circumstance, or interpersonal dynamics. This is particularly true for elderly individuals who are navigating grief, isolation, or complex family relationships.

> **CAUTION** Use the term *"dementia"* with great care. It's a label that is far too easily applied by people who have no qualifications — and sometimes by those with questionable motives. Once that word is spoken, others may begin doubting your independence long before any proper assessment is made. Even with a diagnosis, your legal rights remain intact, but the way people treat you can change dramatically. This is why staying informed, staying mentally active, and safeguarding your decision-making authority as early as possible is so important.

— A retrospective thought before that troubling event potentially unfolds —

Imagine, as difficult as it may be to contemplate or comprehend, almost within an instant you've gone from making sound decisions as you have done your whole life, to suddenly being seen as someone who has lost their faculties. Whether or not the diagnosis of dementia is true, it becomes irrelevant to those with greed in their eyes, who have now achieved their aim. You then suddenly find yourself spoken to in a condescending and almost childlike manner, even though you know with absolute certainty that your mind remains as coherent and intact as ever.

If you believe you have fallen victim to a type of medical diagnosis exploitation, demand a second opinion. Speak up, make yourself heard, and seek an ally to stand by you. Don't let anyone convince you that your mental capacity is diminished when you know, with absolute certainty it is not.

While others may dispute the specifics of such a prognosis, the decision ultimately rests with you. If you still possess clarity of thought and conviction, act now—sooner rather than later. Take steps to safeguard your freedom and autonomy while your voice remains strong and your trust in human nature remains intact.

If you are a genuinely caring and loving family member, or a trusted friend, aware of someone who may be in this predicament, this is your opportunity to also exercise your rights by offering assistance.

— A far cry from the days when the term 'becoming a little senile' was commonly used and accepted as a natural degenerative cognitive progression. As mentioned, we often hear that all too convenient and familiar word dementia, a tone that has a more intense authoritarian and frightening appeal aligned to it. Not unlike the times when people were referred to as lepers, another type of social ignorance. —

Swap that crossword for legal advice

It is important to remain aware that in some countries, a guardian or administrator can be appointed on your behalf in certain situations, often without your knowledge. This underscores the necessity of having your assets and possessions *securely* protected through a robust, ironclad will. Again, in your will you can designate executors and trustees to manage your estate, trust accounts and other assets. By doing so, ensuring they are safeguarded from ambiguity, potential disputes and legal challenges.

As it does to accept the fact that although it's -in all likelihood- the elderly's sons and or daughters—who have the most to gain— maintain their integrity, worldwide statistics confirm that those you raised are more prone to abusing and misusing their power. This is particularly true if they feel they may be deprived of what they consider their rightful inheritance.

– That adage, 'if you want something done, do it yourself –

Fortunately, there are elderly people in this world who will act decisively and take professional advice <u>early</u>. Many of whom make secretive decisions that don't prove too popular with the family by signing everything over to a charity of their choice, perhaps an animal refuge. However, by doing so, it alleviates any stress about having to make awkward decisions and worrying about other people's personal views - especially having to decide who is worthy and who isn't.

Keeping the previous paragraph in mind serves as a vital preventative measure, shedding light on the ignorance that exists within us all. This awareness can act as a safeguard against internal conflicts, preventing siblings from mistreating one another and becoming estranged. Tragic outcomes that often lead to irreparable relationships and ongoing family disputes, with many spiralling into other forms of domestic abuse. By recognizing the very real possibility of family turmoil early on, you can take steps to prevent future consequences, while ensuring that your will remains private.

As a family member or friend, should you have any doubts or reservations about your involvement or entitlements towards safeguarding the rights of your elderly loved ones, then just pause for a second. Now, imagine yourself lying alone in your bed, perhaps in a nursing or aged care home, realizing you were coerced into signing something you didn't fully understand. Only to discover your human rights and liberties you rightfully and deservedly took for granted, had been stripped away from you, having been told you have dementia. A compelling and gross injustice, you then suddenly comprehend the hopelessness of it all, and the on-going entrapment that now surrounds you.

The mistreatment of many elderly individuals - especially within some aged care and nursing homes - is both deeply disturbing and well-documented. Cases of sexual, physical, psychological, and emotional abuse continue to surface, painting a sobering picture of the enormity of the abuse many older people face in later life. It's essential to prepare for such possibilities, even if you're convinced, you'll never enter residential care. Life can take unexpected turns when there are unforeseen forces at play. It is wiser to think through and explore any worries or doubts you have now—while your mind is clear and you have this book as guidance. Other than ignoring them and later ending up in a situation wishing you had and feeling completely helpless and unhappy.

Security must mean everything to you

One of the best ways to ensure your current safety is to investigate the type of home security that best suits your personal circumstances and make the necessary changes and improvements. Including the installation of proper purpose locks, cameras and alarms, and for those living in aged care homes to have an internally installed camera and enhanced audio system. Ensure a caring friend or family member assists you with this important task, sooner than later.

This will in most cases capture any type of abuse, should an elderly person not be capable of making a complaint themselves. Family members, friends, or executive power of attorney should ensure that these recommendations are carried out. Never assume it's a waste of time, because when security cameras and audio are working correctly, humans almost invariably get caught.

It continues to be one of the biggest problems associated with abuse on seniors, that being, it generally goes unreported because it's undetected. Attention to detail is unfortunately not one of human nature's strongest points, therefore the truth of the matter can be altogether different. – Always be mindful of suspicious behaviour.

The Elderly

As unthinkable as it may seem, sexual abuse amongst the elderly is also unquestionably a problem since it is very real. Again, due partly to elderly vulnerability as is their inability in many instances to comprehend events. As a result, many of these establishments adopt the 'nothing to see here mentality'.

All because of the lack of proper training, implementation of better robust safety control measures, monitoring and auditing. Along with the undeniable facts that surround the inadequacies and lack of compassion by many employees.

— Sadly, many people who obtain these roles as care givers do not have the natural attributes associated with someone who possesses both caring and compassionate characteristics-

Ques: "What type of security do you suggest?"

Ans: "Start by contacting the many businesses and services available, including 'My Aged Care' and make enquiries. 'Live life alarms' - a government-funded pendants & watches with fall detection, GPS, and emergency response. 'Services Australia' - Elder Safety: Offers guidance on home safety, elder abuse prevention, and emergency contacts. Discuss with a trusted family member or friend to assist you or make calls to other professionals who install other smart monitoring devices. Offering emergency alerts, real time visual and movement tracking with motion sensors. These are just a few of the modern devices that can provide real-time notifications, alerts, protecting the elderly better than at any time before. - Get proper protection."

— For better security, keep abreast with technology, regardless of your age. —

As humans progressively grow older, they become more isolated and relaxed, becoming easily intimated, even more easily persuaded, believing mostly in the good of humanity, becoming less inquisitive, offering little objection. This is a consequence of life's ageing process, which sadly demonstrates a state of weakness. Consequently, it becomes identified as a green light for further exploitation by unscrupulous behaviour, all because many elderly people have a developed mindset in simply wanting to help other people.

Trust and boundaries!

We all need to be on our guard in life, particularly now that the digital age of scams has put a new meaning on being taken advantage of, and in so many ways. As mentioned throughout this book, it's poor control over our human emotions being the weakest link, during highly sensitive and complex matters, that can cause poor decision and choice making.

All because of the loving and caring nature of the many decent elderly people, where for many it has become normal practice to again simply agree and say yes, with little thought about deception.

There's probably no other type of situation in life that raises more eyebrows and gossip than when the elderly consider starting a new relationship. As stated in the earlier chapter on-line dating, social media and dating platforms show the relative ease of becoming potentially profiled for all the wrong reasons.

He's likely had past relationships which makes it all the more important to understand his history—and why he reached out to you at this time. That insight matters. Pause and reflect on his true intentions and make a conscious effort to uncover them. At this stage in your life, the last thing you need is to let someone with hidden motives - a type of charlatan - disturb your peace. Especially when a man presents himself as grounded, only for you to discover that beyond his charm and confidence, there's very little substance.

Should it be the case you decide to end the relationship and move on, is one thing. However, to rid this person once you have allowed him into your life and possibly your home can be an entirely different matter altogether. They may include various forms of abusive behaviour such as early stalking, financial manipulation, verbal or emotional abuse. Each causes unnecessary stress and anxiety at a stage in your life, when it's the last thing you ever need.

The Elderly

Transparent verification

It may seem to some as being a little dramatic, however, ask yourself this: why are police checks there to begin with? The answer is to provide information on whether a certain person has a criminal record. Therefore, if the person you intend to see has a previous domestic violence record, wouldn't you want to know about it? Let's assume you have been in a previous abusive domestic relationship, wouldn't the possibility of it happening again cause further anxiety. It's not too much to ask of anyone wanting to get close to you, to provide a police clearance check, keep in mind, if a male has nothing to hide, he will be forthcoming with your request.

Several companies offer this service, but only with the applicant's consent. While public record offices maintain archived court and police materials, these collections relate to historic cases and are tightly controlled. They do not provide access to current police databases or recent criminal history, which remain restricted to authorised agencies.

Again, imagine the shock of discovering that a new romantic partner has a criminal history, particularly one involving past domestic abuse. In such a case, early awareness is crucial—far better to uncover the truth at the beginning of a relationship than to learn the hard way when the damage is already done.

Therefore, it's best to remind yourself that now is the time to reflect on any past mistakes you may have encountered, during earlier relationships. So, without sounding patronizing it's recommended that you read the first three chapters, on dating, courting and engagement. Think of it as a refresher as well as the opportunity for perhaps some reminiscing and a few laughs. Not surprisingly, if you haven't dated for a while, you may discover very little has changed on the human side of nature when it comes to finding true love. Other than the types of scrupulous conduct now associated with some forms of on-line dating.

Ques: "I lost my husband some years ago and although I would like to have male company, I'm just not sure about the possible gain versus the pain. I sometimes ask myself if I should bother trying to find another partner?"

Ans: "The legacy of being in a former relationship and finding yourself alone as you well know, can be daunting but shouldn't act as a deterrent to finding a decent man. If you're worried about the degree of possible pain, then don't just fall for human charm and persuasion. Instead opt for making discoveries on merit and his true motives, for being interested in you. Again, any man in his later years who isn't prepared to provide a woman with a criminal history police check, either has something to hide, or is potentially revealing his true intentions towards you. Either way carry out your due diligence very carefully."

As we discussed during the on-line dating chapter, the same precautions apply when speaking to a stranger over the phone, another widely known and accepted digital form of communication. Yet it remains a space where con artists hide and thrive, relying solely on the power of anonymity and persuasive conversation. These confidence tricksters masterfully alternate between subtle intimidation and emotional manipulation, influencing their targets who ultimately become their victims.

If you don't have the phone protection you need, then ensure you get someone to organise it for you, including your service provider, to stop any unwanted unsolicited calls. Unfortunately, there will always be elderly individuals who either ignore or cannot recognize the warnings signs. The moment many of the elderly hear a voice on the other end of the phone; they can become entranced—especially when the caller adopts an authoritative tone or presents themselves as warm and trustworthy. In many instances by claiming to represent a government department or company, these scammers exploit their victims' sense of duty, making them feel obligated to comply and ultimately pay up.

Instead, learn to interrupt the caller by saying "No thank-you" and hang the phone up. Or take down their details and make enquiries or ask a responsible person to do so on your behalf, before agreeing to anything.

The Elderly

But never, ever provide payment on anything that you're not one-hundred percent sure of, as importantly ensure it's something you feel good inside about.

It doesn't matter who they claimed to be, or what they claimed to want, it's all about your peace of mind, your stress and anxiety levels. Falling into confusion is dangerously easy. Before you realize it, you've handed over credit card details, and after hanging up the phone, you're left unsure of what just happened. The consequences often only become clear when you discover your bank account has been compromised. The victim of yet another scam. In today's world, such fraud has become alarmingly commonplace, and it would appear our money transactions were a lot safer before the digital world. If banks still exist!

Therefore, ensure you have made every effort, having put all safeguards in place, particularly requesting verification codes sent to you, regularly changing username and passwords. Better still, continue with the old fashion method of going into the bank—if possible—where there's high degree of accountability that offers a much greater level of safety and old-fashioned service.

This is the kind of vulnerability and the daily abuse that many elderly people face: being scammed through the rising tide of digital fraud, now the preferred method of exploitation worldwide. It's a threat that affects us all, yet one that could so easily be prevented with a touch more common sense. Whether through your own vigilance or with the support of a trusted family member or friend who can help manage your financial affairs.

We are all aware of the temptations and of course the ease that exists when purchasing online, but let's remind ourselves of the stress associated with financial abuse. Instead let's also remember the enjoyment of heading out to shop, never knowing who you might meet.

If in fact you can leave your home, isn't it better to interact and engage with real-life human beings, experiencing the satisfaction that comes with having made a personal and safer transaction while receiving an instant bona fide receipt? Along with the possible excitement of instantly receiving possession and taking home your goods, all the while having had an experience without the fear of being financial abused.

In the event you can leave home, isn't it better to interact and engage with a real-life human being, and experience the a caring person will help you purchase online from a reputable supplier, but again, don't try doing it yourself unless you feel you are competent enough.

Remember, unlike in the days gone by when decency and accountability meant so much more, when greed wasn't as arguably as prevalent or seemingly as fashionable as it is today, you must take extra precautions in everything you do.

SUMMARY

- Elderly individuals should be respected for their lifelong contributions, yet many face neglect, abandonment, or exploitation, sadly by those closest to them.
- Elder abuse takes multiple forms, including financial, emotional, and physical mistreatment, with family members and trusted individuals sometimes acting dishonorably.
- Lawyers/Executors/Power of Attorney and indeed trusted family members and friends can all play a crucial role in ensuring a senior's wishes are fulfilled, requiring diligence in handling assets, debts, disputes, and legal obligations.
- Seniors must remain cautious about being unfairly declared mentally incompetent, in many cases for control and financial gain. Seeking second opinions and legal intervention is vital.
- Early preparation—through legal frameworks, selecting trustworthy executors, and drafting a clear Will—is essential in preventing exploitation and ensuring security.

The Elderly

- Elder abuse often arises from entitlement and greed, with family members being statistically more likely to take advantage of their elderly parents.
- Seniors should act proactively, even if decisions—such as signing assets over to charity—prove unpopular with family members.
- Aged care facilities can be sites of mistreatment, including physical, emotional, and even sexual abuse, often because of poor oversight, inadequate training and care.
- Enhancing home security and installing hidden cameras are crucial measures, providing evidence when protecting the elderly.
- Unreported abuse remains a significant issue, as family members may dismiss, or not recognise signs of mistreatment. Careful monitoring and proper protective measures can help prevent harm.
- Some aged care institutions adopt a "secretive" approach, failing to address abuse, due to the loss of reputation, litigation issues, and basically a lack of integrity and compassion.
- As individuals age, they become more trusting, increasing their risk of manipulation, financial fraud, and exploitation.
- Digital scams present new dangers for seniors, requiring vigilance and awareness to avoid deception.
- Elderly individuals seeking relationships should remain cautious, discreetly assessing potential partners for their ulterior motives including financial exploitation.
- Conducting background checks before committing to a relationship can prevent emotional, financial, and physical harm.

Preventing and Ending Domestic Abuse

- Seniors must reflect on past experiences and apply lessons leant when forming new relationships, particularly remaining vigilant when using online dating platforms.
- Early awareness and protective measures allow seniors to maintain independence and peace of mind in their later years.
- As seniors age, their trusting nature makes them more vulnerable to manipulation, leading to financial or emotional abuse.
- Scammers use phone calls, emails, and false claims to deceive elderly individuals into handing over money or sensitive information.
- Learning to say, "No thank you" and immediately ending suspicious calls can help prevent falling victim to fraud.
- Visiting banks in person rather than relying on digital transactions can provide a greater level of security.
- Extra precautions—such as verifying purchases, requesting authentication codes, and avoiding impulsive decisions—can safeguard financial well-being.
- Fraud and scams are growing in prevalence requiring vigilance and proactive measures to protect against deception and exploitation.
- We need to acknowledge the difficulty in this industry and remind ourselves of the genuine care and compassion that does exist by the many people working in hospitals, aged care and nursing home facilities.

The Elderly

PERPETRATOR

Since you choose to take advantage of the elderly, what is your area of betrayal? Find your preferred method below and discover how your conscience is about to challenge you like never before. When that reckoning arrives accept it, not as punishment but as a signal, a warning to start your journey to end your style of abuse. This is your opportunity to become a decent human being. Once that happens your transformation takes you to a place of integrity where you experience peace of mind, a place you will never want to leave.

Types of abuse...

Financial Exploitation

- Abuse of power of attorney: Misusing legal authority to access or control assets.
- Inheritance impatience: Pressuring elders to transfer assets prematurely.
- Scams and fraud: Targeting elders with fake investments, romance scams, or identity theft.
- Improper use of funds: Caregivers using an elder's money for personal gain.
- Unpaid bills or missing essentials: Despite having resources, elders may be denied access to their phone and money.

Psychological and Emotional Abuse

- Verbal intimidation: Threats, humiliation, or manipulation to control behaviour.
- Isolation: Preventing contact with friends or family to increase dependency.
- Gaslighting: Undermining memory or perception, especially in those with dementia.

Neglect

- Failure to meet basic needs: Not providing adequate food, hygiene, or medical care.

- Unsafe living conditions: Leaving elders in environments that are unclean or hazardous.

Physical Abuse

- Intentional harm: Hitting, restraining, or physically intimidating an elder.
- Overmedication or withholding medication: Used to control behaviour or reduce care needs.

Sexual Abuse

- Nonconsensual contact: Includes inappropriate touching, forced nudity, or assault.
- Violation of dignity: Mishandling during personal care or bathing.

Institutional Exploitation

- Undertrained or overworked staff: In care facilities, this can lead to neglect or mistreatment.
- Low standards of care: Poor oversight and unsafe environments increase risk.

Whatever your reasoning behind your betrayal it is crucial for you to confront it, then by doing so you will get a better understanding of the profound impact it has - not only on your victim but also on you.

The elderly are among the most vulnerable in our society, having lived their lives filled with contributions, sacrifices, and love. They are parents, grandparents, mentors, and friends, with many possibly having already lost their lifelong partner, therefore highly vulnerable to isolation. Yet, in their later years they face challenges such as declining health, isolation, and financial insecurity, all of which they can prepare for. Unfortunately, what they fail to prepare for are cowards like you, either through family association and believing your self-entitled, or perhaps you're incapable of making your own way in life. All the way through to being a callous spiteful individual who indulges in physical and mental harm.

There is nothing admirable about taking advantage of an elderly person — it leaves you with nothing but emptiness and the quiet sting of your own

The Elderly

conscience. Yet when you choose the opposite path, something remarkable happens, you discover a feeling you may never have experienced before. A deep, genuine sense of fulfilment that comes from doing something kind for someone so vulnerable, a feeling that lifts you, not burdens you. Again, unlike the guilt and self-loathing that always follows you when your conscience finally catches up with you.

Maybe you're the type who prefers the unscrupulous behaviour of conspiring through intimidation to find a way to falsely diagnose the elderly victim with dementia. Stripping them of their autonomy and seizing control of their assets - isolating them from those who could have offered protection, turning their vulnerability into your opportunity for financial and personal gain.

As mentioned, sexual abuse is another heinous and degrading violation that shatters the elderly's sense of self-worth, leaving deep lasting emotional scaring.

While you may believe that your actions carry no consequences, life has a way of turning the tables, therefore try to understand the value in every human life, including your own. This journey will foster growth, connection, and love, therefore by choosing to change, you not only free your victims from suffering, but free yourself.

This is your opportunity; you have the power to become someone so much more than being a perpetrator that holds no value in human life. Start now and discover real self-satisfaction, by giving rather than taking away, and experiencing the rewards. It's not too late - step away from the shadows and into the light, stop wasting your time on such cowardly betrayal. Listen to your conscience, become the person you know you would rather be….

– The choice is all yours. –

DRUGS AND ALCOHOL

Drugs and alcohol carry a pervasive stigma—one that intensifies when linked to addiction and domestic abuse. This stigma affects not only individuals but ripples across society, shaping perceptions and attitudes. These often-synthetic substances remain deeply controversial, especially when misused. For those who self-harm, the consequences can be profound—impacting mental health, emotional stability, and overall well-being, often with devastating outcomes.

Drugs and Alcohol

-Although drugs and alcohol are legally accepted in society, they carry a long-standing reputation for fuelling and intensifying domestic abuse-.

Alcoholism is a well-known issue that frequently unfolds within the family home, often appearing deeply rooted in daily life. Tragically, innocent victims of someone else's drug and alcohol abuse - many of them very young - find themselves trapped, forced to fend for themselves within the confines of their home, enduring severe emotional and physical trauma. A ticking time bomb! It comes with frightening unpredictability, yet fortunately most humans can be exceptionally resilient. As a result, they try to ignore it by getting on with their lives, until of course the genie's out of the bottle.

There are countless reasons why people turn to substance abuse, each shaped by different pressures and circumstances. Yet one perspective points to a weakened sense of self-preservation at the heart of this behaviour — often arising from a lack of understanding about our own natural human traits and the internal mechanisms designed to protect us. These innate tools come in many forms and support us through every physical and emotional challenge, acting as our personal fortification and source of resilience. We will explore these protective capacities further in the next section on 'fortitude'.

As mentioned throughout this book, our fortitude is an extremely powerful and personalised ally. It's your closest friend yet generally ignored simply because of ignorance. Many human beings have little knowledge of their fortitude or even how to use it to their advantage. Instead, substance abusers can only offer token excuses for their behaviour as they are all too aware there can be no justification for their actions, least of all that has any merit, as hard as they try to convince themselves otherwise.

-Other than the sympathy they now receive from the authorities since our lawmakers have thrown them a lifeline, an area we will take a closer look at later in this chapter-.

Many people regard drugs and alcohol as socially acceptable, whether used for relaxation, stress relief, or to cope with daily challenges—prescribed or otherwise. However, moderation is key, and essential for responsible use, though evidence suggests this is the exception rather than the rule. For many, drugs and alcohol become their justification for continued use that can lead to abuse. Of course, there are individuals who consume these substances responsibly by maintaining moderation.

Ques: "Although my partner drinks to excess at times, he remains civil towards me. How can I convince him of his excessive drinking when I know he doesn't believe it?"

Ans: "By monitoring his intake and behaviour and having your say whenever you believe it's inappropriate. It can be a constant battle for men to maintain their beliefs or rather remain insistent that they drink in moderation. It's not an ideal situation, with many women putting up with this substance abuse under constant protest. However, it's when his behaviour has crossed the line you need to turn your beliefs into demands and follow the approach we continue with throughout this book".

In the first three chapters on dating, courting, and engagement, we emphasized the importance of recognizing key traits in a potential partner early on. This awareness allows a woman to make a conscious decision about a particular type of male and the type of relationship that aligns with her principles and values—long before committing to marriage. In a non-committal relationship, she retains the freedom to cut ties and walk away if necessary.

Unlike the situation for those women who are now married, having discovered his drug and or alcohol consumption has now escalated into abuse. This comes as a sudden shock to many women, knowing the male had previously limited himself to perhaps a couple of beers, and the taking of the occasional illicit drug has now fallen over the edge having increased his intake.

Although there are many reasons for this, the main overarching reason is, the male goes unchallenged—primarily by himself—therefore believing he gets away with it. This allows the male to become more reckless and comfortable, settling into his new world of self-indulgence, with a feeling of being in control.

— Was this a result of the wife being aware but also afraid, or was it that she didn't see it coming? —

This is where a new domestic abuse law ruling should be considered, as follows: DIL – Domestic Intoxication Liability, highlighting the legal accountability tied to intoxication in the family household. Under this new framework, whenever a woman calls the police to report her safety concerns, complaining that her husband/partner is intoxicated or affected by illicit drugs, the police will arrive and carry out a drug and alcohol test. If the male tests positive to illicit drugs or is above the legal limit for alcohol, then he is arrested and charged, and will not be allowed to return home for twenty-four hours. In the event he proves to be negative to the alcohol limit or to illicit drugs, then he will still be prohibited from returning home for twenty-four hours. Under this new ruling the law specifies that on the third occasion should the male be deemed intoxicated or drug effected, the male is no longer allowed to return to the home, until he meets certain guidelines.

Relationship accountability

Beyond its primary goal of combating domestic abuse, this law emphasises personal accountability within relationships. It reinforces the necessity for couples to begin addressing their own issues together as one, proactively in a timely fashion, rather than relying on the many public resources currently available that are being exploited.

As a result, couples in a relationship either resolve conflicts responsibly, or face the consequences. Again, this approach aims to reduce the burden on the legal system, preventing unnecessary strain on public resources and ensuring that intervention happens before a relationship reaches an irreparable state. It further provides immediate action to prevent domestic abuse against women and children.

— To use a simple analogy—once we relied on being served, we now need to self-serve, therefore we must learn how to help ourselves —

Ques: "I have had the police here on my doorstep in the past when my husband has become aggressive from drinking. How do you stop someone that is under the influence? It's so difficult?"

Ans: "As pointed out throughout these pages, the authorities can only do so much. As difficult as it appears, if a woman isn't prepared to step up -if, in fact, she has the capacity to do so, then the male will continue to misbehave, time and time again."

It only takes a woman of substance to turn this type of situation around, whereby she uses the many techniques and remedies as recommended throughout this book - or end the relationship. The latter being the suggested choice, particularly in the event the male continues with his type of behaviour, since he is now all too aware of this new law.

This proposal is in stark contrast to the current band-aid proposal, where the women - often having to flee the home - in many cases during the middle of the night, and convince the authorities to provide a safe house and financial means. As previously mentioned throughout this book, why should a woman particularly with children have to leave their home, having to endure all the inconvenience, trauma and anxiety, when all the authorities need to do is to remove the problem, being the male as now proposed?

Should the male believe he has been treated unfairly, then as mentioned, he should understand that whilst the authorities are there to help, they also want him and his wife/partner to become responsible for their own relationship issues and indeed their own actions. There's further merit in DIL framework, empowering women to resolve these issues more swiftly. This would have a significant impact on women to have the confidence to call the police at will, without the stigma that's currently attached. Whereby many women feel intimidated believing they are wasting the time of the police. Ultimately, this initiative would play a crucial role in addressing and minimising the risk associated with relationship problems, and domestic abuse, through excessive use of drug and alcohol behaviour.

As importantly, it puts the male on notice that he either mends his ways or he will face possible homelessness, fines, and possible jail, ultimately losing his wife/partner/children. These are the just consequences as you follow through with this type of process, because no woman should ever have to put up with a drunk or an illicit drug user, particularly in the family home. It's also a sure way to discover what your man is really made of!

Consequences, the price of accountability

Sure, there will be consequences since you contacted the police for help, therefore you will be issued a show cause notice, in the form of a written statement. This form serves as accountability that will document your reason for calling the police, creating a formal record of events. In the event of further abuse, it provides you with a future pathway for early intervention by the authorities, again a continuing source of vital evidence. On top of receiving a notice to seek counselling for both you and your husband/partner, where the two of you should attempt to get your lives back to what a civilised relationship should represent.

-Do not make the mistake of thinking that somehow you are aligning yourself with the police, because you're not, it's vitally important you understand that what you are doing is for your you and your children's safety, and not having to worry about the effect it has on the abuser-

Should the proposed law just mentioned never eventuate, why not make it your own law? Placing entries into that all important diary from the very first day he shows signs of alcohol and drug abuse whilst in the home. Again, ensuring these recommendations are now part of your new household rules, which he will become more than just aware of, due to the consequences.

You can still call the police every time you feel threatened or concerned about your safety and that of your family. By doing so, you're making it perfectly clear to him of the three strikes and you're out rule, then the relationship will be over. By documenting, referencing, and keeping copies of statements, even voice recordings, it will provide you with tangible evidence in the event you finally come to terms that you can't live with him anymore.

Therefore, it becomes irrelevant whether the male believes he is guilty of domestic abuse or not, since you now have a way of addressing this type of abuse using this twofold system, either the proposed legislative version or your own.

– As long as you follow through –

This new law proposal would ultimately allow the authorities to act decisively in a practical and measured way, as again it will provide immediate safety for all women and their children. By doing so, it sets new boundaries whereby the authorities now have the power to assess not only the male, but also the welfare of you and the children against potential other types of abuse, setting a new precedent for implementing and monitoring domestic abuse across the board, unlike anything before.

Ques: "So after he has been removed from the home on three different occasions, we don't get to see one another again?"

Ans: "Correct, certainly not in the short term. However, I'm assuming you don't want it to get to that stage. If so, then isn't it time you both sat down and discussed like mature adults where you are both possibly heading and making some changes to avoid that happening. Even if the proposed law doesn't take effect, here is your opportunity to avoid this potentially soul-destroying situation. Whereby the two of you can look back one day, counting your lucky stars, that you both woke up in time, and your relationship survived".

This proposal has real merit, although it will undoubtedly meet with opposition like so many proposals do. However, just think about the very real behavioural change for many males who go home under the influence of substance abuse knowing they must behave or instead draw adverse attention to themselves in their own home. If he behaves and doesn't cause any concern for his wife to call the police, he has nothing to worry about. Other than you, asking yourself how much longer you are prepared to put up with this type of behaviour.

This type of necessary intervention directly results from a man's failure to rehabilitate himself, showing total disrespect towards himself, their wife/partner and family. Therefore, if and when the three strikes are up, he's off to jail, and the relationship is possibly over. Of course, this is all totally avoidable for both of you, if only you both come to your senses.

Remembering this proposed law reform addresses abuse of drugs and alcohol in the home, however it has real merit and can easily become legislated to apply in other forms of high-risk domestic abuse as mentioned. This includes aggressive and physical abuse, sexual abuse, where the male becomes subjected to an assessment in line with the complaint, either being arrested or refused entry back into his own house.

You may be saying, "That's what the police do now". Yes, to a degree, but it doesn't go far enough. Again, at present there's no decisive accountability with many of these couples acting like its business as usual, with the police calling around to the same premises time and time again. This new proposed law provides women with a greater sense of accountability and protection under the law — other than the current feeling of helplessness — a new law with real consequences.

The advantages of this new domestic abuse law reform far surpass the disadvantages; if a man as mentioned feels unfairly targeted by the police, he should address those issues in his relationship with his wife or partner. That's how it should be, putting responsibility back on couples through this early intervention initiative. Ending this notion that the authorities and public taxpayers will both fund and resolve personal issues, that society itself has had more than enough of. The only reason it continues to happen is the law has no answers, well now -in part- they have, meantime couples are all too aware of what they are eligible for, almost to feel self-entitled.

Laying misguided assumptions to rest

It's currently a natural progression for many males in a relationship, believing their wife will gradually put up with their drug and or alcohol abuse. Having the opinion 'she won't leave', 'she has no money', 'she has nowhere to go', 'she won't leave the children'. Does that ring a bell?

A commonly held belief by many men, and regrettably many women accept it as fact – partly because men seldom face the same challenges as what women do. But that's all about to change, because instead of being blindsided by that possible daunting expectation as just described, you have some exceptionally good options. Perhaps the type you have never thought about before, which we will delve into, along with the planning on how to carry them out, both safely, once and for all.

Preventing and Ending Domestic Abuse

Having doubts, just ask yourself if you are prepared to put up with this type of behaviour for the rest of your life, because no man is worthy of remaining in a loving family environment having fallen into the abyss of self-inflicted drug and alcohol abuse. Along with making constant excuses all in a vain attempt to retain his position at the head of the table.

Unless he changes his ways through the options and processes available to him, such as using his fortitude, receiving professional help, or listening to his wife/partner. Or perhaps the all-too-common occurrence, when men come home only to discover an empty nest, then realising they can't live without their wife and family. Then further believing it's probably just all too late, becoming desperate and promising to do everything and anything, if only his wife/ partner and family would return home.

It's a revelation, that every woman should be prepared for — when the man who previously became threatening under the influence of drugs or alcohol often reveals a stark contrast—his aggression masks a deep vulnerability. That of the fear that surfaces when he imagines that you are no longer in the home. The same person who once intimidated you is now in despair at the thought of losing you forever.

When emotions intertwine with a sense of loyalty, the traditional expectation of marriage can take its toll. However there reaches a point in every woman's life where it's just not enough to remain loyal, where instead the time has also come for her to understand life doesn't just revolve around her man. If that means the end of the relationship, then so be it, but only under certain conditions - with your safety being the number one priority. This can be accomplished through both planning and procedures, including thought-out and realistic strategies, along with rehearsed control measures.

Ques: "Every time I think about leaving him, I get so depressed and overwhelmed with everything that needs to be considered, there must be some type of criteria to follow?"

Ans: "There is. But first, never allow yourself to be all too consumed. As suggested throughout this book, a woman must start with acknowledging there is a problem. Then she can build on her self-esteem, finding the desire, courage and strength, along with adopting all-important patience. Then to discover through her diary the direction in which she needs to take. If it's love, that's one direction, if it's over, then that's another. So, for the time being, work on those pathways and it will all fall into place. There will be hurdles to face that you will climb over by keeping in mind the end goal, to rid yourself of domestic abuse behaviour and for all time."

Not unlike challenging other types of abuse, there is a right and a wrong way, particularly regarding your safety, personal circumstances and looking closely at what your options are. From removing the male from the house, or helping him end his abuse, or to just pack your bags and walk straight out that door with the children. With the latter being the better option to end this nightmare, but only as long as a woman is in a reasonably good financial position. However, those without financial means should plan further, and above all, remain calm and again patient.

Women have a much better resolve along with the natural ability to remain rational and compassionate. However, in these circumstances a woman must first look at her own sense of wellbeing, her realistic capabilities and that of the safety for her children.

> **CAUTION** – Of all the different forms of abuse, nothing compares with the more sinister, distorted and frightening actions of a male who is affected by drugs and alcohol.

If you're thinking about opening up, remind yourself of that adage, *loose lips sink ships*. Because as previously mentioned, too many women who go looking for someone to confide in, can become double crossed. You may well decide to confide in a family member that has a relationship with someone, that knows someone else, who knows the male in question. So be extra careful, humans inherently love both stories and gossip, sadly it causes trouble.

Your diary is your personal account, so try to have fun with it, and not allow yourself to think of it as being a burden, because it's a reference, an account and, above all, a documented reminder of what took place. When and where, and what was said, then summarise your writings with heartfelt entries, because you don't want to read over simple matter-of-fact details later. This is your life. It's about you, your innermost feelings and secrets, regarding your relationship living with drug and alcohol abuse, so don't hold back.

It's important to make a duplicate of your personal accounts, therefore, if technology is your thing, create a diary on your digital device and backup on a secretly hidden thumb drive or find a professional to hold on to it for you. It may sound somewhat pedantic, but ask any woman who is now free from the clutches of domestic abuse, or in this case a drug and or alcoholic abuser, that if she had her time over would she have methodically kept a record? Whereby you will receive a resounding affirmation to your question, because it's the history of events that will have significant bearing and undeniable support for any legal claims you may have to make.

— Think of your diary as your very own personal insurance policy, so don't find yourself in a position when you wished you had kept one—then getting caught out without it, like so many women have done with great regret. —

Ques: "I have been in a rocky relationship for many years, but prior to that I had always kept a diary. I get a lot of satisfaction writing about my life, especially when I turn back the pages and reminisce. If only I knew how to go about the future?"

Ans: "You can — because each and every one of us carries our own personal crystal ball. It's the innate ability to envision what lies ahead. Yet that vision only gains true clarity through reflection — when we look back and gaze into it, not with hope but with hindsight, having already reached the milestones we once imagined."

Also keep in mind that by making a handwritten statement about events or photocopying your diary and making a formal complaint provided as a statement to the police. This will ensure the authorities have an account of events, which can be used as further evidence. It cannot be overstated that you will be sadly disappointed with yourself if the matter of divorce goes before the courts in the future. While he perhaps has a paid-up lawyer, you try to defend yourself using legal aid without having put those simple processes in place. By doing so you will have made a persuasive and significant impression on the court's decision.

Being discreet is an absolute necessity, as it is to put away some money as often as possible without raising suspicion. Particularly if you are working and able to remain self-sufficient having gained your own financial stability. Although for many women they rely on handouts from their husbands, and it's for that very reason, wanting to get out of a committed relationship is difficult - yet still achievable.

Ques: "Although as a family we struggle financially, my husband always has money to buy alcohol, where I have hardly enough money to make ends meet. He's always telling me we are broke. Is there a way to get around this without him getting mad?"

Ans: "A common situation for many women, and one that becomes all too real once married. It's a sad reflection of your relationship when you're too afraid to discuss your finances with your husband. However, this situation needs careful thought and planning. It's not wise to have a long-term cunning kit, instead, as difficult as this sounds, it comes down to that adage— 'if you want something done, do it yourself'. This means looking for a job, if only part-time, setting up your own account and never handing over any money to him unless he is genuinely deserving. Build on your self-esteem, and if his drug and alcohol abuse were to intensify, then consider your options in life, of which you have many. Don't become trapped in life with someone that is disrespectful and therefore unworthy of you. Always remember being financially independent provides you with the freedom you deserve. Discovering that freedom outside of a relationship harnessed with having personal goals and using your resilience, sets you on a pathway to find your true self."

So, rule number one is to get both the diary and a cunning kit, i.e. *secret stash of money*, happening as soon as possible, keeping in mind that the full disclosure of all money and assets—*in your possession*—during divorce proceedings is the law. Remember that, and while there's no suggesting you squander any money or assets, courts will show leniency to any woman who proactively planned for her future survival to escape an abusive relationship.

Keeping in mind, you will need records of all accounts, any settlements, and, of course, statements of past abuse, which are extremely important.

It's during this realisation of having no financial independence, or any real means other than desire to walk out the door with the children to start a new life, where a woman truly understands she is all alone. Therefore, she must become the centre of her own universal and that of her children. Time to make plans for intervention or you will remain a part of a living hell that many people would only describe as unimaginable. This type of person will only drag you down to the lowest depths that life can offer.

Hence the need for the three-strike rule!

This highlights a profound sociological failure, since too many women have been conditioned to accept domestic abuse as a natural consequence of marriage. Such conditioning borders on psychological manipulated coercion, distancing those beliefs from the truth. It's essential to confront this reality head-on and dismantle any misconceptions by allowing it to persist.

You should understand that although you may feel your situation is common; it is uniquely different and therefore must be handled as such. It's for your ultimate safety that you always remain mindful of this and never allow complacency to become your biggest adversary.

Ques: "My husband has an aggressive verbal nature, particularly when he has been drinking, so I just leave him be, or I go to a girlfriend until he settles down. Isn't this the best cause of action under the circumstances?"

Ans: "Although it's easy to be critical here, at least you have taken steps. That said, many will be asking, 'Why would anyone willingly

> stay in the same house with such a person?' While it may seem unfathomable from the outside, we should acknowledge that every individual makes difficult decisions, sometimes without rhythm or reason. Observing other households, we would be shocked by the lifestyles some people endure, willingly or in fear. Because those caught up in domestic abuse, whether it's the perpetrator or the victim carefully hiding their actions behind closed doors."

Whilst in his presence and as difficult as this may be for some women, try to gauge his pattern of behaviour when he is under the influence of alcohol and or drugs. Although a difficult exercise to undertake, it's far better to humour him, to discern any rising tension, given the inherent unpredictability.

So regardless of your situation, it's imperative you realise you are in a highly precarious position, and your life could well be in peril. A troubling thought, for the many females who simply continue with their lives, preferring to ignore the warning signs. Many of whom remain in denial, when suddenly it all becomes just far too late. Having procrastinated, not realising that time has come and gone, to be as far away from him as possible.

As mentioned, it is crucial for women to recognize the potential serious risks when informing a man—particularly one under the influence of drugs or alcohol—that she is leaving and taking the children. This type of communication can escalate an already potentially unpredictable and volatile situation, too often leading to tragic consequences. This risk often stems from impulsive reactions and a lack of awareness about how such news may affect someone in a heightened psychotic or unstable state. Therefore, it is essential to approach such decisions with your new mantra- being to pause and think before acting.

Drugs and Alcohol abuse poisons the mind!

For those people that partake in drug and alcohol abuse, they do so for many reasons, of which a large percentage could never provide a plausible reason or explanation for, other than they just do it. There are those who succumb to peer pressure, whilst others believe by stepping up their intake will enhance the effects of pleasure, which invariably ends in disappointment, having received the opposite to the desired effect.

However, in many ways humans are misguided and sadly unaware, they possess their own feel-good drug, naturally produced without any cost, and readily available when simply called upon.

Endorphins—naturally occurring chemicals in the body—play a vital role in alleviating pain and stress while also enhancing pleasure. Unlike medications, they cannot be prescribed by any practitioner, yet they have the remarkable ability to be activated at will, sometimes even producing a euphoric state of mind. Despite their powerful effects, many people remain unaware of, or simply do not appreciate, what their own bodies are inherently capable of. Understanding this natural process can lead to a greater appreciation of life, as it highlights the body's ability to regulate emotions and support overall well-being.

Have you ever wondered how it's possible to feel happy, overly excitable, or even burst into spontaneous laughter without the influence of any external substance? This experience is a testament to the power of the human mind when it works in harmony with our emotions. Our thoughts shape our moods — as we know all too well, when we focus on negativity, we can easily find ourselves feeling sad. Conversely, by consciously choosing positive thoughts, we can lift ourselves into joy, sometimes even into a state of euphoria. This mental shift, supported by the natural release of endorphins — the body's own 'wonder drug' — highlights the remarkable ability we have to influence our emotional well-being.

Ques: "I gave up alcohol some years ago because of my husband's nature when he drank alcohol and I found out I could influence myself naturally to be happy and sociable without the need to drink alcohol. Now an avid believer in the power of the human mind, I often ask myself, was my decision not to drink alcohol responsible for the respect my husband now shows me'?"

Ans: "That's an interesting point—perhaps his conscience is at work, quietly releasing endorphins to inspire compassion without his awareness. It happens when we least expect it or when we consciously seek it. For those who don't wish to give up alcohol, there's value in learning from those who have discovered the balance—integrating the effects of drinking alcohol into their positive thought processes. All the while experiencing near-euphoric sensations while again maintaining moderation and avoiding excess. As for you believing in the power of your mind, you do so because you have learned it's benefits in terms of pleasure, whilst always remaining in control."

It is deeply unjust that any woman should have to endure the immense challenges of dealing with a husband struggling with abuse and addiction, especially considering the profound impact of drug and alcohol abuse on the human brain. These substances severely impair judgment, leaving the individual unable to engage in rational conversation and avoid any coherent decision-making. They also trigger extreme mood swings and, as mentioned, unpredictable behavioural changes. In many cases, substance abuse in men is linked to aggressive and violent tendencies—forms of domestic abuse that no woman or child should ever have to face.

That all-too-common adage; 'one drink is too many, a dozen isn't enough,' stands true. Or another all too familiar phrase, boy do I need a drink', a sometimes subtle and softening excuse for an alcoholic beverage, but for the abuser he uses that phrase as part of his vocabulary for justification. Most people have heard, 'one more for the road', another sure sign of not wanting to give it up—just yet—without understanding the effects that are already taking place within the body from the recent intake of drugs and or alcohol. However, his comment has underlying intentions, again, to justify to himself and those around him that another drink is perfectly acceptable. This all too easy excuse supports his self-indulgent and persuasive belief that excessive drinking and becoming inebriated is ok.

Until the body finally reaches overload and shuts down. Which in many incidences inadvertently prevents that person from drinking themselves to death, or overdosing on drugs, whichever the case may be.

Having considered—in this instance—that your feelings for him are still positive, and you remain in love with him, you feel safe to stay in the family home. With that said, you are either confident with good cause, or it's possible you're about to make a big mistake, because there is little room for error in making these types of decisions.

It's time to put a plan together - and not just any plan, but one that addresses the severity of the problem, ensuring it doesn't perpetuate. Therefore, there must be sheer decisiveness in your planning, as any tip toeing around this issue will not provide you with any long-term comfort.

Again you must be truthful regarding your true feelings toward this person, if in doubt then you must do some sole searching, because far too many women feel an overwhelming sense of duty, that goes against better judgement. Do you love him or don't you. Do you want to help him become rehabilitated, or not? In this scenario, we can assume this male has crossed the line in the extreme, post marital, which is a common occurrence in many relationships. A case whereby the male during pre-marriage kept his substance abuse to himself, then selfishly believing once he gets married, he can produce children, along with maintaining a wife to wait on him, while he continues with his drug and alcohol abuse.

What is the level of risk?

If, on the other hand, you have serious doubts, and you're unable to have him removed from the house, then you must consider leaving the home, along with the children. That's because although there's strong advocacy for women to remain secure in their own homes, their safety and that of their children is paramount and should never be underestimated or in question.

Ques: "I have been thinking about this for some time now, and I don't want to be bothered with confrontation, I am over it, what do you suggest?"

Ans: "Reach out to family services, legal aid, or a lawyer, depending on your financial situation—it's essential to seek professional help. After a consultation and receiving guidance, you'll feel much more assured. It's completely understandable that many women simply want to break free, but circumstances vary. Take in the advice from professionals, align it with the recommendations in this book, and your own understanding. By integrating these elements, you can formalise the necessary processes and procedures discussed earlier.

So, remind yourself, it's normal for a woman to have some doubt about her feelings or understanding of her husband's/partner's behaviour and indeed his true intentions. Play it safe, by prioritizing your safety and that of your family, by moving forward, having accepted advice to end this type of abuse once and for all.

Again, attempting to remove a male from his castle instantly evokes immediate and serious concerns, as he will feel the forces are now closing in. One might argue that a woman's departure from the family home provides the man with a false sense of righteousness and reassurance, a feeling rendered meaningless if she plans not to return.

It's a juggling act, and one that requires making proper assessment before making decisions with good choices, which takes great courage and determination. This book does not pretend to have all the answers, it provides awakening, initial awareness, inspiration, along with finding the motivation, for all women of all ages.

-*Regardless of your circumstances, ensure you first Pause, Reflect, before Engaging anything high-risk, and should that risk be high, take the time to find the best control measures*-.

Having made the decision to move away from the home, not knowing what your true intentions are, be assured that in most cases he will be attempting to contact you constantly, as he is now in desperation mode. This is normal behaviour for the male, all the while you are now concentrating on receiving legal help, so when he rings you explain what you are doing and why you are doing it.

Do so without getting off track, and don't hold back, as he needs to fully understand the seriousness of the situation he has created. So, make those calls to the help lines, along with going into a police station and applying for a police protection notice, that can be tailored to your specific needs and circumstances.

The police can also assist you in this matter, however during the process stay away from your home until the protection order has been granted and papers have been served to your husband/partner, the respondent'. Take this advice seriously. When these papers are served on your husband/partner, he will feel the full weight of the consequences for his behaviour and will most likely get angry- That is why having made these arrangements without his knowledge is so important.

– Sadly, there are women who are now deceased because they never gave this matter enough thought and certainly underestimated how violent the male could be, once he received this type of news –

Drug and alcohol abuse is no trivial matter and requires a calculated response to remedy against, therefore, by challenging him whereby he is now fully aware of what is happening, putting him on notice. This places you in a favourable position to resolve the matter, particularly should he immediately wake up to himself, being your goal, and his salvation.

Tough love!

Although on the surface, the situation may appear to be going well, keeping in mind 'talk is cheap'. Using charm and desperate conversation, and looking for forgiveness, by the male is all too common. Only time can verify the sincerity he must show you. By seeing it through and waiting on that protection order whilst listening to his apologies, is showing your ability and courage to remain strong. And also listening to his remorse, that again may only be on the surface for now, however may prove a positive step in the right direction.

So, the ball is now well and truly in his court, so follow through, and again if you feel comfortable in talking with him on the phone so be it. However, give it some time before being coerced into meeting with him, and if you do, it's to be at a time and place arranged by you. So, keep your emotions under lock and key, as it's important to exercise tough love, otherwise it's all for nothing. Should that happen, make one thing perfectly clear to him, that if he should meet with you under the influence of drugs and or alcohol, then it will be another month before you will consider another meeting. This is essential, because it provides you with much needed space, whilst keeping your ear to the ground on his behaviour.

If he seeks forgiveness during a phone conversation and appears to be remorseful, explaining he can't live without you and the children, and it will never happen again, then chastise him further by explaining how close he is to losing you and the family. Also explain to him, he will be losing everything he ever worked for, because that's the direction his drug and alcohol abuse is taking him. Now is the perfect time for him to attend rehabilitation sessions to cure his habit and abuse; by insisting he enrolls and provides you with the proof.

– Remember, tough love must not become wishy-washy –

You cannot afford to be blindsided on such an important issue, where your entire life could be in jeopardy if you cave in, so don't think for a second that can't happen. Many women throughout history and continue to do so, had good intentions, finally find themselves defeated, because of failing to control their emotions. Men who knowingly engage in substance abuse, are masters of deceit and cunning, so keep that thought at the forefront of any inclination to feel sympathetic. – It's imperative.

Ques: "I've heard it all before, all the grovelling, the apologizing and the promises to change, and here I am back where it all started. Why is it so difficult, when it shouldn't be?"

Ans: "Whilst we want to believe, words alone don't prove change—only consistent actions do. Talk is cheap, whilst charm or desperation can mask deeper issues. Stay strong, stick to your boundaries, and follow through with the order of protection regardless of his promises. If you choose to meet him, do so in a public space where you feel safe. Make it clear that his drug and alcohol abuse is no longer acceptable and ask him directly what he plans to do about it. If he's truly committed to change, he should enroll in a *rehabilitation program within two days and provide proof, if he doesn't, move on with your life."*

Tough love means standing firm—don't cave in to emotions or let guilt override your need for change. A sincere man will take action to repair the damage, while an insecure man will try to manipulate the situation. Your role is to observe, document, and ensure accountability. The truth will reveal itself in time, and your job is to protect yourself and your family above all else."

In this scenario, he is trying to convince you he will change, and although that may sound encouraging along with some trepidation, we should also acknowledge it's far better to hear something sounding positive than to hear him remain in denial. So be sure to remain balanced in your assessment, as difficult as that may appear to be, and follow the processes, and you will succeed.

> **CAUTION** – This protection order has well and truly thrown the cat amongst the pigeons, a vital positive strategy on your part. Take nothing for granted as it will flush out the truth as to whether he genuinely wants to sort his life out, and indeed the truth regarding his feelings towards you and the family.

A line has been drawn in the sand!

Another important tactic is to ensure those all-important consequences are taking effect, therefore you first want tangible proof he signed all the paperwork issued by the police and further proof that he enrolled in a drug and alcohol rehab course, where he permitted you to monitor his attendance and progress. – Again, vitally important.

It cannot be over emphasised the importance of both his and you're understanding that there needs to be tangible and genuine accountability whereby you view (not hearsay) all the evidence as stated. Otherwise having become fool-hardy and moving back into the home prematurely will create more problems than just uncertainty.

Drugs and Alcohol

Work on his conscience, explaining that you believe in him, and that he doesn't need to make excuses or lie about his condition. Instead, tell him it's now out in the open, whereby you will both accept his problem and manage them together. However, making it perfectly clear to him what will happen if he doesn't. If he intends to fight his abuse and get you and the children back, he will do so knowing you are behind him, leaving him with no excuses not to follow through.

Consequently, he will feel less likely a failure, having hopefully gained some courage, along with finding self-respect and motivation to turn his life around. Or he will possibly remain in the same mindset with your present intervention having had little effect, in which case he will probably continue with his drug addiction and alcohol abuse.

– In the event of the latter, it's time to seriously consider ending this relationship and place more emphasis on your future happiness, and that of your children. –

In this scenario, the male has shown remorse and although he has indicated he wants to turn his life around, there must be even further consequences for his actions. By performing a further independent weekly drug test- away from the rehabilitation center you organised along with receiving the results. This may seem pedantic, however, it's also where a woman can either succeed or fail, and it's usually the latter, having neither instigated nor followed through on monitoring such important matters.

Unless a woman wants to teach her husband/partner a lesson, put her past behind her and start fresh with different surroundings, why should she have to be uprooted and made to feel she should move on. This comes with an unjust feeling of failure and somehow being responsible, causing the victim to experience many forms of unjust emotional abuse.

But what about if he doesn't want to leave the home, even with a protection order in place, the atmosphere where opposites live under the same roof together can be taxing. Unless you are a strong-willed woman who can go about her life with a new sense of meaning. Being of course, without the feeling of intimidation, it may well be the better option to strongly consider moving on or again looking at ways to have him removed from the home.

Again, hence the new DIL proposal. Domestic Intoxication Liability.

Preventing and Ending Domestic Abuse

Ques: "I'm considering filing a protection order against my husband, but we still live together. How can I ensure I'm making the right decision and holding him accountable without compromising my safety?"

Ans: "Assess his behaviour closely and set firm boundaries. Before returning home, ensure he has signed all legal paperwork and enrolled in rehab, with proof of attendance. Weekly drug tests add further accountability. If he resists change, prioritising your safety—legal options like occupancy orders may help. Keep detailed records of protection orders, rehab progress, and police reports. Ultimately, a man who refuses responsibility must face consequences. Stay firm, follow through, and protect yourself. If in doubt-get out."

In many countries, it is possible to apply for an occupancy order, which allows one partner to remain in the home as the sole occupant. These orders are often granted when there is evidence of domestic abuse, including drug or alcohol misuse in the home, or when the safety of the woman and children is at risk. Seeking legal advice—often available through Legal Aid—can be far more practical and affordable than attempting to secure alternative housing. A lawyer can assess your circumstances and advise on the likelihood of being granted sole occupancy of the home.

Once again, reiterating the importance of keeping a diary, along with copies of police statements, affidavits, voice recorders, protection order paperwork, medical certificates. Along with any other types of proof regarding his abuse, including his rehabilitation course details, drug and alcohol results? Because without it, abused women will struggle to be believed, because to know the truth, is simply not enough.

– To defeat this behaviour takes real commitment –

Never assume that because this person said this and that, they have your back, because chances are they don't, instead they are just doing their job. It's up to you to carry out all your checks and balances, ensuring all your ducks are in a row from day one. Most couples don't want to acknowledge their marriage as a type of contractual agreement when they decide to get married, however when divorce is pending, most couples scramble to find out where they stand legally.

— Hence the ability to walk away when in a non-committed relationship —

Time to take a closer look at yourself

If you are having trouble coping, don't fall into the trap of substance abuse yourself. Unfortunately, this happens for some women who have allowed the situation of someone else's demise to tarnish their own. Instead of remaining in control and continuing to address your problems using your fortitude and readily handling disappointment along with finding solutions bringing you a greater sense of personal accomplishment.

By cultivating a positive mindset supports resilience, your brain naturally becomes stimulated and releases all those endorphins we spoke about. Powerful hormones that profoundly enhance your well-being. This natural process is irreplaceable, and far more superior to the effects of harmful, artificial illicit substances, as mentioned. A natural overwhelming variety of sensations, delivered and controlled at your requested level. That's the big difference when introducing artificial substances into the body function, humans become susceptible to the overpowering uncontrolled effects.

As mentioned, endorphins, when released, boost self-esteem, ease stress, anxiety, and depression, and in turn improve overall wellbeing. Isn't it time you discovered the gifts you were born with — to uplift yourself and share with your partner when feeling low? Through the simple practice of positive thinking, you become better equipped to handle every situation emotionally, physically, and mentally.

During these circumstances, anyone who believes they need to rise above their current level of feeling naturally euphoric, with excessive amounts of alcohol and drugs are corrupting themselves. They do this by failing to control themselves. It's a recipe for disaster that never ends well.

Ques: "I have found myself drinking alcohol even when I'm not socialising, I don't know how to break free. Every time I try to take back control, it never seems to get any easier and I end up feeling worse. How can this be when I truly want to change?"

Ans: "Feeling the way you do isn't helping, you need direction, and the fact that you're discussing it is a powerful first step. Breaking free begins with shifting your mindset—understanding that whilst your emotions are valid, they don't have to define you. Finding healthy ways to cope, whether through professional support, engaging in activities that bring joy, or fostering positive social connections, can help redirect your path. You deserve a life where you feel valued, respected, and in control, and every small step toward healing brings you closer to that reality. Discover the cause of why this is happening and address it. If you believe it's your way to address your husband's/partner's behaviour, you have your answer. If not, then it's time you understood and reached out to your fortitude, your inner strength with magical like powers."

Over time, many individuals who have self-harmed through substance abuse come to recognize the futility of their actions. They eventually confront the unsettling truth of self-degradation, much like smokers who quit nicotine and reclaim control over addiction.

Fortunately, many come to recognise and admire those who've upheld moderation and preserved their self-respect with dignity. These individuals drew upon their inner strength—reaching for discipline, willpower, and courage—even while others, though aware of the senselessness surrounding them, chose not to.

Peer pressure has both positive and negative aspects; however, in this instance of abuse, it is particularly potent, especially towards the uneducated. Therefore, failure to understand the negative aspects of peer pressure, and becoming coerced into taking drugs and alcohol, has serious ramifications for those people. Many of whom were initially suspicious and indecisive, then agreed to partake in something they wished they hadn't, with many having become addicted, divorced, unemployed, jailed, homeless, even deceased.

That may sound a little extreme, but not when we acknowledge the heartbreaking loss of a perhaps a young life and the pain endured by loved ones who have lost someone to a preventable tragedy. Gaining a deeper understanding of how substance abuse affects the human body can provide both you and your partner with valuable insight.

We all have opinions about what's right and wrong when it comes to drugs and alcohol. What is for certain is that every human being can take charge of their own life by the decisions they are empowered to make.

Insight is just delayed hindsight

There are people that discovered at a later stage, they were oblivious to exactly what had been happening around them. Certain things that should never have been overlooked or missed, that were so important. Just ask the countless women who are now in marriages while their partners or husbands continue to carry out their alcohol and drug abuse behaviour, and now these women curse the very day they set their eyes on him.

Just imagine being in that situation, having sentenced yourself to a life of uncertainty, when it could so easily have been avoided had you kept your emotions in check and read the signs. This is the brutal reality for many women right now around the world who never had the foresight—the forward thinking—or be it the knowledge. All because of the lack of education, to have made better choices to start with. Who now suddenly realise the precarious situation they find themselves in, believing they have little choice but to succumb and accept their fate.

– Or do they? –

That's the reality in the modern world, further exasperated due in part to minority sympathisers of drug and alcohol use. Having convinced the authorities to provide injection rooms or as they are known - shooting galleries allowing illicit drugs to be administered by the public, a so-called type of reform process. Along with sobering up shelters for those having consumed excess alcohol. These resources are paid for by the taxpayer allowing substance abusers to continue to abuse themselves.

-Who really needs educating the most - the people or the authorities?

Preventing and Ending Domestic Abuse

Ques: "I am one of those people who blindly married a drinker and God only knows what else he takes. We have been married for many years with grown-up children, and I have come to accept my life for what it is. How could anyone be sure it wouldn't happen again in a new relationship?"

Ans: "You're not alone in feeling this way. Many people who have lived for years with a partner who drinks or uses substances come to believe that chaos is inevitable and that choosing differently is impossible. But the truth is this: what happened in your marriage was not a failure of your doing — it was a failure of his behaviour. Abuse, neglect, and addiction are choices he made, not signs that you are destined to repeat the same story. No one can guarantee what another person will do in the future, but you are not the same woman you were when you first married. You now recognise the warning signs you perhaps once overlooked. You understand the patterns you once excused. You have lived with the consequences, and that experience becomes its own form of wisdom. The question is not 'How can I be sure it won't happen again?' The real question is 'What will I do differently if I see the same behaviours?' And the answer is: you will act sooner, trust your instincts faster, and protect your wellbeing with far more clarity than you ever had before. A new relationship is not a gamble when you enter it with open eyes, strong boundaries, and a deep understanding of what you will and will not accept. You are not condemned to repeat the past. You can choose differently, and you deserve a life where safety, respect, and peace are the norm — not the exception."

When the male returns home he feels vindicated by simply saying, "It's ok love, I just went to the injection room supplied by the government, and they gave me needles to inject myself with drugs I supplied" or "It's fine love, I just needed some time to sober up, so I went to the sobering up rooms that are provided by the government'.

Drugs and Alcohol

How ironic, when a male who abuses drugs, alcohol and their family is shown sympathy by the authorities, who can then go home feeling quite chuffed with himself and taking his abuse to the next level. Why? Because he now feels vindicated, having been provided with preferential treatment and now feeling special. Yet in the family home, there's no one to provide the same type of protection, or offer any sympathy to the one person who now needs it the most. That would be the forgotten defenseless woman, the wife/mother/partner. - The victim- and let's not forget the children.

Of course that's not quite true, because when they lower a woman's body into her grave, all that preferential treatment, along with all the resources and sympathizers, will all be there - they just arrived far too late.

The following section -- under the heading perpetrator - is directed at the abuser, so why not consider asking him or perhaps someone you know to read through this all-important section. Or indeed other passages of the book, giving him an insight and opportunity to find out more about himself, and what he truly represents. Make it perfectly clear to him that he understands how important it is to you, for him to do this and not allow your emotions to get the better of you. This is a serious matter and again a real opportunity for your man to step up and challenge himself openly to address his substance abuse. Therefore, unless he has something to hide, in which case he declines your offer, you have your answer, then you really need to re-evaluate your relationship.

As you will also find interesting extracts from other chapters to help you hopefully make the correct decisions, particularly within the chapter of marriage. Which provides explicit details on the imperative safeguards every woman must take when contemplating confrontation or having discussions with a male on such sensitive issues that involve abuse.

Finally, and as mentioned, never ever mention that you're leaving in front of a male under highly emotional circumstances. By doing so incites extreme anger in the male, resulting in physical violence, causing death. This is so vitally important to remember, so when feeling like you want to just let it all out, don't. Instead, remember to pause and reflect before engaging.

There is a right way, and there's a wrong way, with too many women no longer alive, because they went the wrong way, so heed this warning.

SUMMARY

- Understand early on the dangers associated with human beings who indulge in drug and alcohol abuse.
- Seek early Support: Call help lines, apply for a protection order, tailored to suit your needs.
- Law enforcement can help, however remain mindful of your exposure to abuse, when that help isn't immediately forthcoming.
- Risk Assessment, before obtaining a protection order, monitor his behaviour closely and evaluate potential on-going risks while still living together.
- Protection orders have serious consequences, but he may react angrily. Avoid contact until arrangements are completed. Many women have lost their lives by not recognizing the signs for potential violence in these moments.
- His substance abuse requires direct confrontation and accountability. Use the three strikes and you're out rule and remain steadfast. Any male who cannot comply, is not worth having a relationship with.
- Tough Love Approach: Words alone are insufficient actions to prove sincerity. Stay firm and ensure legal steps are followed.
- If meeting him, do so in public spaces like a coffee shop. Never return home with him.
- Stay Strong & Vigilant, don't allow your emotions to cloud your judgment. History shows many women have faltered by giving in to charm and coercion.

Drugs and Alcohol

- Risk Assessment, before obtaining a protection order, monitor his behaviour closely and evaluate risks while still living together.
- Delay returning home until you have proof all paperwork has been signed and witnessed, including rehabilitation classes and D&A testing.
- Addiction fosters lies and deception—don't become hoodwinked.
- Encourage Accountability: Make him aware he must accept his problem and take ownership of recovery, encourage him to engage in conversation on this topic.
- Prioritize Safety: Ending the relationship may be the best option for you, don't become dependent on your situation.
- Living Arrangements: If he refuses to leave, legal options like occupancy orders can provide security.
- Remember to Pause, Reflect before Engaging: Impulsive reactions can lead to poor decision-careful analysis. This is essential when dealing with domestic abuse on this scale.
- Cultivating a positive mindset releases natural endorphins, enhancing well-being and creating a positive aura around you.
- Breaking free from emotional pain: mindset shifts, seeking support, and building healthy connections can help.
- Hindsight & Awareness: Many women find themselves in toxic relationships because of missed warning signs.
- An area you need to remain aware of, many policies provide support for substance abusers but fail to justify the struggles of the wife and partners.
- Avoid mentioning leaving directly—this can trigger dangerous reactions, resulting in possible death.

- Seeking other solutions by paying less attention to your man's needs and more of your own, including spending less time in his company.
- The impact of substance abuse affects not only the individual but the entire family, so take extra care and heed the warnings.

PERPETRATOR

It is important to recognize there are those individuals who would have wanted to read the following passages, who have reached a chronic stage in their drug and alcohol abuse—that are now sadly beyond reach.

A situation you may find yourself in unless you are completely open-minded and start to be honest with yourself. Try to accept that the time has come to understand what you represent, in order for you to take back control of your life. It's unlikely you will find a better opportunity than now.

So, let's concentrate on you, the male, portraying yourself as the everyday husband and father, whilst maintaining problems with substance abuse. Whether you are in denial or seriously wanting to turn your life around, this section along with the information from the start of this chapter on drug and alcohol abuse will help you adjust to a new way of thinking.

— *Although this section primarily targets males with partners, husbands/partners, if you're a single man without a partner, you may still find inspiration to turn your life around.* —

You probably don't believe you are excessive in your drug and alcohol intake, since you have never been challenged by anyone, or indeed by yourself? But now you can and hopefully you will become so disgusted in acknowledging the truth. Whereby you receive that light bulb moment, that unexpected epiphany you would never have experienced otherwise. A way of finally being taken to task, only this time by something with exceptional influence - your conscience.

As a married man sharing a home with your wife and possibly your children, only you truly know the extent of your substance use. That awareness is yours alone. The moment has come to listen to your conscience — that inner compass we all possess, urging us toward purpose, responsibility, and what we instinctively recognise as the difference between right and wrong. Begin working with your conscience. Harness your new mantra, assess the risks you create, put controls in place to mitigate those risks, and draw on your own fortitude to provide every tool you need to assist you. These are the first steps toward genuine rehabilitation.

Ask yourself, do you feel any real satisfaction from taking drugs and alcohol, or is the truth more troubling, being that you're caught in a cycle of self-destruction. Those around already suspect what's going on even if you try to keep it hidden. Do you ever question your own sense of morality after indulging? If so, that could be a sign that the weight of self-abuse—understanding the impact it has on your family—is taking its toll. This is the first step toward accepting change.

A growing number of individuals have become overly dependent on prescription medications, often easily obtained during visits to certain doctors. This trend is partly driven by the challenges of diagnosing complex or inconclusive conditions, especially when patients are seeking pain relief. While many genuinely suffer from symptoms that warrant appropriate treatment, there are also those who exploit the system, deceiving physicians to acquire opioids and other drugs by navigating loopholes and exploiting medical ambiguity. - Are you one of those people?

The situation is undoubtedly a double-edged sword, particularly for those who are drug-dependent for the wrong reasons and may already have fragmented mindsets. Their vulnerability makes them easy targets as they are obviously aware certain drugs are part of everyday life and legally available over the counter. Therefore, their mentality tells them purchasing street drugs for them is equally acceptable.

They do so without considering the consequences or understanding the risks, having failed to engage their conscience. Let's assume you are not affected by drugs or alcohol at this time, if so, try this - the second something comes into your mind where you want to say or do something you know you shouldn't, try to practice your new mantra. First by pausing (and holding that thought), then reflect on (between what's right and wrong) before engaging, your conscience will guide you in the right direction. Your fortitude will empower you with the inner strength providing you with the tools we spoke about earlier including finding your courage, willpower and discipline to defeat any further negative thoughts or other temptations. – Just give it ago

With these gifts you can accomplish more than you ever imagined, defeating the urge to abuse yourself and your family without being badly influenced. Along with achieving personal goals, overcoming setbacks with dignity and creating a life of meaningful happiness in your relationship. - Imagine that.

With all these resources you only need to engage again in positive thoughts that will activate prudence, by intertwining and acting not unlike an antidote that controls any temptation against being mentally corrupted and manipulated — thereby remaining true to your new principles and values and no longer allowing outside forces to influence you any longer.

Give it a go, then discover whether the decision you eventually make – having paused, given thought before reacting - was in hindsight the better choice having used your mantra. Unlike the wrong decision that would have otherwise kept you under control by those dark forces you need to defeat. In layman terms- you are gifted in a way that safe- guards you against any harmful thoughts, but only when you use what you have been given, to act as your protector. By becoming more in tune with what you just learned, other than instantly being reactive to how you think you feel, what you see and hear is the best mindful judgement process there is.

Substance abuse carries devastating consequences that infiltrate every part of your life, eroding your self-respect, ethics, integrity, and moral compass. It becomes an overwhelming burden—one that ultimately takes control of you, much like an albatross hung heavily around your neck.

Yet frustratingly, you know what you are doing is wrong, because your conscience always gives you a poke, reminding you once again to carefully consider whatever your thinking of doing is either right or wrong. Therefore, you are aware to the extent this type of bad influence and the effects of drugs and alcohol have over you. Since you know that to be true, why on earth would you want to be controlled by something so hideous, putting yourself and your family through hell. That said, it's not a personal attack on you, rather a means for you to acknowledge the truth hurts or at least it should, and again if you're feeling that way this very second, then your conscience is working just fine, as it should.

It's also true that your better nature and judgement have become corrupted, now impaired and shadowed by rebellious defiance and susceptible to anger causing irrational behaviour including verbal outbursts. Including taking it out on defenseless people who love you unconditionally, your family. But that's about to change because you now have the power to stop, take back control, and finally break free.

When we talk about substance abuse, for many it's recognised as being in a higher category than merely just having a habit. Therefore, again the authorities arguably would have us believe it requires a greater sense of acknowledgement and status, hence providing shooting galleries and a sober up safe house. Therefore, do you believe your behaviour deserves a more sympathetic approach and appreciation, as if it were some type of diagnosed deformity or disease.

This ideology is a big mistake, allowing you and many other substance abusers to believe you're the chosen few when there are so many people who are struggling with illnesses, they cannot cure themselves. This is false representation of the truth that plays out on the mind of perhaps yourself, someone already struggling with the effects of substance abuse. Don't let yourself be fooled; you aren't special, certainly not in that context. You can control your abuse yourself; you just need to reach out and start using what you already possess.

Therefore, see through these programs what they are, a mere token of a government acknowledging your behavior. All in an attempt to keep you off the streets whilst attempting to pacify the public, which doesn't provide any convincing solution. There is no indication of a decrease in the number of users taking illicit drugs in these government facilities, in fact quite the opposite. Therefore, the scheme only offers a claytons acknowledgement.

-But not you, because you now are starting to understand the truth-.

Fewer issues are more contentious than the idea that treating serious drug addiction can involve replacing one substance with another. In some countries, authorities advocate for methadone to curb heroin use believing it will reduce cravings. However, methadone comes with well-documented risks, including ongoing dependence, tolerance, and the potential for overdose. It doesn't get much more contentious when the authorities believe so-called remedies for serious drug abuse are a simple substitution of one drug for another.

If an addict were to say they wanted to give up heroin, they need to be honest with themselves about the choices they're making. Injecting rooms exist to keep people safe yet choosing to walk into one while saying you want recovery creates a contradiction that's impossible to overlook. You can't move forward while still clinging to the behaviours that are holding you back. At some point, you have to decide whether you're using these services as a bridge to a better life, or to delay the hard truth that change begins with you. If you're serious about rebuilding your life, your health, and your relationships, then the first step is choosing actions that match your intentions. Keep in mind, this is about your awareness and ultimately your recovery, allowing you to rebuild your life and reconnect with your wife and family. Isn't that the life you truly desire?

Many individuals—perhaps even yourself—accept this questionable system without being in the right mindset to fully evaluate the reason behind it, or its true effectiveness. As a result, again people like yourself simply go along with it. Meanwhile, those with greater awareness and critical thinking will hopefully recognize its flaws, question its effectiveness and legitimacy, and push back against it, understanding that this is not the path to true freedom from substance dependence.

This controversy—while speculative—raises a deeper concern. Some young, impressionable users have the mindset in believing that moving from oral drug use to injecting is simply a natural progression, especially when they see government-funded facilities providing clean needles. To them, it can appear as though experimentation is happening openly, even safely, within these supervised spaces. This perception can create the troubling illusion that authorities are indirectly normalising or enabling future generations to continue using drugs. Again, contentious as it is subjective, however the belief itself can be powerful—and dangerous, particularly for someone already vulnerable, or addicted, perhaps someone like yourself.

– Is this really the type of rehabilitation program you want or need? –

There will be many people who believe providing safe houses for drug users works, and that's fair enough. However, there are those people who also believe that by allowing people to inject themselves with illicit drugs is nothing more than demonstrating irresponsible behaviour. Again, nothing more than a ruse to keep addicts off the street whilst failing to understand the connection between substance abusers and domestic abuse. As a direct consequence, failing all those involved, including you, your family, and the whole of society

You have nothing to lose and everything to gain, so just try to understand that you're not getting anywhere with substance abuse, other than this absurd notice of trading short-term gain for long-term pain. By doing so you are beating yourself up time and time again. So, allow yourself to become inspired and hold the course and don't make the mistake of sweeping it under the carpet and insulting your own intelligence. Particularly now when your conscience is giving you a clear signal that something significant in your life is about to happen, a change is coming, and all for all the right reasons.

The big picture is that you're a decent person who's simply lost his way, so it's time for a new journey that empowers you to reclaim your life. As a result, you will then discover and continue to experience the true nature and meaning of receiving natural highs that are associated with everyday living, that drugs and alcohol could never emulate.

By looking into what you currently perceive in terms of pleasurable experiences when under the influence of illicit drugs and alcohol, to what you will receive naturally and whenever you want, is just a case of simulating your own mind, with a little practice. It's so important to understand how easy it is to achieve and discover just how your body works and functions, as this book continuingly advocates for.

Remember, every human being has unique idiosyncrasies that shape their distinct character and personality. In other words, these individual qualities make you who you are, although at present you are neglecting them, partly because of ignorance. However, you are far from alone; many people in your situation have never truly recognized just how unique they really are as an individual.

To truly understand what you've become and the potential to become the person you want to be, it's essential to acknowledge and process past childhood experiences. This is especially important if you're dealing with past or present trauma even if you're not fully aware of its presence.

In some cases, unresolved trauma can subtly shape daily life, influencing personality traits, habits, and decision-making patterns without the individual realising the connection. People may struggle with unexplained emotional duress, difficulty forming relationships, or experience heightened sensitivity to certain triggers, all of which can stem from past trauma unbeknown to you, or anyone else.

If left undiagnosed, post-traumatic symptoms can lead to long-term mental health challenges, however with proper support recovery is very possible. This is important to understand because if you suspect there could be an underlying reason for your substance abuse, then the time has come to reach out to your wife / partner and together find professional support.

Whatever you do, don't think seeking help is a weakness, because it's not, it's a show of strength that your fortitude is displaying on your behalf. Think in terms of wanting to reach out for help when being badly injured, a) you're not about to refuse medical assistance are you, and b), because you want help you are inadvertently calling on your fortitude to provide you with strength and courage, that's how it works. Your GP will ask some simple questions, that is the time to just give in and become forthcoming, delving into the unknown and taking up the challenge. By agreeing you will be put in touch with professionals as follows: -

Psychologist – Specializes in therapy and behavioural interventions to help manage mental health challenges.

Psychiatrist – A medical doctor who can diagnose and treat mental illnesses, including prescribing medication if necessary.

Counsellor or Therapist – Provides emotional support and guidance, helping you navigate personal struggles.

So again, sit down with the one person who likely understands you and wants to help you the most—your wife or partner. Together, you can then decide your next steps, managing your substance abuse together or seeking professional help as recommended. Whichever you decide, dig deep and reach for your inner strength and you will find your desire, your courage, discipline and willpower, also waiting for you to get started.

While prescribed drugs assist in managing and healing our health needs, the next chapter introduces a drug-free approach designed to maintain a healthy mind, body and soul, all naturally.

Did something come over you when you thought about the possibility of making a fresh start with your wife or receiving the help of a professional to start your rehabilitation? If so, you brought that feeling upon yourself naturally, your fortitude provided you with the desire and the pleasure that comes with imagining that you could become the person you always wanted to be. When that happened, you felt a feeling of happiness and joy that can remain with you for as long or short time as you wish.

Never believe you can't be that person because you can, and it's a lot easier than you might think. You are now on a mission -and hopefully soon to be in remission- to prove to yourself and to your family to first regain and re-install your self-esteem and self-respect, which isn't unknown to you, since you had it once. So, dismiss any of those negative thoughts that test us all from time to time, and remain positive. Then discover how you begin to look at life in a completely different way.

Your self-esteem provides motivation, moving you in many directions, instinctively prompting you to use your courage to become more and more confident within yourself. You will then make informative decisions, consciously and on a larger scale, concerning the bigger issues. Then, as mentioned, you will suddenly realise you have also regained your self-respect, a natural progression when lifting yourself up, and finding pride.

By appreciating the fact there are those people who are so less fortunate than you, having been born with mental and/or physical disabilities whilst carrying out daily struggles that ordinary people couldn't comprehend, yet they do so without having to abuse themselves.

You have it all, an able body, a wife and family that love you, all of whom want to respect you, but you're not letting them. Probably, you have no answer why you have treated yourself so badly, which is fine, because it happens. Again, since you are most likely someone who has lost their way, isn't it time to go in a new direction. Start by taking a serious look at how you treat yourself. Becoming kinder to yourself, appreciating your life and what you have, as importantly, thinking about what you are missing out and more importantly what you could lose.

There are so many opportunities available for you to become inspired in so many other ways. As an example, imagine doing the sort of work you have always wanted, then turn that dream into reality and go after it, and you will get it. You only have to call on your silent partner- your new mantra and recognizing your fortitude - by finding that desire and determination to achieve what it is you want in life. Once you step aside from being controlled by something other than yourself, you will accomplish great things and enjoy life like never before. Then to discover your own influence

Drugs and Alcohol

has branched out affecting so many people, especially when you see the faces of your wife and family that will reinforce your beliefs.

Time to put our step-by-step plan into action, with easy procedures to provide you with both direction and guidance. All of which are very much achievable in practical terms, and not designed to be overwhelming or exhaustive, so just relax and maintain open-mindedness. To bolster your good intentions, carry the thoughts of your wife/partner and family with you as you continue reading, giving you further inspiration to achieve your goal. Remain aware of how you would feel, living alone without your family, which is sadly the way you were heading had you not discovered there is a much better road ahead.

This next section on fortitude will reinforce the idea that everything you need in life is already within your reach, freely available for you to use. The choice is yours, and once you embrace it, you will finally break free from the heavy burdens that have weighed you down. You can now move forward without relying on artificial substances, freeing yourself to truly live without any further restraint.

- Start by avoiding the need to socialise with those people who possibly drag you down.
- Never lose sight of how you would feel without your wife/partner and family at your side.
- This is a perfect time to talk to your wife/partner and let it all out by opening up about your plans to go in a new direction.
- Learn the benefits of being kinder and more compassionate to yourself, to your family, and feel the effects it has on you.
- Experience the feeling of being in control of yourself.
- Instantly swap any negative thoughts with positive ones.
- Discover your passion and look towards achieving those goals.

So, what's it to be, the above or more substance abuse?

Let's now explore the natural attributes you already possess, qualities you may not even be using—by examining the powerful tools within your fortitude that we discussed earlier. These tools can operate instinctively, simultaneously, and often with little conscious effort. That is the real strength of your fortitude: it supports you as you navigate every thought and decision. And once these inner powers begin working on your behalf, their impact becomes unmistakably clear.

When you abuse substances without first engaging your mantra or indeed calling upon your fortitude, you have lost control and become submissive, often seeking immediate relief—numbing pain, escaping reality, or silencing inner thoughts. It's a path of least resistance, driven by habit, emotion, desperation or addiction. In those moments, you're not confronting your deeper needs or fears—you're bypassing them. There's no challenge, no pause, no reflection, just reaction. It may feel easier, but it comes at the huge cost of long-term peace, self-respect, and genuine happiness.

In contrast to using your fortitude to resist substance abuse, instead you are choosing temporary discomfort, other than facing your cravings and saying, "I want to be in control of myself". That takes courage. It's not just about saying no to a drink, a pill or a needle, it's about saying yes to life, to clarity, to self-worth. Your mantra allows you to pause, reflect, and act with good intentions.

-It's the difference between being controlled by a moment and reclaiming control over your entire future-.

You can make the weaker choice to walk the path that avoids the challenge, or take the other path, embracing it—transforming it into strength. Imagine how proud your wife and family will be when they realise the hopeless drunk and drug user has taken back control, indulging in moderation, or climbed the entire mountain having given up both drugs and alcohol altogether. A truly life-changing experience and one incredible accomplishment.

Ensure you read the next chapter on fortitude, which in part is directed at you, the substance abuser, as it provides thought provoking analysis of how we can interact within ourselves as human beings and reclaim our lives.

FORTITUDE

There is a vital need for you to understand and draw upon your fortitude, because it represents the inner strength that enables us all to endure hardship, clearing the pathway allowing us to meet our goals. When we recognise this capacity within ourselves, we gain access to a quiet resilience that supports discipline, restores self-respect, and strengthens our boundaries. Fortitude becomes the driving force behind meaningful change, <u>*YOU MUST BELIEVE THIS*</u>, allowing us to rebuild, recover, and move forward with purpose. By learning to harness and activate this inner strength we stop seeing ourselves as powerless and begin to realise that the ability to endure and grow has always been within us. It's inherent- that's why humans are such a dominant unrivalled species. That same strength is in you, waiting to be used properly. The question once again now is whether you're up for a challenge.

Therefore, once you've grown accustomed to its powers you will then become comfortable with its unlimited capabilities. When you do, you can fully embrace the many tools within your fortitude that you can use at will. Each one brings has its own specific design and purpose, i.e desire. If desire didn't exist, we would never have that internal spark to pursue anything at all.

When we use these tools collaboratively, they become almost seamlessly integrated. Once put to use, they empower us all to innovate, solve complex problems, obtain our goals and achieve remarkable outcomes. That would otherwise be impossible.

Never underestimate or undervalue this unique human capacity—your fortitude. Instead, acknowledge your need for support in ending substance abuse and embrace that support just as you would embrace life-changing news of being in remission- knowing your about to be given a second chance at life.

By using and aligning the following contents below, from a)-h), along with your new mantra and carrying out risk assessments, you are now on your way into being reprogrammed and empowered, ready to confront any issue you have. That's regardless of how insurmountable you believe it may be, because these tools provide the inner strength for you to accomplish ending substance abuse. So don't be bashful, why not get hold of a highlighter and highlight whatever you want throughout this chapter. Because by doing so you are letting go of being controlled and acknowledging what you are reading resonates with you. Are you ready to give it a go?

Plan A: Self-Respect

Self-respect is the admiration you hold for yourself; it's about treating yourself with kindness, consideration, and with dignity. When you have self-respect, you make choices that honour your principles, values, and well-being, that provide the power to set boundaries that protect you from harm or mistreatment. Without regaining or finding your self-respect it puts you at a disadvantage and at odds with what you need to accomplish, along with the new standards you now need to work with.

If you currently suffer from guilt, even self-loathing, then don't despair, as it takes this type of conscious awareness to first make us all aware of why we need to help ourselves in order to make a change. In life, having realised something has to be done, you only have to stimulate your mind, by explaining to yourself that you want to do this or that, and you will be provided with all the power you need.

As mentioned, this type of positive thought process will fend off bad temptations, since you are now about to use the right tools to achieve and accomplish your goals. Other than allowing your mind to become void and susceptible to corruption.

There's no better time to stay true to yourself than when socialising, don't allow yourself to be swayed or become badly influenced, instead you now owe it to yourself to stick to a new set of principles and values. Why? Because it's what you want, it's not about what you don't want. You are now in control.

Gaining self-respect provides an overwhelming and gratifying feeling of self-satisfaction, that provides decency and wellbeing along with a sense of the personal achievement you feel when receiving respect and giving back that respect to others.

Self-respect is the gateway to how we feel and treat ourselves as individuals, which ultimately exposes our true character and personality to others. –

Plan B: Self-esteem

Self-esteem is having an overall sense of your value or worth, having a positive view of yourself and life in general. Low self-esteem provides self-doubt, responsible for negative thoughts. You are worth more than what money could ever buy so the sooner you realise your true value; the sooner you can tick another box in your arsenal of tools held together by your fortitude.

Without self-esteem, it affects what we want to accomplish, relationships, and overall happiness. Having healthy self-esteem provides positive self-belief, setting goals, and more importantly it's instrumental in wanting to surround yourself with supportive and like-minded people.

Self-esteem is a fundamental part of who you are, shaping your confidence, resilience, and the qualities that define your abilities. It influences how you perceive yourself, how you assess your achievements, and the way you position yourself within society.

You are most likely suffering from very low self-esteem, and although it's not a comfortable place to be, the good news is, the only way is up, so you can now build on your self-esteem to a level whereby your confidence becomes reinstated, returning your emotions to a balanced level.

Feeling unworthy and insignificant, believing you have little to contribute, and choosing to appease others instead of expressing your own opinions and beliefs, you are only holding yourself back. It's time to step out of the shadows and into the daylight and become the person you know you want to be.

By thinking positively, you will build on your self-esteem without turning back, then discovering there's no greater cause for wanting your wife and family in your life. Once accomplished, nothing will ever remain on your mind quite like returning to and remaining your normal self.

Your self-esteem naturally grows as you nurture self-respect and learn to appreciate yourself. Self-respect is synonymous with your inner qualities, your values, integrity, and sense of worth—while self-esteem reflects how you perceive yourself externally, including your confidence and how you interact with the world. Strengthening self-respect creates a solid foundation, allowing self-esteem to flourish.

Shift your thinking habits toward what genuinely uplifts you and seek inspiration in meaningful actions. Use your self-esteem as a driving force to spend quality time with your wife and children, focusing on their happiness and your own. In doing so, you'll begin to experience a deeper, more rewarding sense of belonging—one you may have been missing out on for far too long.

Leveraging your self-respect alongside your newfound self-esteem creates a powerful ripple effect, allowing compassion to deepen and integrity to resurface. As a result, you'll naturally begin to recognize your renewed strengths and courage. These qualities will guide you toward engaging in the things you are good at, so take the time to acknowledge your achievements and witness how your self-esteem thrives on its own.

It happens almost by magic, by simply reshaping how and what you think about, as long as it's in a positive way—there's nothing positive in thinking about substance abuse. As a result, you're boosting your confidence in how you go about daily life, particularly becoming empowered to protect and love your family with a completely new sense of purpose and excitement.

Plan C: Acknowledgment

Side effects of substance abuse, desecrate almost everything considered decent in a civilized society. It is, therefore, also very clear that such a trait is unparalleled in its capacity to be soul-destroying. Accepting and acknowledge this as the truth provides a greater cause for the building of your new foundation.

This will reinforce any doubts that you are on the right track, since it sits well within your conscience. Further acknowledging you are aware of your past experiences that will also provide you with the future resilience to face everyday challenges.

Plan D: Desire

Having the desire to move forward and end this abuse is now crucially important, as it will give you huge personal comfort and satisfaction, since it provides you with further reassurance of the path you are now on—being the right one.

Particularly in the event you should become challenged between your desire to end any further abuse and any urges you may have to resume substance abuse.

Just think about that, by realising it's the truth regarding what your mind is capable of doing, you simply adopt an overwhelming desire to turn your life around. It comes naturally.

This can easily be achieved by manipulating your desire and exercising the decisions you have made, which will now take precedence for the need to make the necessary adjustments. Having learnt how to develop the desires to conquer your demons, you can and will reshape your entire character. Doing so creates an impregnable barrier between your deepest desires, against any thoughts of self-harm, resulting in profound personal self-satisfaction.

Find the desire to do something in your life that you've always wanted to do, perhaps embarking on a new type of employment as we mentioned earlier, finding other interests that stimulate you. That stimulation will result in becoming excited providing more personal satisfaction than any artificial substance could ever give. It's out there, you only have to reach for it.

Plan E: Discipline

Hopefully, you now have a better understanding of the many aspects and virtues of your very own fortitude, that of self-respect, self-esteem, acknowledgement, and desire. All of which will greatly assist you in defeating substance abuse. Having discipline is also vital and necessary to ensure effectiveness and efficiency in reaching your goals. It's just the law of averages. Whenever you fail to follow through, something will come back to bite you. Therefore, the requirement for strong discipline in these circumstances, training yourself to take control is vitally important for your success. It goes hand in hand with what we want to accomplish throughout our life.

The necessity and purpose of discipline is to have a clear set of goals, and to use persistence as another tool for your fortitude to follow through. Stick to a certain set of rules- find direction. Never become disheartened, if the need for additional changes or some further planning is required, it's a simple matter of putting contingencies in place. You've heard the adage, 'if at first you don't succeed…'

To make your life much more well organised, set yourself clear guidelines and oversee them to get the best results. That's discipline. Refrain from becoming distracted and heading into unknown territory. Rather, concentrate on accomplishing those goals and feel the satisfaction that rewards you. Look back on those accomplishments as part of your commitment and success in moving in the right direction. All as a result in believing and instructing your very own personal bodyguard to help you along the way- your fortitude.

Ask yourself how you feel now that you're heading in this new direction, realizing your true belonging and self-worth, being kind to yourself, as opposed to the path you would normally be on?

Once you put your mind to something, remaining motivated and persistent, and following through with dogged determination, means understanding and using your discipline as your body has been designed to do.

Plan F: Willpower

Many people struggle to manage their willpower, yet it plays a crucial role in determining how successfully we reach our goals. While deciding and reaching agreements are common practices, willpower is an inherent part of us—so why not harness it with intention? By doing so, you will be aligning your new goals with what you aspire to achieve? Consider how often New Year's resolutions fade away once the celebrations end. The reason? They weren't that important to begin with. If they had been, discipline would have guided the control of willpower, ensuring follow-through.

By calling on your discipline, particularly now that your desire is never to engage in substance abuse ever again, you can simply call on your willpower to control your behaviour. Then simply remain aware of what you have set out to achieve with reasonable timeframes, and you will reach your goals.

Plan G: Strength and Courage

Strength is not just in resisting the urge to return to old habits, but in facing the emotional and psychological battles that come with it. Every step you take toward rebuilding a life with purpose and determination without indulging in substance abuse shows courage. This path can be difficult, but every moment of resilience and self-belief brings you closer to a future filled with hope, dignity, and self-respect. Embrace the small victories and remember that every day of sobriety is a testament to your incredible inner strength.

Fortunately, you can draw on another type of strength, that of your family that shows courage and support along with their unconditional love for you.

That's a lot of strength and courage for women and young children, despite being aware of your shortcomings-.

By tapping into your strength and courage, you're exercising the full power of your resilience, your greatest asset, now that you've recognized and embraced your challenges for what they truly are. Especially by bringing them into the open, you've ignited a fierce determination to press forward. It's a bold beginning.

It's now time to further build on that mindset of yours and put an end to any feelings that inexplicitly draw you into a depressive mood. In the event you believe you don't get depressed, then ask yourself why you indulge in substance abuse to begin with.

Facts are; while some people believe using drugs and alcohol increases euphoria, it also leads to depression, so essentially, you're only making your situation worse. That's assuming you aren't under any medication for depression. Therefore, it's both logical and realistic to assume that through careful planning, the best way forward is to go cold turkey. Having now become the preferred choice for those males who want to test their fortitude through exercising their courage, discipline, willpower and strength and putting an end this misery of substance abuse as fast as possible.

Admittedly, going cold turkey pushes the boundaries of human endurance, again testing your willpower, but by doing so you no longer have to tiptoe around the challenges you face. Instead, you will continue to make certain headway in a defining way whilst reaching your goals.

This is so achievable, since there are people just like you who are in the same predicament. Having finally understood that there is nothing that they can't achieve, accomplish, or overcome. Since they also have a real understanding of what their fortitude can do for them when put to good use.

Whether to go cold turkey or not is both a personal and professional one, however, it's best to remember that by making continued visits to injection rooms to self-medicate is bordering on pretense. Therefore, creating a type of clayton's intervention. This may prove to be more agonisingly frustrating and difficult than manning up and doing the initial hard yards yourself, by again, going cold turkey- Take the challenge you won't regret it.

Once you adopt going cold turkey withdrawal symptoms are just that, slowly but surely leaving your body, an exorcism of sorts, gradually getting easier as your body adjusts to normality. Because withdrawal experiences vary from person to person, it's essential to acknowledge that drug and alcohol dependency occurs on a broad spectrum, shaped by complex factors such as – method of administration, type and consumption of substance use. If you opt to go cold turkey, consulting your doctor beforehand is strongly recommended to ensure you fully understand withdrawal symptoms and identify the most suitable approach for your individual circumstances.

-Think in terms of the willpower people use when fasting, where they have successfully lost weight through dieting, in part by using their fortitude in reducing their substance abuse. Only in this case the substance abuse is food, which is not unlike the urges you experience. -

When someone is living with substance addiction, the body isn't craving nourishment — it's reacting to dependence on the substance. Unlike food and water, which are essential for human survival, illicit drugs are not. The body can function without them. Meaning the longer you remain steadfast and fight those urges, the sooner the drugs will totally withdraw altogether. Then suddenly your body is no longer dependent, giving you a genuine chance to begin again- starting a brand-new life.

If you are feeling a little overwhelmed, perhaps somewhat intimated by the thought of going cold turkey, then you're not alone. That feeling is perfectly normal. However, there comes a time when we all have to face up to certain things ourselves that we would rather not have to do, and that time for you is now.

Plan H: Acquaintances and Socialising

Although not recognised as major components in our fortitude toolkit, acquaintances and socializing nevertheless contribute significantly, both emotionally and mentally. Therefore, fortitude isn't just about individual strength; it's also about resilience, adaptability, and the ability to navigate life's challenges with support and connection. However, irrespective, acquaintances and socialising are very much a part of life that offer both good and bad influences.

One area we discussed earlier is that of ending your relationship with those people who also substance abuse, who may have attributed it to your demise. When you become stronger in the future, you may even want to help those same people who, like you, may want to turn their life around. Perhaps a conversation for another time.

By acquainting yourself with people of good standing who show integrity is vitally important for your welfare and overall rehabilitation, so never become complacent on this one vitally important issue. You don't want to find yourself in a position having gone one step forward and two steps back, ending up with the wrong crowd.

There's another adage that says, 'you live and learn.' Unfortunately, we do so too often through our mistakes, and although that's not ideal, it gives us the opportunity to learn from them and to ensure we don't make the same mistakes again.

You should also acknowledge the one most important person that you're ever likely to ever have in your life, your wife/partner, so instead of treating her with contempt – which you have been doing- start to treat her with the utmost respect she deserves and watch the changes the two of you will discover when being together. She is your confidante, your mentor, your lover and your best friend. It's time you understood that.

Continue building alliances, again with like-minded people who may have also been subjected to substance abuse, which can also be good therapy. However, tread carefully, there are those people who treat therapy sessions as springboards for the type of session afterwards you no longer want to be a part of.

So, remind yourself if you do participate in therapy sessions to explain what you have been through, because by opening up allows you to hear about yourself in detail and hopefully understand the truth.

Fortitude

Now is a good time to consider your work ethics and start to become more receptive and approachable in the workplace, it won't go unnoticed, instead it will further bolster your self-esteem and confidence, and provide you with the respect you also need.

Continuously build on wanting to be the type of person who feels good within themselves having only good things to say about others and making someone else feel good in return. By adopting this attitude instinctively shapes your character, making you the type of person others come to admire and take notice of.

As you settle into your recovery, remember that you're no longer facing this journey empty-handed. You now have your new mantra 'forever' to — Pause, Reflect, then Engage — a simple but powerful rhythm that allows for positive thoughtful responses before every choice. You have your fortitude, that you now know can work wonders, that quiet inner strength you've carried all along, now ready to guide you when desire comes calling. Along with your conscience, -which you need to start listening to-, the part of you that has always known right from wrong. As your body heals, your own endorphins will begin to rise again, offering natural moments of calm, clarity, and even joy — the kind you once chased artificially. Woven through all of this is the bright light at the end of the dark tunnel, that being the love of your wife and family, a love that has waited, endured, and believed in the man your about to be. When you bring these forces together, you're not just recovering — you're rebuilding a life filled with purpose, connection, and hope.

You can do this — you have nothing to lose and everything to gain.

Good Luck.

SINGLE MOTHERS

While this self-help book centers on domestic abuse and women's safety, it also highlights the urgent need for greater awareness and education to help prevent young women from being abused and becoming single mothers outside of marriage.

> **Awareness** – This type of education should emphasis the risks associated with being young and vulnerable, particularly the consequences of becoming unexpectedly pregnant. These young women—many still in their teenage years—face the immense challenge of raising one or more children on their own. This highlights the need for greater support, other than the authorities believing that providing financial assistance is the only solution.

– It's recommended you highlight areas of interest throughout these pages, including making entries into your diary –

Knowledge is power

Many of these young women repeat the same mistake time and time again, unwittingly allowing themselves to be questionably abused both physically and emotionally. Particularly in terms of the sociological effect it has when many females suddenly discover they are all alone. Again, as a direct result of having never received any social skill education, being, a failure by the authorities to recognize its significance.

It's not enough for people to say, "It's the job of the parents", because although in theory that makes good sense, many times offspring don't take their parents' mentoring as seriously as their mums and dads would like. Therefore, many rebellious uneducated sixteen-year-old females—although at the age of consent—are again at greater risk, a precursor for male unethical behaviour.

Ques: "I have two daughters, one when I was seventeen and again falling pregnant when I was nineteen. Both my girls have never seen their fathers, and I don't receive any child support from either of them. How is a single mother expected to properly support their children without father support and with little financial help?"

Ans: "There's no denying it's a difficult situation. If not having already done so, contact the CSA (Child Support Agency) a division of Services Australia, and make formal claims against the fathers presuming you know who they are. There are males in this world who have no morals, least of all care about your circumstances. If they are unemployed, then chances are they won't be able to pay child support, in many cases they have no intention of doing so either. However, you can turn this situation around if you really want to, start by never allowing yourself to fall victim to believing that because you're a single mum, your life is somehow less worthy, limited, or destined for hardship. Then take a closer look into what this book offers, and you will find what you are looking for, with everything waiting to fall into place".

There's no point being consumed by the thought of being in hardship, you will only remain hamstrung, rather, consider concentrating on carving out a new life for yourself and your children.

Throughout this book there are many inspirational examples for why women should seriously consider reinventing themselves and become a woman of substance. Lift yourself up and discover what life has to offer other than remaining a struggling single mother. Perhaps start by looking into what you enjoy doing and researching how you can turn that interest into a career, perhaps even a small niche business while working from home, remaining close to your young family. There are a thousand and one options for you, with well-trained people on hand to help you get started. Think about this advice as your escape from any further thoughts of doom and gloom, then call on your inner strength again being your fortitude (the previous chapter) and start planning your future for success and happiness.

Start by talking just one step, and a feeling of excitement and further desire takes hold, and before you know it, you become directed towards your goals. You can do this, simply alter your mind set by changing your attitude, giving you the all-important inspiration to move forward, and watch everything else follow. Below is a road map for you to consider for your future independence and whilst it may not be to your liking, most will be of great benefit but only when you become a true believer.

If we focus specifically on independence — not just escaping poverty, but becoming self-directed, self-reliant, and self-confident — the path for a young mother becomes clearer and more empowering.

Here's a framework that speaks directly to independence, not just survival.

The Independence Pathway for a Young Mother

1. Emotional Independence: "Remind yourself you have the strength to stand on my own two feet".

This is the foundation.

- Building confidence through small wins
- Learning to trust her own decisions
- Separating her identity from partners, parents, or past mistakes

- Developing a sense of personal worth

2. Financial Independence: Say to yourself -- "I can support myself and my daughters."

This doesn't require a high-paying job at first — it requires control.

- A steady income stream, however small
- A basic budget
- Avoiding dependence on unstable partners
- Building skills that increase earning power
- A tiny emergency buffer (even $10–$20 a week)

Financial independence grows from being consistent

3. Practical Independence: "I can manage life without relying on others." Having this type of resolve will change your life completely.

This includes:

- Knowing how to navigate services
- Understanding childcare options
- Managing appointments, bills, and routines
- Learning basic digital skills
- Being able to advocate for herself

These are the everyday competencies that create freedom.

4. Social Independence: "I choose my support network." Be mindful of what you want and not what everyone else wants.

Independence doesn't mean isolation — it means healthy support.

- Choosing positive, reliable people
- Letting go of toxic relationships
- Connecting with other young mums
- Building community ties

A strong network increases independence because it reduces crisis moments.

5. Skill Independence: "I have abilities that no one can take away." This type of mindset will provide the inspiration and motivation you need.

This is where long-term change happens.

- A qualification
- A trade
- A digital skill
- A side income she controls
- A job path with growth

Skills are the most powerful form of independence because they create options.

6. Identity Independence: "I know who I am beyond my circumstances."

This is often the hardest part- so read through fortitude again.

- Seeing herself as capable
- Believing she deserves stability
- Rewriting the story, she tells herself
- Recognising her strengths as a mother

When identity shifts, everything else follows.

7. The Core Truth

A young mother becomes independent not by doing everything at once, but by building:

- One skill
- One habit
- One support connection
- One income stream
- One mindset shift

Independence is built on a foundation of small gradual layers.

If only an educational curriculum was in place, this style of mentoring could have equipped young women with the knowledge and insight needed to make more informed choices—particularly the ease with which pregnancy can occur. In turn, this would enable them to pursue paths that foster lasting, positive outcomes throughout their entire lives, other than becoming derailed before their journey began.

Single Mothers

— Whether you're a single mother or a young teenager, if you haven't read the first three chapters, then now is a good time to remind yourself to do so. —

The earlier chapter on dating provides young women with valuable advice on safeguarding themselves when out socialising or indeed seeking potential partners. These young women should understand the power of testosterone—whereby males will go to extraordinary lengths to fulfil their desires, often with little awareness, interest or appreciation of the potential consequences. Such is the heavy burden placed on young females and the reality of life particularly when faced with a male who refuses to take no for an answer. (See chapter on sexual abuse)

Unless young women remain vigilant by managing the male advance together with their own emotions and desires, an unplanned pregnancy can easily eventuate. As mentioned, it only takes one unexpected event to derail the goals of every young female, changing the entire course of her future—at least in the short term.

Commonplace scenarios that many fall victim to, including young virgins that are coerced into visiting a male friend, without considering his intentions, and subsequently finding themselves in a compromising and sometimes frightening situation. There are many who would say, "She should have known better", and "She knew what she was doing". However, for the most part, we are talking about young impressionable teenagers, incredibly some as young as twelve. Many of whom are being taken advantage of, either by promiscuous young males, or older males without any morals.

It is therefore a fact of life that many females fall pregnant because of their pursuers taking advantage, then hide behind the veil of anonymity and legalities. In other words, many scrupulous males knowingly aware it's not against the law to have sex with a sixteen-year-old, are therefore inclined to prey on young females for nothing more than their own selfish-gratification.

We can then correctly assume, there are those males who possess the mentality of only being focused on becoming the first to have sex with a virgin. Having done so, putting their boots back on and hitting the road.

Was she abused, overpowered, did she say no? Maybe she believed it best to remain still and quiet, not fully comprehending what was happening to her, and simply became submissive. Was she therefore raped through coercion?

These are just some of the underlying realities and consequences many young females face, who sadly find they have little recourse. Along with the sudden impact it will have on her conscience, due to the further shocking news of becoming pregnant.

All of which is compounded by the guilt some females experience, with many being fully aware they said no to his advances, that he never adhered to. These are the escalated consequences that many young females are unaware of at the time. Many of these young women are unexpectedly forced to scrutinise their own behaviour, as a requirement to file a complaint with authorities becomes yet another layer of emotional abuse, underscoring the urgent need for early education.

> **CAUTION** – Tragically, many young women fall victim to meeting undesirables -some more than once- who care less about themselves, let alone whether a female falls pregnant or not. He never had a single thought of becoming a caring and supportive partner, a full-time father, or contributing to child support. Nor did he give any consideration associated with the child's upbringing being raised without his/her biological father. Just some of the behavioural patterns that lay awake in the male primal psyche, that every female should become well aware of.

One way or another life is all about education, and whilst there will always be those young women who will pay little or no attention to the advice that's given to them, there will always be those that do—perhaps like yourself—who will therefore be spared from making regrettable mistakes.

Parents also have a moral and ethical responsibility towards their children, and they know it. Unfortunately for many, they only provide token advice, as they themselves- in all probability- never received any proper mentoring or indeed education on the matter. Therefore, the cycle simply continues with many new generations being sent out into the world to fend for themselves. Then feeling unsupported with matters of serious importance that could have been so easily avoided to begin with.

From adolescence to young adults

As mentioned, it's understandably difficult trying to get the undivided attention of a teenager when attempting to provide sound advice on life's true accounts. Particularly during such delicate matters regarding sex, which generally comes down to the offsprings believing they know it all, along with a general lack of respect. Hence the need for formal education.

Arguably children raised in secure, functional, and well-supported environments are more inclined to become well-adjusted to face society. Prioritizing this type of formal education and support would ensure those young females who don't receive any early training are then less likely to become struggling single mothers, raising children without a loving father.

— Failure to address this vitally important social issue can and will continue to have far-reaching consequences lending itself to generational disadvantage. —

Ques: "I am only sixteen and still a virgin with no intention of falling pregnant until one day when I become married. I know I am only still young, but I don't understand how that can be difficult to achieve'?

Ans: "You're right, it is easy to achieve if you are first aware of the many challenges you face along the way, that's the part many young women currently don't understand. In fact, if you had a dollar from every young woman who had the same thought as you, only then to become pregnant unexpectedly, you would be a very wealthy young lady. Hopefully you have read the first three chapters, and don't give up on accomplishing your goals, especially not to become pregnant until you are more mature and stable".

Again, many of these children are destined to grow up without a father, some of whom will invariably be subjected to being raised in a dysfunctional environment. Once they have reached the age to find their own way in life, only to further find themselves on social welfare, becoming impoverished, with a lack of direction, failing to fit into society, and falling foul of the law.

— Part of that cycle we discussed earlier —

The repercussions for struggling single young mothers can last for many years, if not for a lifetime, day by day trying to survive, facing continuous mounting financial hardship, and in many cases poverty. As that young mother grows into a mature woman she will reflect on what could have been, knowing the direction she took could have been so much better had she not been let down, by an absent father, the authorities, and indeed her herself. Fortunately, it was only for her own maternal instincts that provided her with the will to make the best she could out of life for herself and her children.

Fortunately, there are still certain decent men who seek genuine love and are only too happy to embrace a readymade family. For a single mum and her children, the dream of having a complete family is not beyond reach - such men do exist.

There are many single mothers with more than one child who have risen above this type of adversity, and having done so is nothing short of miraculous accomplishment. Providing and ensuring their children have the best possible upbringing is by no means an easy task, with many single mothers holding down a full-time job. A situation most men would find extremely difficult.

— Again, any young woman feeling trapped in this situation has the means and the power to change her life if she so wishes. —

In years gone by, there were women who had large numbers of children, in some cases, six, eight, ten, even more being common. Many of these were single mothers whose partners had since gone off to war or just left, leaving these women to persevere with scarcely enough food and money to make ends meet. Yet these women persisted only like a woman can, and despite the harshest of conditions, she prevailed creating as happy environment as best she could. Whilst doing so many of those children went on to lead respectful and successful lives.

Therefore, there's nothing you can't accomplish as a single mother in the modern era, raising your children with the same hopes and dreams of those who were much less fortunate- back in the day.

This is your life, and by making the most of it, you only need to find inspiration by reminding yourself when looking into the faces of your child or those young children, who never asked to be born. Who will one day reflect on the way you raised them, hopefully with fond memories, compassion, and respect. When they do, you can then be proud of what you have achieved when you realise your legacy will continue, as they will continue providing the same opportunities for their own families in later life.

As a single mum with your newfound confidence, and when the time comes, learn the meaning of delegating, ensuring you receive ongoing help from your children while showing them the love they deserve. This will reward you tenfold, since it takes pressure off you, whilst teaching the children that if they want something they have to work for it. Because raising your family single-handedly without receiving help can potentially become a progressively spiral downturn. In many cases, losing both control and your self-respect, finally coming to a dead end and living in a dysfunctional family environment.

If you find yourself at your lowest, remember that the only direction left is upward. While it may sound like a cliché, it's a powerful mindset to embrace—progressing steadily, step by step, day by day. With no further backward path, focus on staying committed to your responsibilities, and meeting deadlines. Nurturing those around you, teaching children how to show and receive love, as should these actions become part of your daily routine. By doing so you will inadvertently instill a growing sense of self-achievement, reinforcing your journey toward a better place in life.

As it is to persuade women of all ages, regardless of their circumstances to keep a diary, the most comforting secretive confidante a woman could ever possess.

— All of which can easily evoke a warm and fuzzy feeling inside, especially when you realize you've captured your innermost thoughts and again upon reflection, then

experiencing sudden revelations you wouldn't have had otherwise. Transforming past mistakes into guiding lights for the future, something to become truly excited about. –

You might begin this life-changing journey by being completely honest with yourself and letting go of any habits or behaviours you know don't serve you well. The powerful part of this step is that it helps you rediscover — or discover for the first time — your own principles and values. And if you haven't identified them yet, now is the perfect moment to do so.

Write them down so every time you open your diary it becomes a reminder of the direction you made a commitment to follow. As a reminder to pay close attention to where your life is heading, and whether you are maintaining your principles and values. Just remain mindful of the unexpected hurdles in life we all face, and deal with them decisively one at a time. Such as, unworthy males.

Patience and Perseverance

For every young single mother facing the weight of responsibility and uncertainty, remember this: patience and perseverance are your greatest allies. Progress may feel slow, and setbacks may come unexpectedly, but each day you show up—for your children, and for yourself—you are building a future rooted in strength. Patience allows you to grow through the challenges without losing hope, while perseverance fuels your determination to rise above limitations others may place on you. Your journey is not defined by your status, but by your unwavering commitment to creating a life of purpose, stability, happiness and love.

Ques: "As a single mum, I have at times thought about what I should be doing with my life, perhaps even changing my circle of friends, and I now feel encouraged to do so. However, for obvious reasons I also understand that life doesn't always go according to plan, is there something else I need to do?"

Ans: "Not really, what you are expressing is perfectly sensible, however caution is key. Being genuine about re-evaluating and possibly changing your life and indeed your circle of friends can be arduous as it is up-lifting. Adopt the mindset of being, once beaten twice shy and analyse everything you do before following through. Socializing with people who don't share your principles and values can hold you back, therefore consider who may be better as acquaintances only. Just keep your feet firmly on the ground and start living the life you want with your children."

You must be forthright or you're just allowing yourself to remain as you are, which may well appear to be decent enough in principle, but at the moment we are talking about single mothers who might want to break the mold.

Remind yourself of the adage; 'Good things come to those who wait', so consider your wait is potentially over to start afresh.

Sadly, some women believe they are made to feel inadequate, convinced that their life's status in life is somehow diminished. Yet that belief only holds power if it is accepted. The real stigma lies not in single motherhood itself, but in the narrow perceptions of those who misjudge what it represents. Motherhood remains one of the most vital and profoundly meaningful roles in existence—an institution beyond replacement. Isn't it time we honour its true significance and discard the outdated notion that being a single mum equates to living a lesser life?

Let's summarise what resonates with you. So instead of just reading this chapter one time, read over the highlighted areas you hopefully made and what you have written in your diary. Don't make the mistake of just reading this section of the book and moving on without having received something of value. It really is that important for you to read again and find further inspiration, remembering, this is your life.

SUMMARY

- Never allow men with questionable intentions to take advantage of you, he must show you respect before anything else.

- Begin now by acting on one of your new personal principles, to never sleep with another male, ever again, without taking proper precautions.
- These precautions stem from understanding the potential long-term consequences when not using contraceptives.
- Discover what his true motives, intentions, and feelings are.
- If you're not a single mum, then you now know how easily it can be to become one. Good news is you should also know how to prevent yourself from becoming one.
- Do you understand the unique challenges for siblings growing up together under the same roof having different fathers?
- Let a male earn you over a reasonable amount of time, other than allowing yourself to be an easy lover.
- A single mother can still accomplish everything she ever desired by using her fortitude, it really works.
- Put the word stigma in the bin, and surround yourself with decent people who are caring, respectful, with good morals, ethics and who have integrity, and you are on your way to transforming yourself.
- Remember the old saying... 'First impression', so why not become that woman of substance? Take pride in yourself, perhaps it's time for a change in something as simple as your attire, to provide inspiration, lifting you out of the doldrums.
- Maintain a high degree of self-respect and feed your self-esteem, discovering what's possible to improve your quality of life.
- Try socialising at better establishments and refrain from mixing with people that offer little in value, other than remaining as an acquaintance. Then discover how much more confident you feel, meeting likewise people.

- If you have become a single mother without completing your education, you won't do better for yourself than to resume your studies. Finding the time to upskill will be an enormous personal challenge and accomplishment, driving your discipline and willpower to new heights.
- Perhaps as mentioned, establishing your own small business, working from home, having discovered that niche market in something you love to do- 'unknown to anyone else'.
- There are educational institutions waiting to help you achieve your goals to find financial relief, other than having to scratch around looking for a dime, only to find a nickel.
- It's all part of the reinvention process in discovering what's possible, even when you're a single mother, because, if anyone can make this transformation happen, a single mum can.

Take the time to read the chapter on dysfunctional families and use that knowledge to ensure you never allow your family to live any other way than being respectful to themselves, their families and to others.

PERPETRATOR

Are you the type of person who targets young impressionable teenage girls to have sex with? Or maybe you have in the past with the knowledge you have fathered a son or daughter without any intention of ever raising or contributing to that child's welfare.

Whatever the case, you should know you must live with your conscience, which incidentally is working on bringing you too account. That's how life works, whether the authorities get involved or not. It's of no real consequence whether you're young and immature or an older male, because without clearly understanding what you're doing both morally and ethically, it has the potential to deliver many years of heartache for everyone. Make no mistake, that also includes you.

Therefore, you either need a refresher or perhaps you have never been aware of their meaning. Here's your chance to take the time to read the following then on reflection question yourself to your behaviour and let your conscience do the talking for you.

Morally – refers to the principles associated with right and wrong. It's about personal conscience and what one feels—good or bad. You know the difference between when something is either right or wrong. It's inherent to us all. Under normal circumstances there is no misunderstanding, therefore there can be no excuses.

Whilst ethically – refers to the rules and standards of your conduct as seen as being acceptable in our society. It helps to provide guidance for all human beings to act in a civilised manner.

If you've never given this subject much thought, you're about to receive a valuable true-life lesson, by confronting the virtues of the poisoned chalice, which we will now explore.

Before we do, and for the sake of this explanation, we will look only at the naive young man and leave the more scrupulous older male to one side for now.

Whilst every young man is entitled to seek out a female partner for consensual sex, without contraception he is playing a very dangerous game. Dangerous, because that naivety rarely considers the consequences of a potential pregnancy, or the heavy burden that may weigh on his mind for the rest of his life.

That is the poisoned chalice — a legacy of ignorance that can create lasting emotional and financial hardship for him, the mother, and the child. When sex is on your mind, men who fit your description are often focused on only one thing, not the consequences that become painfully clear nine months later. A moment when he may be knocked over by a feather upon hearing, he is a father. Then comes the instinctive denial, the thoughts of terminating a potential early life, and the sudden realisation that he now has a biological child.

The stigma of an "illegitimate" child, the looming child-support obligations, and the overwhelming question of "What now?" all collide at once. A man who avoids responsibility for his child may experience psychological distress rooted in guilt, shame, or unresolved identity conflict. Even if he outwardly denies it, the internal consequences can be profound.

Now the meaning of the poisoned chalice becomes clear.

Aren't you glad you're not in that position- or are you? because there are many males who continue to live having failed to understand the consequences, now learning to fight their conscience. It wasn't so long ago that when a man knowingly fathered a child, would stand tall and do the honorable thing, as it were. He would marry the mother of their child and make an honest living, learning how to live together as a family, and discovering love as life intended.

Imagine removing that poison chalice (of course metaphorically speaking) as you now live your life without the weight you placed on your shoulders. You no longer begrudge having to spend money on your family since you're together, you no longer live in denial, your conscience is clear, and your identity remains intact. But what's the true benefit here? – again, its discovering love.

However, in times gone by, there were equally challenging situations, particularly when the male simply ran off, with the young mother unfairly coerced into giving her child up for adoption. Not that the mother couldn't have adjusted to raising that child with family support along with her maternal instinct—not at all. Rather the self-inflicted selfish mentality, a sign of the times - being the cause of that stigma, orchestrated by the young women's parents who became grandparents. Cost of which- having disenfranchised themselves- by never seeing their own grandchild. All because they valued their social status more than the welfare of their own daughter and grandchild. A family travesty based on ignorance.

On the other hand, you may be the scrupulous male having found yourself in too deep, abandoned a female or several females you have made pregnant. Whether you perceive those relationships as one-night stands, it doesn't discount your behaviour of selfish abandonment. All of which amounts to neglect and emotional stress — a pattern of behaviour that constitutes both ethical and moral abuse.

There would be many people who would brand you in a far harsher way, other than an abuser, but that won't help. Nor will it make for better understanding for the reasons why you have adopted the mentality of believing you should run and hide. Whatever the selfish reason, spare a thought for that child, wanting to be a part of your life, wanting you to be their dad- forever.

Therefore, if you're paying alimony to a single mother that's honourable, but have you considered being there for your child and his/her mother permanently or has that never crossed your mind? Because many men run away not understanding why. Regardless of the current situation between you and the mother, there was an ignition of sorts to begin with, if only for lust or indeed sex. Again, is that not something worth trying to reignite, for the sake of that child, and the mother —perhaps wanting your love, your presence and your support? It's perfectly understandable for couples not to be in love to begin with, however love can grow, with only one way to find out. – by putting your mind to it.

Shouldn't your child's feelings and that of their upbringing be more important than anything else in life? Have a think about that for a while. Look at what you are potentially missing out on, raising a child or children you were responsible for bringing into the world. Otherwise, children will grow up always wondering what it could have been like had their dad been around, as the day will come when it suddenly hits you- and hard. These are the types of consequences when producing human life without fully understanding the serious implications later in life.

If you are the type whereby you deliberately dodge alimony payments, whether as a result of failing to accept being the father, or due to a separation or divorce, then ask yourself how you would feel if your own father did the same to you. Failure to make financial contributions for your offspring is generally in spite, lack of funds, or just being irresponsible.

Put your ego to one side, think less of yourself, and stop being afraid, even if a long-term relationship with the mother is off the table. Discover the joy of making financial contributions to raising your own biological child, your own flesh and blood and the personal satisfaction that comes with all being together. Then it starts to happen, being able to look at yourself in the mirror, and not having to look over your shoulder perhaps for the first time in a long time. Knowing you never surrendered your conscience or allowed your child to carry the burden of your absence or indeed live in hardship.

A man without conscience is a man without virtues, a man without virtues is a man who remains empty. Having never grasped morality, therefore unable to show compassion or demonstrate empathy. That's everything that this self-help book advocates and aspires to, providing you with what you need to learn and hopefully become inspired by. Becoming someone who is now willing to shape up and accept their responsibilities.

Nothing could ever describe having better morals, ethics and integrity in these circumstances like a man finally stepping up and becoming accountable for his own actions.

CONCLUSION

As we conclude this journey together, it's crucial to reflect on the width and breadth of the topics we've explored in our mission to prevent and end domestic abuse. Each chapter has offered insights, strategies, and support, tailored to different stages and circumstances of life, all with the aim of fostering awareness, safety, empowerment, and healing.

We began with the foundational aspects of dating, courtship, and engagement, emphasizing the importance of recognizing healthy relationship dynamics from the outset. By understanding the signs of respect, communication, and the mutual sharing of principles and values, we lay the groundwork for a future free from abuse, with a pathway to love and discover happiness.

For those navigating the complexities of living alone, we provided guidance for staying safe and building a supportive network. This phase of life offers a unique opportunity for self-growth and resilience, enabling individuals to fortify themselves against potential risks. Our exploration of marriage and divorce addressed both the joys and challenges inherent in these significant life changes. We discussed ways to foster a loving and respectful marriage and offered resources for those seeking to safely leave abusive relationships and rebuild their lives post-divorce.

The chapters on coercion and control, sexual abuse, and the impact of drugs and alcohol delved into some of the most insidious forms of abuse. By bringing these issues to light, we aimed to empower survivors with awareness, along with the knowledge and tools to recognize and escape these harmful situations. We also focused on the needs of the elderly and single mothers; two groups that are often vulnerable to domestic abuse.

Providing targeted support and strategies, we sought to ensure that no one was left without hope or help.

Throughout this book, we also highlighted the importance of understanding, intervention, and the planning processes for confrontation. Yet these pillars are most effective when anchored to our own fortitude, the inner strength that enables us to rise above adversity. By equipping ourselves with knowledge and fostering a community of empathy and action, we awaken the resilience within each of us. Fortitude is more than endurance; it is the catalyst for becoming who we truly inspire to become.

Remember, the pathway towards safety and empowerment doesn't end here. Continue to seek support, share your experiences, and stand firm in the belief that everyone deserves a life free from fear and violence. Together, we can create a world where domestic abuse is not just addressed but eradicated, through the power of teaching.

I genuinely hope this book has offered you moments of reflection, encouragement, and connection—just as writing it was a deeply personal and heartfelt journey for me. My mission was to write each chapter spontaneously without prior dialogue, which may not necessarily agree with everyone, but written with the hope of inspiring change and offering comfort. Above all, my greatest wish is that the insights and strategies shared within reach those who need them most—especially the children—and of course all women, and indeed the perpetrator himself. We all deserve a life, free from the shadows of domestic abuse, instead filled with love, peace, and happiness.

This isn't the end; it's just the beginning!

"Consider gifting someone this book, destined to keep on giving 👫".

Epilogue

If you or someone you know is experiencing sexual abuse or family violence contact:

- National Sexual Assault, Domestic Violence Counselling Service 24-hour helpline **1800 RESPECT** on **1800 737 732**
- 24-hour Emergency Accommodation helpline on **1800 800 588**
- Safe At Home helpline on **1800 633 937**
- National Violence and Abuse Trauma Counselling and Recovery Service on **1800 FULLSTOP (1800 385 578).** They also have a specific line for the LGBTIQA+ community called the Rainbow Sexual, Domestic and Family Violence Helpline on **1800 497 212**
- SHE (free and confidential counselling and support) on **6278 9090**
- Sexual Assault Support Services on **6231 1811**, or after hours **6231 1817**
- Family Violence Crisis and Support Service on **1800 608 122**
- Bravehearts – Sexual Assault Support for Children on **1800 BRAVE 1**
- Kids Helpline is for young people aged 5 to 25 on **1800 551 800**
- Don't go it alone. Please reach out for help by contacting **Lifeline** on **13 11 14**
- Men who have anger, relationship or parenting issues, should contact the **Men's Referral Service** on **1300 766 491 or** the **Don't Become That Man** helpline on

Disclaimer: This book is intended for informational purposes only and does not substitute professional legal, medical, or psychological advice. The content reflects perspectives and recommendations based on lived experiences, and advocacy efforts, acknowledging that domestic abuse affects individuals in diverse ways.

Since experiences of abuse are deeply personal and context-dependent, readers are encouraged to interpret the material in a way that aligns with their own beliefs. This book does not claim to provide definitive solutions covering every circumstance, but rather aims to offer support, raise awareness, and provide guidance for those seeking opinions, direction, or help.

If you or someone you know is in immediate danger or experiencing abuse, please contact local authorities, emergency services, or a qualified professional for help. The authors and publishers disclaim any liability arising from the use or interpretation of this book's contents.

www.ingramcontent.com/pod-product-compliance
Lightning Source LLC
Chambersburg PA
CBHW031054080526
44587CB00011B/683